The Great Transformation
Supply-Side Structural Reform

Series on Chinese Economics Research*

(ISSN: 2251-1644)

Series Editor: Fan Gang *(Peking University, China)*

Published:

Vol. 22: *The Great Transformation: Supply-side Structural Reform*
by Ma Xiaohe

Vol. 21: *China's Economic Development Strategies: Transformation and Innovation*
by Liu Rui

Vol. 20: *China's Rural Labor Migration and Its Economic Development*
by Liu Xiaoguang

Vol. 19: *Environmental Economics Research and China's Green Development Strategy*
by Zhang Youguo
translated by Xu Hao, Xie Linlin

Vol. 18: *The Transformation of China's Economic Development: Perspectives of Sino–US Economists*
by Yang Wandong, Zhang Jianjun, Huang Shudong and Zhu Andong

Vol. 17: *Income Distribution and China's Economic "New Normal"*
by Wan Haiyuan and Li Shi

Vol. 16: *Research on Efficiency and Fairness of Resources Allocation by China's Governmental Administration*
by Sheng Hong and Qian Pu

Vol. 15: *Industrial Overcapacity and Duplicate Construction in China: Reasons and Solutions*
by Li Ping, Jiang Feitao and Cao Jianhai

Vol. 14: *Reforging the Central Bank: The Top-Level Design of the Chinese Financial System in the New Normal*
by Deng Haiqing and Chen Xi

*For the complete list of volumes in this series, please visit
www.worldscientific.com/series/scer

Series on Chinese Economics Research – Vol. 22

The Great Transformation
Supply-Side Structural Reform

MA Xiaohe
Chinese Academy of Macroeconomic Research
National Development and Reform Commission, China

Translated by
YANG Limeng

World Scientific

NEW JERSEY • LONDON • SINGAPORE • BEIJING • SHANGHAI • HONG KONG • TAIPEI • CHENNAI • TOKYO

Published by

World Scientific Publishing Co. Pte. Ltd.
5 Toh Tuck Link, Singapore 596224
USA office: 27 Warren Street, Suite 401-402, Hackensack, NJ 07601
UK office: 57 Shelton Street, Covent Garden, London WC2H 9HE

Library of Congress Cataloging-in-Publication Data
Names: Ma, Xiaohe, 1955– author.
Title: The great transformation : supply-side structural reform /
Ma Xiaohe, Chinese Academy of Macroeconomic Research, National Development and Reform Commission, China ; translated by Yang Limeng.
Description: New Jersey : World Scientific Publishing, [2020] | Series: Series on Chinese economics research ; vol. 22 | Includes bibliographical references.
Identifiers: LCCN 2019045019 | ISBN 9789811209338 (hardcover) |
ISBN 9789811209345 (ebook) | ISBN 9789811209352 (ebook other)
Subjects: LCSH: China--Economic policy--2000- | Industrial policy--China. |
Supply-side economics--China.
Classification: LCC HC427.95 .M3345 2020 | DDC 338.951--dc23
LC record available at https://lccn.loc.gov/2019045019

British Library Cataloguing-in-Publication Data
A catalogue record for this book is available from the British Library.

大转型：供给侧结构性改革
Originally published in Chinese by China Social Sciences Press

This book is published with financial support from the Chinese Fund for the Humanities and Social Sciences

For any available supplementary material, please visit
https://www.worldscientific.com/worldscibooks/10.1142/11527#t=suppl

Desk Editor: Tan Boon Hui

Typeset by Stallion Press
Email: enquiries@stallionpress.com

Foreword

"While appropriately expanding aggregate demand, China will strengthen supply-side structural reform." This was first proposed at the 11th Meeting of the Leading Group for Financial and Economic Affairs in November 2015. In a period of more than one year, the "supply-side structural reform" has become a popular term talked about in all regions, fields, and sectors and on all occasions throughout China. However, this term is not as all-inclusive and omnipotent as a basket.

The supply-side structural reform is the key point of the Chinese government's economic management during the "13th Five-Year Plan", so it will be of great theoretical and practical importance to correctly understand and grasp its background, contents, essential features, thoughts, and goals. Nevertheless, there are a range of questions that need to be explored and addressed urgently, including how to understand the supply side and the demand side, why the supply-side structural reform is proposed at the current stage, how to implement and what is to be changed by the supply-side structural reform, what else should be taken into consideration, what policy to be taken, etc. For this reason, the Academy of Macroeconomic Research set up a research group of major research projects in 2016. More than a year of hard work headed and organized by Vice President Ma Xiaohe and researchers from the Administration Office, Economic Research Institute, Institute of Foreign Economics and Trade, Industrial Research Institute, Institute of State-owned Land, Social Research Institute, Market Research Institute, and Institute of Sports Management finally produced 1 abbreviated draft, 1 general report, 6 reports on special topic, and 4 reports on policy recommendation. During the research work, all staged achievements made by the research group were published in some internal magazines including *Situation Briefing* of the Academy of Macroeconomic Research, NDRC, *Economic Briefing* of the Development Research Center of the State Council, and *World Economic Survey* of Chinese Academy of Social Sciences as well as some foreign periodicals including *Economic Daily* and *Insight China*. In addition, the research group members were well received for their tutorial lectures on supply-side structural reform commissioned by NDRC to the Counselors' Office of the State Council, the Rocket Force of the Chinese People's Liberation Army, and the special training class for national NDRC directors at the prefecture level.

About the Author

Ma Xiaohe (1955–) graduated from the Renmin University of China and received his doctorate from Nanjing Agricultural University. He is a professor and the former vice president of the Chinese Academy of Macroeconomic Research, National Development and Reform Commission. His main research areas and research directions are economic development strategy, industrial structure and industrial policy, urban and rural economic relations, agriculture and rural development policy. His major publications include *The Scientific Outlook on Development*, *Structural Transformation and Agricultural Development*, *The Supply-Demand Balance of China's Agricultural Produce after the Accession to WTO*, *Research on the Rural Tax and Fee Reform in China*, *The New Stage of China's Agricultural Development*, *The Grain Question in 21st Century in China*, *Contradiction of Dual Structure in China & Choice of Industrialization Strategy*, etc. His main papers include "Issues of Current Economic Development and Recommendations on Macroeconomic Policy", "International Experience of Industry Nurturing Agriculture and Policy Adjustment in China", "Several Issues on Building a New Socialist Countryside", "Poverty Reduction is the Strategy for China's Economic Development", "China's Food Industry Development Strategy during the Eleventh Five-Year-Plan Period", etc.

About the Translator

Yang Limeng (1966–), Associate Professor and translator. He has been a freelance translator since 2004 and has translated over 5 million words till date, mainly in the field of construction projects (e.g. tender documents) and confidential military materials. Since July 2013, he has been working as an associate professor translator in a private translation company in Xi'an, responsible for quality control and allocation of translated works, training of translation team members, development of translation software and platform, directing and managing large translation projects, and conducting quality review of translated works by other individual translators or groups.

Contents

Chapter 1

Basic Theories and Institutional Framework for Promotion of Supply-Side Structural Reform

Ma Xiaohe, Guo Liyan, Fu Baozong, Li Dawei, Liu Xianwei, Bian Jing and Guan Bo

Academy of Macroeconomic Research

Abstract

China's current economic operations are encountering several contradictory problems at both the supply side and the demand side, but the root of these problems lies heavily in the supply side. Since the root problem on the supply side is the sluggish reform of institutional mechanism, it is necessary and inevitable to promote supply-side structural reform in China. The supply-side problems will be addressed in three aspects: intensive and economical supply of production factors, efficient and high-quality supply of products, and efficient supply of institutions, where top priority is given to supply of institutions. China's supply-side structural reform differs essentially from that in western countries including the UK and the USA in the theoretical basis, practical background, institutional environment, policy instruments, and dynamic mechanism, and it cannot be viewed as a replica of western supply-side economics. During the supply-side structural reform, we need to properly handle four important relationships: between supply and demand, long term and short term, government and market, and the domestic and international. The supply-side structural reform is a systematic project that involves all aspects of the socio-economic development. Successful implementation of this project depends first on whether we can quickly seek out new engines for economic growth as the traditional engine fails and second on whether we can create a new engine for economic growth by carrying out reform in institutional mechanism to ensure efficient supply of institutions. In this respect, reforms should be deepened on five systems and mechanisms such as administrative management, state-owned enterprises and monopolized industry, technical innovation, tax and finance, and related fundamental systems. The supply-side structural reform can also be promoted by expanding openness to the outside world.

At the 11th Session of the Central Leading Group on Financial and Economic Affairs, decision-makers proposed that "while moderately expanding the aggregate market demand, we will deepen the supply-side structural reform, improve the quality and efficiency of supply system, enhance the engines for sustainable economic growth, and raise the overall level of China's social productive force". Later on, it was explicitly stated in the "13th Five-Year Plan" outline issued by the State Council that "while carrying out the supply-side structural reform, we will increase efficient supply and meet efficient demand so as to accelerate formation of systems, mechanisms and pattern of new normal development". In the next 5 years, therefore, the supply-side structural reform will be prioritized in the economic management of the Chinese government. However, here are some problems concerning the supply-side structural reform that need to be investigated: How to understand concepts of supply side and demand side? Why the supply-side structural reform is proposed at this stage? How to carry out and what are the contents of the supply-side structural reform? What should be considered and what measures will be taken during the supply-side structural reform? This is what will be covered in this book.

I. Background of China's Supply-Side Structural Reform

Since the first quarter of 2010, China's economic growth rate has slowed down from 12.2% to 6.7%; especially at the new normal development stage, there appeared a prevailing trend of structural slowdown boosting the pressure of economic downturn in China. At this time, the underlying structural contradictions facing China's economic development could hardly be eradicated from the demand–supply method alone; instead, macro-management needs to be utilized to find a new way out and build a new policy system.

1. *Discontinuity between new and old engines for economic growth due to the structural disequilibrium between the supply side and the demand side*

Currently, both the supply side and demand side of China are faced with a severe structural disequilibrium that features weakening traditional engines and underpowered new engines. From the perspective of the demand side, on the one hand, the narrowing investment space and diminishing marginal benefits of public investment have led to a sharp decline in the driving force of unit investment for economic growth while the continuously falling rate of return of the real economy and the gloomy business prospects have led to low demand for social investment; on the other hand, the irrational income distribution structure and low level of welfare system, including social security, have led to inadequate impetus for growth of consumption that further leads to a distorted transmission chain between consuming willingness and consuming behaviors and to incomplete release of effective social demand. From the perspective of different income brackets, moderate- and low-income citizens have sufficient consuming willingness for mid- and low-end products, but their willingness is depressed by their incomes while medium- and high-income citizens have the consuming capacity for high-value-added and high-end products, but their new needs can hardly be satisfied by slow upgrading of China's industrial structure and product supply structure, because of which their consuming potentiality is suppressed. Under the existing system, the structural contradictions arising from the demand side are virtually caused by the lagging reform of institutional mechanisms and reflect insufficient system supply.

From the perspective of supply side, over the years, the central government has excessively intervened in industrial development and allocation of relevant resources and factors. On the one hand, contrary to the law of economic development, local governments were propelled by the pursuit of higher GDPs to vigorously build various industrial parks and blindly implement the industrial subsidy policy; as a result, a mass of capital and resources flowed into mid- and low-end industries, thus giving rise to low-level construction, repeated competition, and severe overcapacity. On the other hand, the lack of fundamental systems such as equity and credit, insufficient protection of innovation incentive and entrepreneurial spirit, irrational setup of industrial access threshold, and barriers on entrance of capital, technology, and resource factors to mid- and high-end industries led to slow growth of new industries and insufficient impetus for upgrading of industrial structure. Under such circumstances, the failure of the product supply structure to adapt to the changing structure of social demand resulted in the fact that the mid- and low-end products and those with lower technical content and value added were oversupplied while the mid- and high-end products and services with higher technical content and value added were short of supply.

2. *Industrial transformation and upgrading severely restricted by high cost of institutional transactions*

Over the years, the underlying structural contradictions in construction of fundamental systems have been involved deeply with vested interests, which imposed much obstruction on reform. In some industrial sectors, for example, there were administrative monopoly, irrational allocation of production factors, tedious administrative regulations of the government, too many approvals, and lengthy intermediary services. As a result, enterprises were disqualified from taking part in economic activities due to continuously rising costs of institutional transactions, fund-raising activities, land acquisition, and some hidden fees. In the *Survey on Business Environment* report issued by the World Bank in 2016, China only ranks 84th among 189 economies evaluated, indicating that Chinese enterprises still face various institutional barriers in business start-up, registration of property rights, and application for construction permit. According to a survey, it usually takes 31.5 days to start a business in China after dealing with 11 procedures; in OECD countries, however, these figures average at five procedures and 9 days. The high cost of institutional transactions due to the lagging reform of systems and mechanisms has become an obstructive checkpoint for the normal operation of enterprises, forming a bottleneck constraint on industrial structural transformation and innovation-driven development, and has severely weakened the industrial capacity of effective supply and microscopic vitality of enterprises.

3. *Economic downturn pressure unrelieved due to weakening effect of demand-side management policy*

Since the year 2010, in order to relieve the economic downturn pressure, the Chinese government has taken a series of demand-stimulating policies, such as enlarging the size of fiscal expenditure, increasing public investment, cutting interest rates and required reserve ratios, and raising money supply. First, from June 8, 2012 to October 24, 2015, the Chinese government conducted structural reduction of required reserve ratios and interest rates for 7 and eight consecutive times, respectively. Second, from 2010 to 2015, the Chinese government continuously increased the supply of money, with M2 supply increased from RMB 72.585 trillion to 139.23 trillion. The money supply in this period was 2.01 times the economic growth; if calculated at the prices of the indicated years, an increase of 1 unit GDP production needed an increase of 1.07 unit of M2 supply in 2010, which rose to 3.3 in 2015 and kept rising in 2016. Third, since September 2014, the Chinese government successively carried out 12 key project packages to stabilize economic growth and benefit the people, which absorbed RMB 7.4 trillion of fixed asset investment. Finally, the Chinese government adopted the proactive fiscal policy for consecutive years; in 2015, for example, the budget deficit was expected to be RMB 1.62 trillion but the real deficit amounted to RMB 2.3551 trillion. Practice proves that the more the marginal efficiency of various demand management policies declines, the more insignificant its effect on "stabilizing economic growth".

Under the new normal of economic development, insufficiency of effective supply and excess of ineffective supply are two main restrictive factors impeding long-term and steady growth of Chinese economy; besides, it is apparent that perseverance of the macro-policy accentuating demand-side management is incompatible with the new situation. For this reason, the Central Government of China decided to initiate supply-side structural reform as the focal point of its macro-policy for a long period in the future since November 2015 in order to break through the underlying structural contradiction and institutional barriers on the supply side. This will also help unleash the potentiality of economic growth, foster new impetus, and pave the way for high-level and effective connectivity between supply and demand.

II. Basic Theories and Analysis Framework

1. *Analysis of the supply-side and demand-side theories*

(1) *Macroeconomic theories on supply side and demand side*

In microeconomics, the supply–demand analysis is the basic framework for economic behaviors of micro entities and operating rules of market economy — two aspects of economic activities that are conditional and indispensable to each other. Supply means goods or services which producers are willing to provide within a given time and under given conditions, including quality and quantity. Demand means goods or services consumers are willing and able to purchase in a given period and at a given price level.

Based on supply–demand relation, microeconomic theories have established a partial equilibrium theory and a general equilibrium theory. According to partial equilibrium theory, the supply and demand of any commodity are functions of price; when equalization of this commodity's supply and demand clears the market, there will be a market equilibrium price for this commodity. According to general equilibrium theory, scholars argue that in the perfect competitive market environment there will be a group of optimal price solutions allowing all consumers to maximize utility with a given amount of income and allowing all manufacturers to maximize profits in the input–output combination determined by their production functions. At this point, all markets are cleared.

A thorough analysis indicates that microeconomics uses static equilibrium analysis for supply and demand analysis from the perspective of a price-forming mechanism. Against this background, price is the only factor that determines demand and supply.

Microeconomic theory has also made an analysis of changes in the consumers' utility functions and income level and in the producers' production functions. For consumers, the ascending income level will make the demand curve move rightward and thus increase the commodity demand volume and price; for producers, any changes in the production functions or in the quantity of production factors will make the supply curve move rightward and thus increase the commodity supply volume but decrease its price. In fact, this theoretical framework has provided the feasibility to promote economic growth by moving the demand and supply curves.

(2) *Supply-side and demand-side theory in macroeconomic theories*

Modern macroeconomic theories can be traced back to John Maynard Keynes's *The General Theory of Employment, Interest and Money*, which focused on research of the overall process of national economic activities and proposed the concepts of aggregate demand and aggregate supply. Aggregate supply is defined as the total volume of final commodities and services provided by a country or a region at constant prices in a given period, while aggregate demand means the sum of an economy's demands for final commodities and services at constant prices in a given period. When a balance is reached between aggregate demand and aggregate supply, the gross output will be the gross output of national economy.

In macroeconomic theories, the aggregate demand (GDP) is divided into consumer demand (including governmental consumption and private consumption) and investment demand (including foreign demand in an open economy), and a strict mathematical formula is used to define the relations among such economic variables as aggregate social demand, money supply, fiscal expenditure, and interest rate, which has laid a theoretical foundation for the use of the demand-side fiscal and monetary policy instruments to make the aggregate demand curve move rightward and eventually realize growth of the gross output. The aggregate demand in macroeconomics and the demand in microeconomics are related to and different from each other. With regard to their relation, the macroeconomic aggregate demand may be deemed as the sum of all microeconomic demands, as their curves are sloping toward the lower right. However, it must be noted that there is visible difference in their analytical frameworks. If the price is constant, the microeconomic theory argues that the main determinants for demand of each commodity are consumers' preferences and income level, but the macroeconomic theory claims that the main determinants of aggregate demand are such economic variables as money supply and fiscal expenditure. As a matter of fact, consumers' preferences and income level are inevitably under the influence of changes in such macro-variables as money supply and fiscal expenditure, which promote movement of all micro-demand curves and eventually lead to movement of the gross macro-demand curve.

Corresponding to aggregate demand, aggregate supply is the total product of economic society, which means the quantity of products all manufacturers of a country are willing and able to produce under given conditions of current prices, production capacity, and total cost. According to Keynes's macroeconomic theory, the relation between aggregate supply and social prices derives from the fact that short-term macroscopic production function is nothing but the function of labor supply which is influenced only by wage level in the short term.

Under this framework, the macroeconomic theory has concluded that there are two extreme cases of classical aggregate supply curve and Keynes's aggregate supply curve. By analyzing the classical aggregate supply curve, this theory argues that the aggregate supply curve is a vertical line if by default the production function remains unchanged and there is full employment because the changing market prices will not have any influence on the total output, and that Keynes's aggregate supply curve is a horizontal line if price is extremely rigid in the short term because manufacturers may hire any necessary number of labor forces at the current wage level. In reality, however, the aggregate supply curve may slope upward due to viscous monetary wage.

Apparently, Keynes's macroeconomic theory of aggregate supply research lays particular stress on the relationship between aggregate supply and price, the inherent logic of which indicates a close relationship between labor supply and actual wage level. According to this theory, it is clear that if any change in production function leads to enhancement of production capacity, the aggregate supply curve will move to the right, providing theoretical basis for promoting economic growth from the supply side.

However, it must be seen that Keynes's theory aimed to address serious unemployment issues existing at that time in capitalist countries and laid stress on short-term analysis of factors stimulating economic growth.

His research on aggregate supply was focused more on analyzing the relationship among the level of employment, actual wage, and aggregate supply, provided that the input of production factors, such as capital and resources, remained unchanged, and that the total factor productivity also remained unchanged, than on how to expand total output by raising total factor productivity. It is therefore clear that this theory on the supply side seems not so intensive.

(3) *Static equilibrium analysis of supply and demand*

Whether from a microeconomic or macroeconomic perspective, a static equilibrium analysis indicates three possible supply–demand relationships: (a) an equilibrium will arise if all goods or services produced by social production are consumed, where the total social output means the gross domestic product (GDP); (b) a disequilibrium will result if goods or services produced rise above or fall below the level of consumption, where expanding production or reducing demand may be necessitated in a closed economy; and (c) an equilibrium will be eventually reached through regulation of import and export in an open economy.

(4) *Limitations of traditional western economic theory in analysis of supply and demand*

First, western economic theory lacks a thorough analysis of effects on aggregate supply. Assumption by both the microscopic manufacture theory and the macroscopic aggregate supply theory suggests the manufacturer's production possibility curve and the form of macroscopic production function are predetermined and so is input of an overwhelming majority of production factors. In reality, however, the production possibility curve and macroscopic production function are constantly variable. According to an analysis based on the Solow dynamic economic growth model, within a medium and long period, the growth of total output is derived primarily from outward extension of production possibility curve resulting from technical progress. Theory of institutional economics also explicates that institution serves as a decisive factor for economic growth and social development of a country, which is reflected by the mathematical model that different institutions may lead to different production functions.

Second, western economic theory lacks a dynamic, medium- and long-term perspective in analysis of supply–demand equilibrium. A comparative static method is adopted by theory of traditional economics in analysis of supply–demand equilibrium. The relationship between aggregate supply and aggregate demand may appear more complicated if a dynamic analysis method is adopted because a dynamic rather than static equilibrium is necessitated for an economy to realize steady and healthy development while constantly enlarging the size of aggregate supply and optimizing economic structure. Looking at it from the demand side, we have found that the current investment may influence the social labor force, capital, technology, and resources and further influence aggregate supply, and that the current consumption may help to improve the labor force's quality and thus indirectly encourage innovation and further future supply. Looking at it from the supply side, if the future supply structure accords with changes at the demand end, a dynamic equilibrium will be achieved between supply and demand; if not, the disequilibrium between supply and demand will get worse and eventually lead to an obvious slowdown of economic growth. To achieve a dynamic equilibrium between supply and demand, the following two conditions must be met: (1) the supply-side policy objectives must comply with futuristic changes in potential demand and (2) the demand-side management objectives must be in accordance with changes in potential supply capacity.

Finally, western economic theory leads easily to policy preferences at demand-side management. The macroeconomic theory is structurally tight and logically strong in demand-side management, so much so that it has provided a normative logic system for national governments to implement macroeconomic regulation and control. In particular, the demand-side management worked effectively when addressing the economic crisis in 1930s. Since World War II (1939–1945), this theory has therefore become an increasingly "noted school of thought" in economics. Nevertheless, with little reference to how to change production function, this theory disenabled state governments to obtain feasible policy proposals for raising the level of aggregate supply from the supply side, leading objectively to a fact that state governments usually made their macroeconomic policies based on demand-side management.

2. *Supply-side analysis framework*

The demand-side management alone is not enough to support long-term steady economic growth. If the input of all production factors in an economy remains stable and the supply structure remains unchanged for a long time, a disharmony will be likely to occur between the supply structure and the demand structure, as a result of which the supply–demand equilibrium will be hard to achieve and the demand-end policy will be less effective, no matter how the aggregate demand curve moves. Being aware of this limitation in traditional western economic theory, scholars used theories of classical political economics and production function to open the "black box" of aggregate supply under Keynesian macroeconomics in order to optimize the structure and enlarge the size of aggregate supply created by such production factors as labor, capital, technology (institution), and resources and further to find solutions to the supply–demand equilibrium, which include the following:

- First, in-depth analysis of the relationship between tax and aggregate supply is required. Supply-side economists, such as Robert A. Mondale and Arthur B. Laffer, who treated tax as one of the important variables influencing aggregate supply, argued that if the technical level remained unchanged, the rising tax rate would have a strong effect on producing activities and result in insufficient input of most production factors in production so that the total output and the total tax scale decreased due to leftward movement of the aggregate supply curve. For this reason, scholars including Laffer proposed a supply-side policy system represented by massive tax cuts on enterprises. However, the supply-side economists failed to deliver a normative elaboration on the relationship among tax rate, total output, and total tax revenue, and overlooked effects of technical progress and improved factor quality on aggregate supply curve.
- Second, in-depth analysis of the relationship between technological innovation and economic growth is required. Joseph A. Schumpeter,

who lived in the same period as Keynes, adopted the analytic method of political economics to define innovation as "new combination of production factors and production conditions" and create a feedback mechanism consisting of "innovation — efficiency improves — profit increases — give access to large number of competitors — profit decreases — new round of innovation", arguing that innovation was the fundamental impetus for economic cycle and growth. On this basis, scholars including Christopher Freeman and Alexander Gerschenkron analyzed the role of innovation in economic growth and the innovation power of enterprises. Robert M. Solow's neoclassical economic growth theory also introduced technical progress into the economic growth model by reference to classical political economics, and eventually reached an important conclusion that technical progress in economic growth would be the only source of economic growth. By adopting the supply-side analysis method, all these theories have introduced technical progress as production factors or a combination of production factors into product functions on the supply side, and discussed how to promote economic growth through technical progress motivated by policy instrument.

- Third, in-depth research on the relationship between institutional system and economic growth is required. After recognition of weak points in assumptions such as "economic man" and zero institutional cost in classical economics and Keynesian economics, some institutional economists, including Ronald H. Coase, John K. Galbraith, and Douglass C. North, adopted the historical analysis method to conduct in-depth research on the role of institutions in economic growth, and concluded that there was a huge difference in the output of the same production factors under different institutional systems. This conclusion in reality treated supply of institutions and supply of production factors as important parts of production functions, thus providing a theoretical basis for promotion of economic growth on the supply side by institutional changes.
- Finally, promoting economic growth of developing countries through optimizing the structure of factor supply is required. After World War II, many developing countries subject to imperfect market economy and short of factor supply became independent and started seeking

> further development. In this context, economists such as Jan Tinbergen, William A. Lewis, and Hollis B. Chenery, after absorbing essentials of Keynesian theory and classical theory, advocated promotion of economic growth by making up for the shortage of production factors including capital and technology and by optimizing the structure of factor supply. This advocacy has in effect expounded the economic growth mechanism from both the supply and demand sides, and it was reflected in well-known theories such as Chenery's "Two-gap Model" (savings shortage and foreign exchange shortage) and Lewis's "Dual-sector Model" (the capitalist sector and the subsistence sector).

Based on the foregoing analysis, the logic frame of the supply-side and demand-side economic theories is as illustrated in Figure 1.

Differences between the supply-side framework and the demand-side framework include the following: (1) The consumption, investment, and net export on the supply side, as part of GDP, contribute to GDP growth mainly in the current period, whereas, the labor, capital, technology, and resources on the demand side contribute to GDP growth mainly in the next stage rather than in the current period. (2) On the demand side, the consumption, investment, and net export themselves are components of economic aggregate, which may be directly influenced by means of various

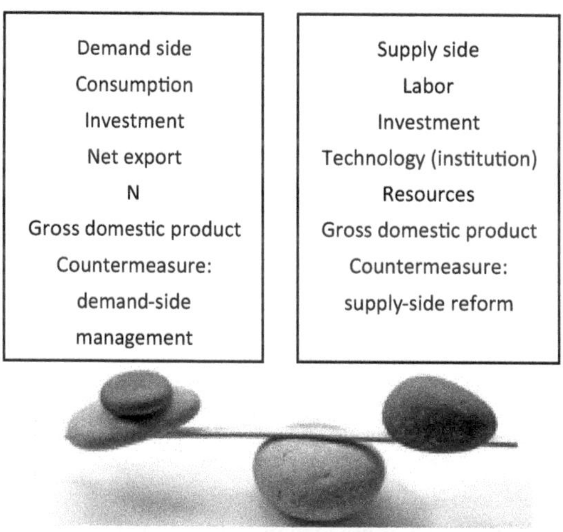

Figure 1. Analytic Framework for the Demand Side and Supply Side.

policy instruments, whereas, on the supply side, production factors such as capital, labor, technology, and resources are inputs in economic activities, where the output structure may be directly influenced by policy instruments through making changes in the quantity, structure, quality, and mode of activity of production factors. (3) The demand-side framework is mainly used to analyze effect on economic growth in a short period, while the supply-side framework is intended to analyze effect on economic growth in a long period.

There is also an essential difference between investments on the demand side and those on the supply side, though both mean inputs of capital in a statistical statement. The former, as an important part of GDP, may be either public investment or productive investment; the public investment may also be either public service investment to directly add effective supply of products or investment irrelevant to supply of products. The latter must be investments in plant, equipment, technical training, water and electricity supply, roads, gas, and Internet access, which are closely related to potential economic growth.

The following functional expression can be used to describe the relation of aggregate supply with such production factors as labor, capital (investment), technology, institutional systems, and resources:

$$Y = f(L, K, R, T),$$

which means supply at three levels:

- **Supply of factors:** Quantity and quality of L (labor), K (capital), R (recourses), T (technology);
- **Supply of products (goods and services):** Scale and structure of Y;
- **Supply of institutions (which involves scale and efficiency of total output generated by supply of factors):** Specific expression of functions.[1]

[1] Many modifications of this analytic method were provided by scholars. Some scholars treated T (technical innovation) as part of functions and argued that this intangible factor was hard to distinguish from institutional innovation and hard to measure, but some classified institutional system as one of production factors. According to this book, technical innovation is treated as a production factor and a form of function to comply with the

In its entirety, the supply-side structural reform needs to solve the problem of supply in the following three aspects:

(1) **Supply of production factors:** The intensive and economic allocation of factors is the premise for effective supply of quality products. Theoretically, the first-order partial derivatives of the total output relative to labor, capital, resources, and technology are greater than zero. Therefore, the key topic of supply-side research will be how to improve the efficiency of factor allocation and how to maintain a steady increase in the supply of production factors such as technology and high-quality labor that are relatively scarce but have a higher marginal output. In addition, the supply-side research also needs to focus on how to eliminate obstacles impeding factor mobility and realize market-oriented allocation of factors.
(2) **Supply of products and services:** The ultimate purpose of the supply-side reform is to provide effective supply of quality products and ensure output of products and services adaptable to the changing demand structure. In reality, the consumer's utility function varies with the emergence of new goods and services. The problem the supply-side reform needs to address is to produce and provide effective and quality products and services in line with the changing demand structure so as to reach a dynamic equilibrium between supply and demand.
(3) **Supply of institutions:** New supply of institutions generated from the institutional and mechanism reform is essential to the supply-side reform. Without new supply of institutions, the supply of factors and products makes no sense. Supply of institutions is a decisive factor to determine what size and structure will result from input of production factors. On the one hand, institutional arrangement must ensure the key role of market in allocation of resources so as to strike a balance between the consumers' pursuit of utility maximization and the

current situation in China, where a technical innovation support mechanism has been preliminarily formed and there are abundant technical factors, and where the currently existing problem is how to promote free mobility and optimal combination of all factors to generate effective supply by means of institutional innovation.

Y =f (L, K, R...) +TFP				
Supply of factors	Capital	Labor force Human resources	(Land) resources	Science & technology
Supply of products	Efficient products		Quality products	
Supply of institutions	Financial system reform Fiscal system reform	Household, social insurance, education, health, employment	Land reform Resource property	Sci-tech systems Innovation and entrepreneurship

Figure 2. Growth Function and Three Levels of Supply.

producers' pursuit of profit maximization; on the other hand, it must ensure the government's roles in promoting the supply–demand equilibrium toward a higher level by directing allocation of factors in production of products and services while addressing the "market failure" problem through reform and policy coordination in such fields as innovation, labor, finance, resource property, land utilization, and education system. Three levels of supply are illustrated in Figure 2.

3. *Contents of the supply-side structural reform*

There are three key words that may help you understand the contents of the supply-side structural reform: "supply side", "structural", and "reform". "Supply side" means supply of factors, products, and institutions as mentioned in the foregoing paragraph to change the macroscopic production functions in China; "structural" means seeking solutions to numerous structural problems that influence the macroscopic production functions; and "reform" means improving supply of institutions by institutional mechanism reform to boost transformation of the old kinetic energy under the new normal.

Therefore, the supply-side structural reform is defined in this paper as "promoting reform of structural problems in economic development on the supply side, the purpose of which is to improve the quality of demand-oriented supply of products, increase effective supply of institutions based on reform and innovation, and through flexible allocation of resources based on market need, eventually create a new economic growth system that will realize efficient and dynamic connection of supply and demand, emancipate the productive forces, maintain a medium and high rate of economic growth and push the industrial development toward medium- and high-end level."

III. International Comparison of China's Supply-Side Structural Reform

1. *Western supply-side economists' advocacy and the structural reform's practice and implications*

In the 1970s, under the influences of the changing international environment and China's structural problems in economic development, economic stagflation occurred in major developed economies and gave rise to many problems, including heavier fiscal burden, unbalanced international payments, declining productivity, slackening structural adjustment, and inadequate Keynesian demand management. After the supply-side economists' advocacy prevailed for some time, the structural reform policy[2] was implemented in the United States (represented by Reaganomics), in the United Kingdom (represented by Thatcherism), and later in other European and American countries.[3]

---

[2]The International Monetary Fund (IMF) treated the structural reform as "those policy measures taken to reduce obstacles of efficient allocation of resources and promote long-term economic growth".

[3]Countries other than the UK and US had exercised the structural reform for more than two decades, including Helmut Kohl's administration in 1982 and Schroder's administration in 2005 in Germany. In the 1980–1990s, Japan's fiscal and financial system reform and Koizumi's "structural reform without sacred zone" were identified as structural reforms.

(1) *Western supply-side economists' advocacy and the structural reform practice*

In the early 1980s, the US Reagan administration pursued the supply-side economists' advocacy to propose the "economic recovery plan" to reduce tax rate, reduce government regulation, and tighten the money supply. At the end of the 1970s, the Thatcher cabinet carried out a series of policies including tightening the money supply, privatizing the SOEs, cutting tax, and reducing government intervention in order to address economic stagflation.

Reducing tax rate to stimulate investment from enterprises: In the United States, after taking office, Reagan reduced the highest marginal rate of personal income tax from 70% to 28%, reduced enterprise income tax from 46% to 33%, and provided preferential tax for investment of enterprises, allowing accelerated depreciation of enterprises. In 1981, he reduced the capital gains tax rate from 28% to 20%, and in 1982, reduced the highest tax rate of non-work incomes, including personal interest and bonus, from 70% to 50%. Reduction of tax rates had significantly increased capital returns and enhanced the residents' and enterprises' willingness to make investment. In the United Kingdom, during Thatcher's ruling period, she reduced the marginal tax rate of high-income earners from 80% to 50% and that of the low-income earners from 33% to 30%.

Tightening the money supply to curb inflation: In the United States, during Reagan's reign, then Federal Reserve Chairman Paul Volcker treated anti-inflation as the main target of monetary policy, so he lifted the interest rate and lowered the money supply to the extent that the federal fund rate soared up to 20%. Though the inflation rate hit a new high of 15% in 1980, the continuous deflation policy eventually changed the public expectation: the inflation rate was controlled below 4% in 1984. In the United Kingdom, after Prime Minister Thatcher took office, her means to curb inflation included increase of interest rate and curtailment of bank facility. As a result, the UK's benchmark interest rate went up to 17% for a time; the unemployment rate rose sharply from 5% up to 10% in the 1980s, but the inflation level fell dramatically from 21% to under 5%.

Loosening government's control to stimulate enterprises' competitiveness: Before and after Reagan took office, the US government reduced its market intervention in industrial development first by loosening government regulation in industries such as aviation, transportation, railways, and natural gas and then by easing market access for service industries such as cable TV, bank, and telecommunication. The government's deregulation had resulted in the significant increase of enterprise mergers and acquisitions, the steadily rising rate of capacity utilization, and the constantly growing efficiency of enterprise operation. While loosening government control and regulation, the Thatcher cabinet carried out large-scale privatization reform of state-owned companies engaging in pharmaceuticals, petroleum, railways, aviation, and transportation, and promoted companies in the state-owned sector to be listed on the stock exchange, including industries such as telephone, natural gas, water supply, and electric power.

Reducing enterprises' cost to enhance competitiveness: In addition to loosening control of enterprises, the UK government canceled government control on foreign exchange, abolished government control of prices, income, and dividend on shares, and reduced the transaction cost for entity enterprises' access to market and participation in competition. Weakening the power and revoking the statutory privilege of the labor union by Thatcher's administration had contributed much to reducing enterprises' labor cost and frictional cost in addressing disputes with the labor union and further to building a competitive and flexible labor market.

(2) *Western supply-side economists' advocacy and results of the supply-side structural reform*

On the one hand, the supply-side advocacy had achieved positive results in the structural reform. In a short time, such advocacy helped the US find a way out of the morass of stagflation. Since 1983, the US economy maintained a high growth rate of around 4% for 8 consecutive years, which even reached up to 7.3% in 1984, with a dramatic decline in periodical volatility of macroeconomic indicators such as real GDP, industrial production, employment growth, and unemployment rate. In the UK, Thatcher's series of policies curbed the trend of hyperinflation, solved the unprofitability of public enterprises, and maintained steady growth of the British economy. Since 1982, British GDP reversed the 2-year downtrend and witnessed a continuous growth for 9 years at a run; moreover, the British economy picked up faster than other countries in the Eurozone, with the main macroeconomic indicators getting less volatile. Despite a higher short-term unemployment rate, the surplus labor force was absorbed by the improved efficiency of all business sectors, so the unemployment rate dropped by a hefty amount after it peaked in the middle 1980s. The British financial situation took a turn for the better rather than for the worse soon after the tax reduction measures were taken. The structural reform in many sectors laid a solid foundation for the economic prosperity of the UK and the USA for a number of years afterward. When the economic expectations stabilized, the government's intervention was lessened and the private sectors were allowed to make better plans for their investment and consumption activities; as a result, the endogenous impetus for economic growth became much stronger.

On the other hand, these reforms led to some negative effects. The failure of Reagan's administration and his successor to reduce government expenditure while cutting tax had resulted in an escalating amount of government debt and the rising rate of deficit. The Federal Reserve's deficit rate remained merely 2.64% in 1980 but rose to 5.87% in 1983. In addition, the tax reduction policy contributed much to the income distribution gap. In the UK, Thatcher's cabinet encountered the fact that the state-owned monopoly was substituted for private monopoly in the process of privatization and breakup of monopolies. Particularly in the public sectors of water, electricity, telecommunication, and transportation, the privatized companies' high profit embezzled consumers' benefits, and the improvement of economic efficiency gave less consideration to social equity. The poll tax policy issued by Thatcher's cabinet in 1989, for instance, was boycotted by low-income groups because it overlooked the concrete economic conditions of each family and imposed an identical amount of tax on all people. It is worth mentioning that the US and UK government's deregulation led to the fact that the virtual economy, including finance, was overdeveloped and became disconnected from the real economy, which served as a delayed action bomb to trigger the global financial crisis.

(3) *Western supply-side economists' advocacy and revelation of the structural reform*

The US and UK governments' adoption of the supply-side economic policy for structural reform seemed pragmatic in addressing the current problems at that time, including the following issues:

- The first was an appropriate supply of institutions that are fundamental to the supply policy. The macro-policy's effectiveness needs to be guaranteed by an institutional foundation that is relatively stable and able to vitalize the enterprises and market. In many countries in Latin America, for instance, the unstable institutional foundation failed to motivate the vitality of enterprises and market, despite their reference to the western supply-side economists' policy views. Therefore, one country may take specific policies in a specific period, depending on its national conditions and developing stage.
- The second was an effective market mechanism that premises what roles a policy will play. Supply-side economists highlighted vitalizing enterprises and enlarging supply. When the market mechanism matured, enlarging supply could be effectively connected to demand because of less administrative intervention in supply–demand information; on the contrary, due to immature market mechanism in some Latin American countries, enlarging supply through administrative interventions usually disconnected supply from demand and resulted in invalid and excess capacity, thus weakening effectiveness of the supply policy.
- The third was the problem targeted by the supply policy. In both the USA and the UK, the supply-side economists' advocacy adopted to address the long-term "stagflation" problem had achieved positive results. In the United States, for instance, the tax reduction policy reversed the marginal effect of tax reduction on revenue enhancement, thus resulting in the increase of government deficit and the impairment of social equity.
- The fourth was the supply policy's adaptation to the changing economic situation. A policy effective in a period may become invalid and even lead to negative effect after the economic situation has changed. In the United States, for instance, the supply-side economists' advocacy adopted in the 1980s found it hard to play positive roles

during the global financial crisis in 2008, and was even seen as one of the causes of the crisis.

- The last one was the supply policy's coordination with other policies. In the United States, for instance, when the tax reduction policy was enacted, the government also implemented a tight monetary policy and loosened the financial constraints to curb inflation while stimulating economic growth, which had invigorated long-term technical innovation and business venturing.

2. *Characteristics of the supply-side structural reform in China*

While the current supply-side structural reform in China is identical conceptually to the structural reform advocated by the western supply-side economists, the former differs essentially from the latter in the theoretical basis, practical background, institutional environment, policy instrument, and dynamic mechanism.

(1) *Theoretical basis*

Based on the western classical economic theories, the western supply-side economic theory was the product of the western free economy theory in combination with the reality of the European and American economic development in a certain period. The supply-side economic policy emphasized the market's role in allocation of resources and proposed that long-term economic growth rely on the improved conditions on the supply side. Unfortunately, the supply-side economists failed to develop an independent and rigorous theory system, so their theory seemed more empirical, their monetary policy in practice referred primarily to the monetarist theory, their deregulation policy was based on the common sense of modern economics that "competition creates prosperity", and their tax reduction policy was derived mainly from the optimal tax rate analysis framework of the public finance; in particular, the deregulation policy, as well as critique on Keynesian Economics, reflected the neoliberal economics in the United States.[4]

[4] Since the 1980s, for instance, some Latin American countries had carried out radical reform of economic liberalization in light of the neoliberalism, but they were eventually beset with economic and social crises.

The supply-side structural reform of China is a major theoretical innovation based on Marxist theory of political economics through borrowing and absorbing essentials of other economic theories. First, the supply-side structural reform aims to improve the supply efficiency and quality and release potentialities of economic development, which is practical application of Marxist theory of political economics on the relationship between production and consumption, the use value of goods and services, and the value equilibrium relation. The reform has also borrowed and absorbed the idea of comprehensive judgment, namely, the economic growth sources of the economic growth theory. The current economic growth of China is under a transition from the previous scale growth mode that excessively depended on the increase of capital and labor to the present quality-benefit growth mode that depends on technical progress, management innovation, and efficient allocation of resources. Second, the current supply-side structural reform of China highlights optimization and adjustment of economic structure, which represents practical application and development of Marxist theory of political economics on the value structure relation, including the productive relation structure of provision of products or services, the industrial structure, and the product structure. The reform has also borrowed and absorbed theoretical essentials of the development economics on industrial structure, technological structure, and regional structure. Finally, the supply-side structural reform emphasizes the deepening of institutional mechanism reform, which represents application and development of Marxist theory of political economics on mutual adaptation and interaction between productive forces and relations. The reform has also borrowed some essentials of the institutional economics, namely, the institution itself is a productive force.

(2) *Practical background*

When the United States and the UK implemented the supply-side economic policy, they had effectuated industrialization and entered the high-income development stage, where the economic structure and market mechanism had matured. The short-term background for implementation of the supply-side economic policy was characterized by the stagnation of economic growth, the intensification of inflation, and the rise of unemployment rate, which needed to be solved through fiscal and monetary policy and structural reform. The long-term background featured predominance of Keynesian theory and excessive government interventions in market, which resulted in low economic efficiency and needed to be solved through reform and release of development vitality.

The supply-side structural reform of China took place at a specific stage after transformation of institutional mechanism, where the industrialization remained unfinished, the market mechanism remained immature, and the economic development had not yet entered the high-income stage. The short-term problems that need to be tackled include the slowdown of economic growth rate, the decline of enterprises' profit, the fall of industrial product price, the decline of fiscal revenue growth, and the escalation of potential risks, particularly the financial risk, which can be solved through market mechanism and government adjustment. For this purpose, the sensitivity and efficiency of supply in response to demand should be improved. Unlike economic stagnation in the United States and the UK at that time, China has been maintaining an economic growth rate of up to 6% in recent years, though it tends to fall, ranking at the top among the world's major economies. In addition, China's employment remains relatively stable. In 2015, the number of employed people exceeded 13 million, with the unemployment rate remaining at a low level; in 2016, the unemployment rate maintained at low level of around 5.0%.

(3) *Institutional environment*

Western supply-side economists advocated free market economy, arguing that government interventions should be minimized because they had destroyed the automatic adjustment mechanism of market economy and undermined the economic supply forces due to improper interventions. To address difficulty in economic development at that time, some countries including the US and the UK implemented the supply-side economic theory for the purpose of vitalizing economic development by stimulating investment and business operation while reducing inflation. As compared with improvement of economic efficiency, the supply-side economic theory paid less attention to safeguarding social equity as a result of denying the positive effects of public expenditure and social security system on economic development. In objection to drawbacks in Keynesian economic policy, the supply-side economic policy placed more emphasis on improvement of the resource allocation efficiency on the supply side than on reasonable factors of demand management.

In China, the supply-side structural reform comprises a series of policies and reform measures for China's modernization construction under the economic system framework of common development that combines the public ownership with other types of ownership. The reform is carried out on the principle of efficient market and government behaviors to strike a balance between efficiency and equity by giving play to the decisive roles of market and the government in allocation of resources, and to maintain a dynamic equilibrium between supply and demand by learning lessons from excessive government interventions and overdependence on large-scale demand-stimulating policies in previous years. The long-term objectives of the reform include the following: improving the quality of supply; promoting structural adjustment by means of reform; remedying distorted allocation of production factors; enlarging effective supply; enhancing the adaptability and flexibility of supply structure toward the changing demands; raising the total factor productivity; better meeting the needs of the masses; and facilitating healthy development of the economic society.

(4) *Policy instruments*

The western supply-side economic policy was designed to address the short-term macroeconomic supply–demand imbalance. As western countries had a more mature market system, their policy instruments based on the existing institutional arrangement laid particular stress on macro-policy adjustments, including fiscal and tax policy and monetary policy, which were supplemented by reform of economic and social mechanisms, such as reducing individual income tax and enterprise tax, cutting government budget, reducing social welfare spending, controlling monetary supply, loosening government regulation, promoting privatization, and weakening strengths of the labor union.

China's policy on supply-side structural reform covers a variety of sectors and has more profound effects. As China stays in an institutional transition period, the supply-side structural reform involves not only adjustment of macro-, medium-, and micro-polices but also long-, medium-, and near-term institutional mechanism reforms, which is a complete system composed of target tasks, policy adjustment, and institutional mechanism reform and represents an organic unity of institutional innovations.

(5) *Dynamic mechanism*

During implementation of the supply-side economic theory, the US and the UK had a mature economic structure and system that left little space for structural adjustment and reform, thereby making it difficult to unleash the potential of economic development because of the following: (1) it was unlikely to promote urbanization due to the small difference between urban and rural areas (in 1980, the urbanization rates of the UK and the US reached up to 78.5% and 73.7%, respectively); (2) it was unlikely to make adjustment of regional structure due to small interregional difference when the two countries saw sufficient liquidity of production factors across regions during industrialization; and (3) the market system was mature in both countries. As the cradleland of modern market economy, the US and the UK were two countries with mature market systems in all sectors, where all interest subjects stayed in a relatively balanced state.

In China, however, the current economic development remains at an upper-middle-income level, lagging far behind high-income countries, so there is huge scope for economic growth. At the present stage, the prominent contradictions facing China's economic growth involve imbalance, disharmony, and unsustainability, and many systems and mechanisms are under construction and adjustment. Therefore, structural optimization and innovative reform can unleash huge potential of economic development because of the following: (1) the enormous gap between urban and rural development, and (2) the numerous structural and institutional barriers impeding free mobility of production factors and optimization of resource allocation. For this reason, China is qualified to achieve sustainable economic growth in a long period by carrying out supply-side structural reform to eliminate barriers in allocation of resources and unleash structural potential.

In brief, China's supply-side structural reform is not based on the western supply-side economic theory; instead, it represents significant innovations in theory and policy in line with China's specific social context and development phase and will enrich these innovations during practice of China's socialist modernization.

IV. Four Relationships to Be Properly Handled in Promoting Supply-Side Structural Reform

To further promote the supply-side structural reform, China needs to properly deal with four relationships: between supply and demand, between long term and short term, between government and market, and between overseas market and domestic market.

1. *Relationship between supply and demand*

Supply and demand complement each other, where the latter is the target of and depends on the former. Both are mutually conditioned in a unity, and thus emphasis must be placed on both sides during implementation of the supply-side structural reform in order to realize policy targets. Currently, the supply scale suggests a mismatch between supply and demand due to excess aggregate supply in China, which is caused by the shortage of effective supply to meet personalized high-end demand and by the excess supply of mid- and low-end products. At the present stage, there exist such serious problems as excess supply of high-end products and mismatch between supply and demand because the low-end supply of traditional sectors cannot be digested and the effective demand in sectors of new energy and new materials has not yet been fully unleashed. As shown in Figure 3, when the demand curve D remains unchanged, if supply is enlarged by moving the supply curve S toward the lower right to S′ so that both curves intersect at E1, there will be a problem of oversupply (shaded area between S′ and S), where new capacity means "new surplus" when the demand remains unchanged. To reach a new equilibrium at a higher level, new demand needs to be enlarged at the same time, i.e. pushing the demand curve D toward the lower right to D′; a new equilibrium is reached when the new demand and new supply intersect at E′, where the

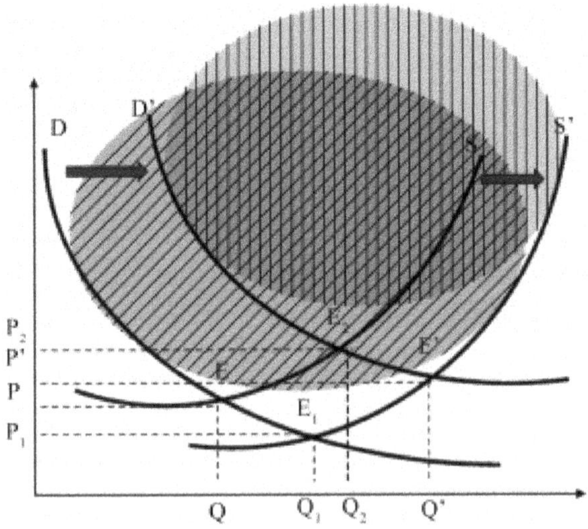

Figure 3. Relationship Between Supply and Demand.

new supply is absorbed by the new demand (the shaded area between D and S′ is narrowed down to the shaded area between D′ and S′).

It is thus concluded that the supply-side structural problem must be solved through structural adjustment on the demand side and that the demand-side structural problem must be solved through supply-side reform. Increasing the supply without the demand being taken into consideration will inevitably generate new overcapacity. In the new situation, therefore, the supply-side structural reform requires considering structural changes on the demand side, orderly coordination on both sides, active promotion of the supply-side structural reform, and constant improvement of the supply-side adaptation and flexibility to market demand.

2. *Relationship between long term and short term*

The short-term demand management and the long-term structural reform have their advantages and disadvantages. In practice, both should be combined to steady the supply–demand relationship and promote the equilibrium conversion of the supply–demand structure from a lower level to a higher level. The supply-side structural reform aims to correct the mismatch of supply–demand structure and the distorted allocation of production factors, to achieve optimal allocation of factors such as labor force, land, and capital through medium- and long-term innovation in technology, system, and management, to improve the supply–demand structure, and to unleash new economic growth potentials. However, the supply-side structural reform may have less effect on economic fluctuations within a short term; besides, measures to cut overcapacity, reduce inventory, and deleverage may intensify the economic pro-cycle contraction within a short time, though they are helpful to medium- and long-term structural adjustment. In comparison, the demand management aims to achieve a dynamic equilibrium between aggregate supply and aggregate demand through counter-cycle adjustment within a short term; nevertheless, the demand management can hardly promote medium- and long-term structural optimization.

Column: Differences between demand management and supply-side structural reform in promoting the supply–demand balance

The macroeconomic aggregate supply–aggregate demand (AS-AD) model is used here to analyze the relationship between long term and short term. Under the economic new normal, with the declining supply of production factors and the rising cost, the short-term aggregate supply curve (SAS1) will move to the upper left to SAS2; the equilibrium point of the intersecting aggregate supply curve and aggregate demand curve moves from E0 to E1, with the yield dropping from Y0 to Y1 and the price rising from P0 to P1 (indicating a possible stagflation). At this moment, there are two solutions to this problem. First, the demand management policy, such as expansive financial policy or monetary policy, is adopted to make the aggregate demand curve (AD1) move to the upper right to AD2 so as to offset the effect of the short-term supply curve's upper right movement. At the same time, the equilibrium point of the aggregate supply curve and the aggregate demand curve changes from E1 to E2; as compared with yield at E0, the yield at E2 comes back to the potential level of Y0, but the price rises from P1 to P2. This indicates that the demand management policy may prevent dramatic recession within a short term but it may give rise to inflation. Then, the supply-side structural reform is carried out to promote technical progress or optimization of production factor allocation and make the long-term supply curve (LAS1) move rightward to LAS2 (increasing potential yield), thus pushing short-term supply curve's rightward movement from SAS1 to SAS2, the equilibrium point of the intersecting aggregate supply curve and aggregate demand curve's movement from E1 to E2, the price declining from P1 to P2, and the yield increasing from Y1 to Y2. As compared with the demand management policy, the supply-side structural reform takes a longer time to strike a rebalance between aggregate supply and aggregate demand due to the price stickiness and the pressure of economic downtrend and long-term stumbling along the bottom (see Figure 4).

In the short term, the supply-side structural reform needs short-term demand management to create a favorable environment for reform and requires the economic growth to stabilize in a reasonable range. If the short-term demand management measures are not in place or too feeble leading to excess slowdown or continued downturn of economic growth, the supply-side structural reform will be deprived of the opportunity for reform; in case of excessive application of the short-term demand incentive measures leading to an excessively rapid or high rate of economic growth, the distortion of industrial structure will be intensified to the extent that it adds much difficulty to the supply-side structural reform. For these reasons, the short-term demand-side management needs to be moderate, namely, neither excessively stimulating nor excessively tightened.

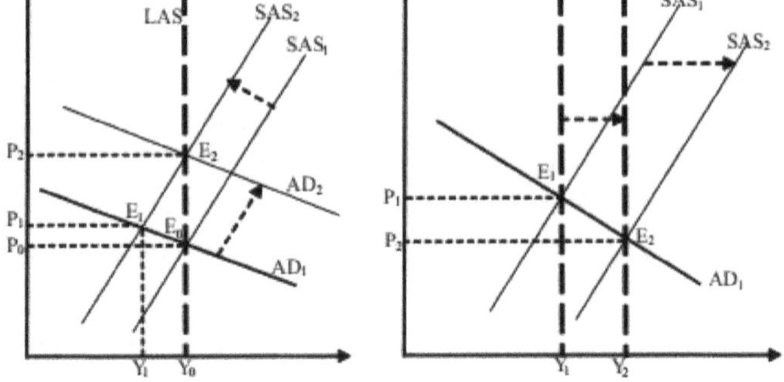

Figure 4. Column Diagram: Demand Management (left) and Supply-Side Adjustment (right) Promoting Rebalance Between Supply and Demand.

3. *Relationship between government and market*

As neither the government nor the market can be omnipotent, they need to play their respective roles. The supply-side structural reform does not mean to restart the planned economy, so the government's interventions need to be reduced. Generally speaking, the market seeks efficiency while the government pursues equity. The government's improper interventions in competitive sectors by utilizing public rights and public resources will definitely lead to distorted market and inequity on market. During the transition from planned economy to market economy over the years, some decision-makers intentionally or unintentionally magnified the consequences of market failure as excuses for government interventions and overregulation of market; as a result, improper use or misuse of administrative power, redundant administrative approvals, promotion of buyer, and monopsony as well as aggravating burdens on enterprises had adverse effect on allocation of factor resources and disturbed the market competition order.

On the contrary, the supply-side structural reform does not aim at extreme marketization due to unprompted or blind market adjustment that produces a great deal of asymmetry, monopoly, and negative externality. The bursting of two asset bubbles in the United States, the "middle-income trap" in Latin America, and economic recession in some emerging economies are enough to demonstrate that extreme marketization may weaken or even negate the government's positive roles in economic governance. In economic operation, therefore, we should be fully aware of the possible consequences of market failure, strengthen and improve the government's macroeconomic control, market supervision, public services, and social governance, effectively prevent systematic risks, prevent and dissolve negative effects of the cyclic economic fluctuations, maintain fair market competition order, and promote healthy economic development.

Take the government's provision of public services for society and imposition of taxes on producers and consumers for an example. In general, the government needs to collect a certain amount of taxes and dues from producers and consumers in order to maintain market order and ensure stable operation of economic society; nevertheless, if such collection goes beyond a reasonable range, it will impair the vitality of

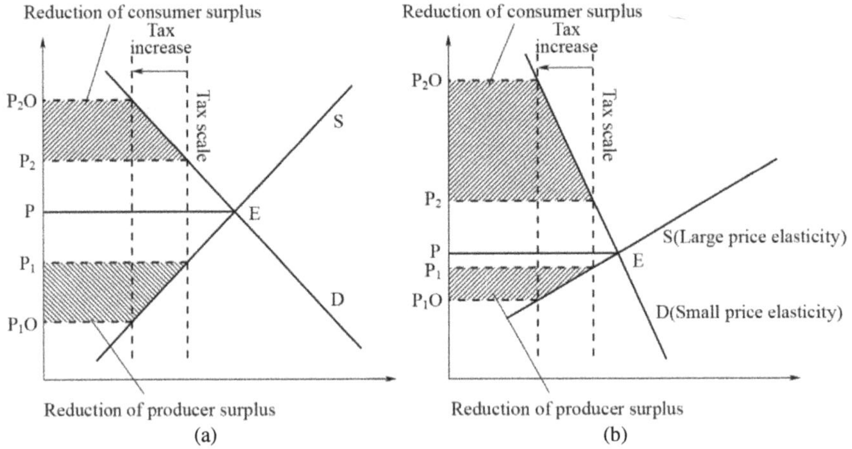

Figure 5. Influences of Government's Additional Taxes on Social Welfare.

economic development. According to Figure 5(a), if the government's collection of taxes stays within a reasonable range and the supply curve S and the consumption curve D share a same curve slope, the triangle section where the dotted line before tax collection and two curves (S and D) intersect will represent the taxes and dues paid by consumers and producers to the public services provider (government). However, if the government wants to intervene in market in addition to providing public services and the cost of such intervention can be borne by producers and consumers merely in the form of taxes and dues, the dotted line (representing taxes and dues) will move left and the shaded area as indicated in Figure 5(b) will represent additional cost borne by producers and consumers. As known to all, there is a cost for the government to collect and spend taxes and dues; therefore, if the government spends all additional taxes and dues in improving benefits of producers and consumers, then what the producers and consumers have lost is the cost for collection and spending of these taxes and dues. If the taxes and dues are used for impractical project construction, the increase of taxes and dues will do nothing but impair benefits of producers and consumers. In fact, as compared with developed economies, China has a large population base and remains at the late stage of industrialization, so the price elasticity of demand is smaller than that of supply as shown in Figure 5(b), and the increase of taxes and dues will cause more loss to consumers' benefits than to producers' benefits.[5] It is thus clear that the increased taxes and dues will have a "squeeze-out" effect on producers and consumers, whether or not they are used for benefits of producers and consumers. Particularly, if the slope of the demand curve D changes, the household consumption and even the social consumption will be inhibited. In the supply-side structural reform, therefore, cutting taxes and dues will help relieve burdens on enterprises and stimulate social consumption.

4. *Relationship between domestic market and overseas market*

The supply-side structural reform should depend on the reform and opening up policy. As an open economy, China has blended into the world economic system through globalization and liberalization of international trade. Next, China will renovate its traditional industries, foster emerging industries, and push all industries toward middle- and high-end levels, so the international markets are essential for China to obtain all necessary advanced capital, technology, and labor force and to meet new demands on overseas markets with new supply generated by new economic engines in the future. In addition, as a major trading nation in the world, if China wants to take part in global governance and in making economic and trade rules, it needs to carry out reform of some systems and mechanisms inadaptable to new changes on international markets and participate in international affairs under the direction of new concepts, new mechanisms, and new modes so as to raise its power of discourse and influence in allocating international resources and making rules for international investment and trade. Apparently, the supply-side structural reform must be carried out through "opening the door" to the outside world in order to achieve the abovementioned goals. If the reform is conducted by "closing the door", there will be serious excess of supply when supply exceeds demand or serious

---

[5] The indirect taxation system currently adopted in China is composed primarily of value-added tax and turnover tax and secondarily of income tax. Consumer surplus as shown in Figure 5(b) is reduced significantly, including tax collected from production and shifted to consumers.

shortage of supply when supply fails to meet demand. Consequently, the connectivity between domestic and overseas markets as well as resources on both markets is vital to deepening the supply-side structural reform.

V. Thoughts and Institutional Framework of Promoting the Supply-Side Structural Reform

There are two key points for the supply-side structural reform at present and in the future: to foster new drivers of economic growth when the traditional drivers are weakening, and to generate effective institutional supply as a new engine for economic growth through institutional mechanism reform.

1. *Fostering new drivers of economic growth*

During the transition of China's economic growth from high speed to medium-high speed in the future, attention should be paid to eliminating backward industries, transforming traditional industries, fostering new industries, and constantly expanding the space of consumer demand.

The transformation of traditional industries should avoid the "hollowing out" phenomenon when eliminating outdated and low-end capacity and take new opportunities generated by the new round of industrial technical revolution in the world to renovate traditional industries with new technology, new processes, and new management modes, and create intelligent, green, and high-end industries.

The development of emerging industries should focus on three points: first, six pillar industries, such as a new generation of information technology, new energy automobiles, biological technology, green and low-carbon technology, high-end equipment and new materials, and digital creativity; second, four strategic industries, such as space and ocean, information network, life science, and nuclear technology; and third, new superior products, including new aircrafts and spaceships, a new generation of work platforms and integrated observation systems of space and sky, quantum communication technology and the Internet of Things, synthetic biotechnology and regenerative medical technology, and a new generation of nuclear power equipment.

The concept of regional linkage development should also be used for transforming traditional industries and fostering emerging industries to make development resources converge at advantaged areas of economic growth and create the economic growth poles and zones. In China, for instance, there will be three north–south and two east–west economic growth zones, at the cross point of which there will be a number of growth poles.

The expansion of consumer demand requires reducing the portion taken by the governments at all levels from household residents, enlarging their portion in national revenue, cutting down public investment outlays in government expenditures irrelevant to potential productivity, and increasing direct spending on moderate- and low-income residents so as to enhance residents' actual consumption capacity and provide consumer support for transformation of traditional industries and growth of emerging industries.

2. *Creating new engines for economic growth through the institutional mechanism reform*

The institutional mechanism reform aims to foster new drivers for economic growth, properly handle four major relationships (short term and long term, supply and demand, government and market, and domestic market and overseas market), break restrictions in the flow and optimized allocation of factor resources in key sectors and steps, and remove institutional barriers in structural transformation and industrial upgrading. Specifically, the reform is designed to do the following: (1) accelerate the reform of administrative system, transform government functions, delegate power to authorities at lower levels and call off items subject to administrative approval, and loosen administrative interventions in market; (2) accelerate the regulatory system reform of state-owned assets and enterprises, deepen the reform of monopolized industries, loosen government control, break market monopoly, relax market access of private enterprises, and expand space for private capital investment; (3) accelerate the reform of innovation systems, promote market-oriented reform of factors such as talents, technology, and technical innovation, improve incentive system for personnel training and innovation, and arouse the vitality of social innovation and entrepreneurs; (4) deepen the reform of the financial system to ensure the fiscal policy's positive roles in "cutting overcapacity, reducing excess inventory, deleveraging, lowering costs and strengthening areas of weakness" and the financial policy's levering roles in conversion and continuity of the old and new economic growth drivers; and (5) further improve basic systems, including property rights production system, social security system, social honesty system, and management system for resources and environment protection, to provide fundamental institutional support for middle- and high-speed economic growth (see Figure 6). In addition, the supply-side structural reform will also be promoted by opening the market wider to the outside world.

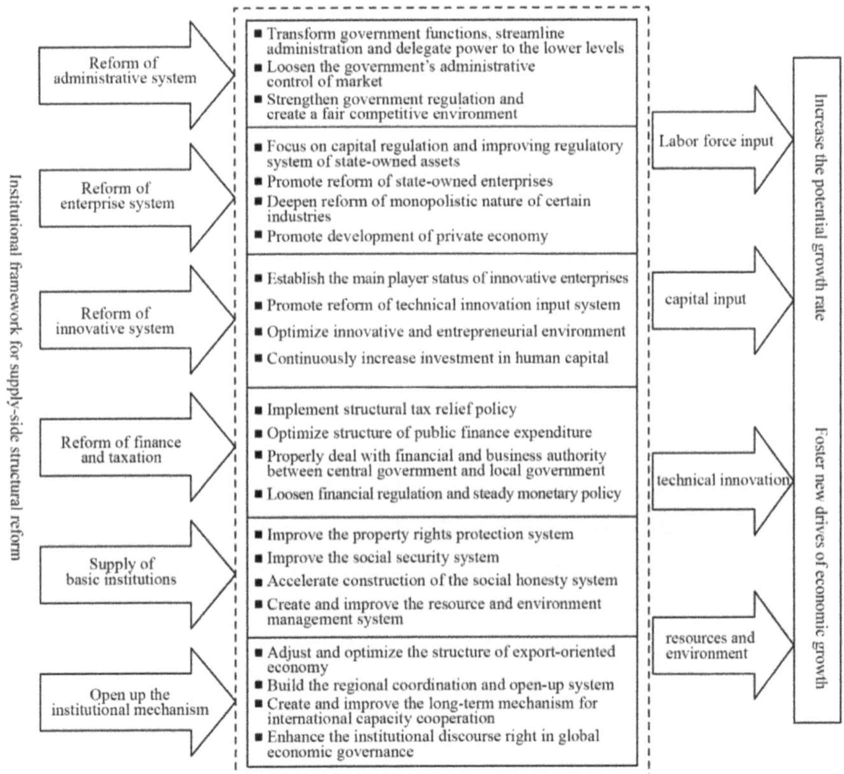

Figure 6. Institutional Framework for Supply-Side Structural Reform.

3 *Improving supporting measures for the supply-side structural reform*

(1) *Accelerating administrative system reform*

Promoting the supply-side structural reform requires the government to streamline administration and delegate power to the levels, reduce interventions in market, deepen administrative system reform, increase valid supply of institutions, and provide more targeted and efficient public products and services: further transform government functions, continuously streamline administration and delegate power to the levels, optimize public services, improves government service efficiency, and stimulate vitality of market and creativity of the society; accelerate the reform of approval system, strictly regulate the approval behaviors, and prohibit disguised approval in the name of intermediary service and "filing"; speed up the reform of registration system, make use of the national uniform social credit code system, and simplify the registration process; improve government power list, market access negative list and responsibility list system, define administrative function boundary, eliminate gray area of authority, and eliminate and decentralize administrative approval management matters beyond the listed scope.

Strengthen functions and public service functions of the government: shift administrative resources from pre-approval to in-service and post-execution supervision, speed up construction of the modern market regulation system where rules are complete and clear, the decision-making mechanism is transparent, and the supervision and responsibility are in good place; improve the social management functions and speed up formation of the social management mechanism that features fundamental governance, dynamic management, and emergency disposal; improve public service function, perfect arrangement of people's livelihood system, increase financial investment, and construct the basic public service system that covers urban–rural areas, is fair and reasonable, and improves the inclusive standards; expand the scope of public services purchased by the government, perfect the system design for government to purchase public services, and refine specific procedures for bidding, enquiry, and commissioning.

Innovate inter-sector and regional coordination mechanism: formulate the road map for major reform issues by the central and local governments and functional departments, and establish the joint conference system, coordination system, mechanism supervision and accountability system, and the positive incentive mechanism for personnel so as to promote inter-sector and cross-region comprehensive reform; seriously investigate and punish the behavior of substituting short-term emergency measures for established reform routes, and prevent against fragmentation of reform.

Innovate the performance appraisal evaluation mechanism: strengthen participation of third parties, form a scientific and professional reform performance appraisal institution based on People's Congress and the Chinese People's Political Consultative Conference (CPPCC) at all levels, establish a comprehensive and accurate reform performance evaluation mechanism, and promote scientific and comprehensive evaluation of reform performance; speed up the reform of the cadre's political performance appraisal system, develop scientific evaluation index system for effective implementation of the reform responsibilities, and appropriately increase the weight of the people's assessment in the cadre assessment mechanism as an important reference basis for promotion and removal of cadres; gradually establish working mechanisms such as conflict of interest prevention, democratic supervision, error correction and fault tolerance, and provide institutional space for cadres at all levels to make errors during the reform.

(2) *Deepening the reform of state-owned enterprises and monopolistic industries*

State-owned enterprises occupy a large amount of economic resources and have formed an obvious buyer and seller monopoly, which increases the cost of buyers and sellers. Therefore, deepening the reform of the state-owned enterprises, reducing or releasing the monopolistic industries will be the key task for the supply-side structural reform and will accelerate implementation of the new round of reform of the state-owned enterprises: strengthen state-owned assets supervision, reform state-owned capital authorization and management system, set up state-owned capital investment operation companies, improve the market competitiveness of state-owned enterprises with capital regulation, and improve the efficiency of state-owned capital operation; promote centralized and unified supervision of state-owned assets, incorporate the state-owned capital of enterprises and institutions into the supervision system, and allow qualified companies to become the state-owned capital investment and operation companies; promote enterprise merger and reorganization and mixed ownership economic development, regulate and perfect modern enterprise system, improve state-owned capital allocation and operation efficiency, and enhance the vitality and competitiveness of state-owned enterprises.

Improve internal governance mechanism of state-owned enterprises and accelerate "de-administration": deepen the management system reform of state-owned enterprise leaders, gradually cancel the administrative rank and administrative treatment of state-owned enterprises and their business managers, and establish a new mechanism of direct selection, appraisal and management of the Board of Directors; normalize the responsibility scope of the shareholders' meeting, board of directors, board of supervisors, and business management according to the modern enterprise system; make use of the state-owned enterprise executive contract system, annual salary system, tenure system, and market-oriented selection to implement the professional management system of state-owned enterprises, and create a professional manager team of state-owned enterprises to meet the requirements of modern enterprises through "marketization" and "de-administration"; construct the professional manager market management system, and create a unified, open, competitive, orderly, and professional manager market; promote market-oriented reform of the human resources of state-owned enterprises, and improve flexible internal manager system of the state-owned enterprises; implement market-oriented selection of managers and employees of state-owned enterprise, improve incentive and restraint mechanism, and rationally determine the salary level and job treatment of state-owned enterprises and workers.

Accelerate strategic adjustment of the state-owned economic layout and accelerate optimization of state-owned economic structure: increase state-owned capital investment in the important industries of national economic lifelines and key areas to ensure realization of national strategic goals and give full play to the leading role of industry; withdraw state-owned capital from a general competitive area or competitive link to ensure expanding broader space for private capital investment; accelerate reform of the state-owned enterprises, improve quality and efficiency, actively dispose of the zombie enterprises, and effectively solve the problem of surplus capacity and the backward production capacity of the state-owned enterprises.

Unleash restrictions on private enterprises in finance, telecommunication, energy, transportation, education, culture, health, and other sectors, and widen the development fields for private investment: identify the natural monopoly and monopolistic business of the traditional monopolistic industries, gradually release business links and businesses, eliminate tangible and intangible barriers, and actively introduce private capital; accelerate the pilot reform of mixed ownership of local state-owned enterprises engaging in electricity, telecommunications, civil aviation, railways, petrochemicals, energy resources, tap water, gas, heat supply, and urban infrastructure, and attract private capital into these sectors; further relax controls in finance, telecommunications, cultural media, education, and medical services, and encourage the development of services that are synchronized with consumption upgrading so as to form new economic growth points as soon as possible.

(3) *Optimizing the environment of innovative mechanism*

Innovation is a new developmental idea for the supply-side structural reform. In view of the outstanding problems in China's innovation system, we should mobilize all kinds of resources and all parties' initiatives, increase innovation input, and improve weak points: Further strengthen the status and leading role of enterprises in innovation, encourage enterprises to carry out basic, key, and frontier innovation research, improve involvement of enterprises in decision-making of national science and technology plans, application-oriented major scientific and technological special programs, establish the demand-oriented and enterprise-led technical breakthrough system in key areas of social procurement, universities and scientific research institutions, and development services; strengthen the support for key demonstration projects such as industrial infrastructure and intelligent manufacturing, green manufacturing, service-oriented manufacturing, and their industrialization.

Promote the integration and development of universities, promote the comprehensive participation of institutions of higher learning and vocational colleges in the construction of a national innovation system, and provide support for a group of universities and colleges to form interdisciplinary and interdisciplinary scientific research teams: speed up construction of the industrial innovation centers and networks for enterprises, universities and colleges, civil and military organizations to collaborate and share results, vigorously develop new research and development institutions, and promote collaborative innovation among different regions and industries; set up a number of high-level national labs to enhance technical innovation capability in national strategic fields so as to meet the strategic needs of China and pursue international sci-tech frontiers.

Optimize the development environment of private economy, give them full market freedom and fair competition space, stimulate innovation activity, improve innovation ability, and speed up innovation and development of private enterprises: improve the innovation and entrepreneurship support policies, set up the sharing mechanism of innovative results and benefits, and release the innovative potential of all kinds of talents; optimize the market competition environment, and ensure equal protection of all kinds of enterprise rights and interests and legitimate property rights; respect and strictly protect intellectual property rights, implement strict intellectual property protection system, perfect an intellectual property ownership system that is conducive to stimulating innovation, establish and improve intellectual property operation trade and service platforms.

Cultivate and protect the entrepreneurial spirits, improve the spirit of artisans, respect knowledge and talents, perfect the market-based talent resource allocation mechanism, and increase the motivation of innovative talents with high quality: improve the incentive mechanism of scientific and technological innovation, implement transformation of scientific and technological achievements, fully decentralize the right to dispose, use, and earn income from innovation achievements, raise the ratio of the scientific research personnel in sharing benefits from transformation of technical achievements, and support the part-time and off-duty transformation of scientific and technological achievements of scientific research personnel.

Continuously increase all kinds of education training and human capital investment at all levels, and accelerate cultivation of practical and innovative talents: further consolidate the basic education, higher education, vocational education, and innovation education, cultivate a large number of scientific and technologically innovative personnel to meet the need of talents in construction of open and innovative systems; promote the reform of the educational system so as to improve the quality of population and promote the transformation of educational system to practical education system; promote education to open wider to the outside world, encourage the introduction of international high-quality educational resources, liberalize social capital in running schools, increase the supply of high-quality educational resources, and accelerate the construction of diversified and efficient education investment and supply patterns.

(4) *Deepening the reform of fiscal and taxation system*

Promote the supply-side structural reform, further optimize the structure of financial fund expenditure, give full play to the function of financial resources to improve weak points, and invest more financial funds into people's livelihood security and basic public service: Increase investment in transportation, energy resources, municipal infrastructure, public service facilities, livelihood facilities, and ecological and environmental protection facilities; increase the support of inclusive tax policies for innovation and improve the total factor productivity; speed up the fiscal and taxation policies that promote the upgrading of traditional industries, strategic emerging industries, and the development of service industries.

Further rationalize the relationship between the central and local financial responsibilities, moderately increase responsibilities and reduce financial authority of the central government, moderately reduce responsibilities and increase financial authority of local government, optimize taxation structure of local government, get rid of land dependence and stimulate enthusiasm of the local government: establish clear and mutually exclusive transfer payment frameworks, redefine and divide the current financial transfer payments other than general transfer payments; adjust and improve the transfer payment system to equalize basic public services; promote the overall planning of compulsory education, basic medical care, and basic old-age pension, eliminate barriers on human resources among regions and sectors, and promote the unified market construction of the labor force in the whole country; deepen the medical system reform, implement the national medical insurance network as soon as possible, and integrate the urban and rural residents into the national unified medical security system.

Implement structural tax relief and optimize the tax structure: reform the personal income tax system, establish and improve the compensation for human capital investment and the effective incentive mechanism, and promote the quality of rational utilization of human resources; perfect the tax preferential policies supporting the enterprise innovation, consider appropriate reduction of the value-added tax rate of enterprises and the tax rate of the enterprise income tax, integrate the stage of enterprise and product innovation, such as pre-tax deduction, tax relief, and reduction of tax rate, and ensure that the tax policy supports the whole process of innovation activities through preferential tax methods; improve the land use tax policy, perfect the ecological tax system, comprehensively advance the resource tax reform, gradually expand the tax range of the resource tax, pay the independent environmental tax in a timely manner, and increase the types of taxes.

Actively promote the reform of the financial system and increase the effective supply of financial products and services: actively promote the supply-side reform of the financial industry, enrich the financial institution system, establish different sizes, various modes, and diversified business institutions, develop medium-, small-, and micro-sized financial organizations, and solve the financing problems of medium-, small-, and micro-sized enterprises; expand private capital into the banking sector, actively encourage the development of medium-, small-, and micro-sized financial institutions; expand pilot range of private banks and gradually reduce and cancel access thresholds for financial institutions such as banks; standardize the development of Internet finance and promote comprehensive operation of financial institutions; promote development of private finance, regulate the micro-loan and the financing guarantee institution, and improve the management level and the quality of service of the financial institutions.

Improve the multilevel capital market system and vigorously develop direct financing: accelerate improvement of multilevel capital market, gradually establish and perfect the transition mechanism, and quit mechanism among the main board market, small and medium market, growth enterprise market, and the NEEQ market; give full play to active roles of all kinds of venture capital, improve the economic efficiency of financial capital service entity, support the economic transformation ability, boost enterprises to improve the innovation ability, accelerate the transformation and upgrade process, improve the debt structure, and increase the share of equity capital; promote enterprises, especially traditional enterprises and excess capacity industries to gradually reduce leverage, financing costs, and financial risk pressures in a controlled manner and pace; expand the scope and scale of foreign capital convertibility; establish a more convenient, open mechanism for cross-border capital flow; improve the RMB exchange rate forming mechanism, promote RMB internationalization, and raise RMB's international status; strengthen comprehensive financial supervision, prevent and reduce regional and systemic financial risks; define goals of the monetary policy and establish a relatively independent monetary policy system; accelerate the market-oriented reform of RMB exchange rate and formation mechanism of benchmark interest rate.

(5) *Improving the basic public service system*

The effective property rights protection system is an important prerequisite for giving full play to the function of property right incentive, restriction, and resource allocation: perfect the property rights protection system; accelerate improvement of the property rights protection system to protect all kinds of property rights according to law; improve the administration system of property right protection, speed up the transformation of government functions, enforce the administration according to law, strengthen property rights protection, and prevent public right infringement of private rights; improve the legal system of property rights protection, perfect the legal system of equal protection of all kinds of property rights, ensure the judicial authority and the integrity of the judiciary, strengthen the top-level design and coordination, adhere to the principle of equity, efficiency, equality, and balance, and accelerate construction of the institutional mechanism of property rights protection in key areas such as private property right, state-owned property right, collective property right, and intellectual property rights; pay considerable attention to protection of the private property rights and the property rights of entrepreneurs in accordance with law so as to stimulate entrepreneurship and innovation.

Social security is the stabilizer of social operation and the accelerator of social civilization progress: perfect the social security system; accelerate establishment of a more equitable and more sustainable social security system, strengthen the national overall planning of basic pension insurance and medical insurance, and gradually realize the national unified social security standards and social security system; speed up the implementation of the full coverage plan and basically realize the full coverage of statutory people; stick to the actuarial balance, improve the fund-raising mechanism, and make reasonable division of responsibilities of the government, the enterprise, and the individuals; moderately reduce the social insurance rate and improve the social security system; perfect the old-age insurance system, and appropriate some state-owned capital to enrich the social security fund; expand the investment channel of the social insurance fund, strengthen risk management, and improve the return on investment; fully implement the insurance system for urban and rural residents, reform the way of medical insurance payment, give full play to the medical insurance control, prevent urban and rural residents from being poor due to illness and returning to poor due to illness; solve the problem of medical reimbursement in different places, realize the direct settlement system of medical expenses in different provinces, and promote the free flow of people across the provinces.

The market economy is the credit economy, and the sustainable development of economy requires a fair, transparent, and stable social environment: accelerate construction of the social honesty system; speed up establishment of a nationwide unified social credit system platform, and strengthen the collection, collation, and application of credit information; establish an incentive mechanism for the trustworthy people, increase recognition and publicity of the trustworthy behaviors, and commend enterprises in good faith and the exemplary individuals; establish and perfect the joint disciplinary mechanism of dishonest people, give full play to the comprehensive regulatory effectiveness in the fields of administration, justice, finance, society, and so on, establish cross-sectional linkage response and dishonesty restraint mechanism, limit or ban the illegal dishonest people according to law, and impose punishment on dishonest people in all aspects; promote the formation of social constraints and corrections, improve the information recording and disclosure system of the dishonest people, and impose limitations on these people in market activities; promote the integrity culture and integrity spirit, perfect the supervision mechanism of public opinion, establish the reward and report system for dishonest people, implement the reward of the whistle-blowers, and protect the legitimate rights and interests of the whistle-blowers; develop various credit service institutions; establish the multilevel and all-round credit service system where the public credit service institutions and the social credit service institutions as well as the credit information infrastructure services and value-added services complement each other.

The resource and environment management system plays an important role in optimizing resource allocation and promoting the supply-side structural reform: improve the resources and environment management system; clarify the environmental property right, establish the market trading mechanism, let the market play its decisive role in the allocation of resources, and realize the optimal allocation of eco-environment resources through property rights transaction; make the ecological environment protection play its roles in cutting overcapacity and overstock, deleveraging, and in improving weak points; improve environmental access threshold and promote industrial structure adjustment and optimization; improve the implementation mechanism of the resource environment legislation and regulations, implement more stringent use of resource environment, and protect the red line system so as to ensure that economic growth is not at the expense of excessive resource consumption and environmental pollution; speed up the establishment of property right system of natural resources assets, determine the subjects of property right, and innovate earning form of property rights; protect the owner's rights and interests of natural resource assets and share the income of natural resource assets fairly; improve the system of resource tax and environmental protection, and truly realize "who pollutes, who pays, and who manages, who benefits"; increase resource conservation, environment-friendly technology, and promotion of products, support the establishment of green low carbon cycle development industry system, and promote green development and construction of "beautiful China".

Chapter 2

Fiscal Taxation System and Policy Framework Under Promotion of Supply-Side Structural Reform

Guo Chunli and Liu Fang

Academy of Macroeconomic Research

Abstract

The current fiscal and taxation system affects the workforce, capital, land, optimal allocation, and technological innovation of energy and mineral resources. Moreover, the indirect tax structure and the misallocation of financial funds are not conducive to the optimization of the industrial structure; the weak tax regulation function is not conducive to the expansion of consumer demand; and the lagging reforms in the division of power, expenditure responsibility, and financial power are not conducive to the smooth progress of the reform in the fields related to land and household registration. In order to promote the structural reform of supply side, we should speed up the perfection of the preferential tax policy to encourage the improvement of human capital, optimize the investment direction and mode of financial capital, perfect the land use tax and fee policy, perfect the ecological tax system, increase the support of the inclusive fiscal and taxation policies for innovation, and strive to improve the total factor productivity. We also need to accelerate the perfection of fiscal and taxation policies that promote the optimization and upgrading of traditional industries and the development of strategic emerging industries and services, expand the consumption capacity of urban and rural residents and promote the upgrading of consumption, and promote the efficient combination of supply and demand. We will further straighten out the relationship between central and local financial powers and administrative powers and establish a system that is compatible with the central and local powers and responsibilities for expenditure, so as to create conditions for the smooth advancement of reforms in such areas as land and household registration, which are closely related to the factors of production.

I. Introduction

The supply-side structural reform aims to promote structural adjustment, rectify the distortion of factor allocation, expand effective supply, improve the adaptability and flexibility of supply structure to the changing demand, and improve total factor productivity while moderately enlarging total demand. Compared with the past period when China mainly emphasized demand management, the supply-side structural reform emphasizes both supply and demand. At the same time, we should strengthen the supply-side structural reform to see improvements in the supply structure as the main outcome, realize the low-level balance between supply and demand, and strike a high-level balance between supply and demand. The ultimate goal is to promote the long-term sustainable and stable development of the economy.

The fiscal and taxation system can influence the investment of enterprises from the demand side, residents' consumption, and import and export structure. It can also influence innovation behavior, industrial structure, capital accumulation, and total factor productivity from the supply side. Furthermore, the system has much to do with the reform of land, household register, and social security, which are closely related to the allocation of production factors. Thus, it is closely related to the supply-side structural reform. In supporting the supply-side structural reform, the finance and taxation system has a unique advantage. We should give full play to the basic function of the fiscal and taxation system and to the related policies, in the process of deepening the supply-side structural reform. Scientific and perfect fiscal and taxation systems and policies are important guarantees to improve the allocation efficiency and total factor productivity of labor, capital, and land; to promote the innovation of product supply and upgrading of industrial structure; to promote the expansion of consumption demand and upgrading of consumption structure of urban and rural residents; and to promote the smooth advancement of the reform of land, household registration, and social security systems. In the aspect of optimizing the allocation of factor resources, the quality of human resources can be improved and utilized reasonably by exerting the function of tax adjustment and distribution and perfecting the tax policy to encourage improvement of human capital. By optimizing the investment direction of financial funds, more financial funds will be invested in the fields of emerging industries and public services as improving the way of government investment can further stimulate social investment and guide the optimal allocation of social funds. By improving the land use tax and fee policy, we should guide the efficient allocation of land resources and increase the support of inclusive fiscal and taxation policies, such as increasing the efficiency of allocation of scientific and technological resources, increasing the support of fiscal funds for enterprise innovation, expanding the scope of support and perfecting the support methods, and forming tax policies covering the whole process of innovation activities. We can also encourage product and technological innovations and further improve total production factors by constructing and perfecting the ecological tax system to utilize resources efficiently and protect the ecological environment. In terms of optimizing the industrial structure, we will optimize the taxation system and further improve the taxation policies that promote the development of strategic emerging industries, service industries, and the transformation and upgrading of traditional industries; improve the production and operating environment of enterprises; influence their investment decision-making and guide their investment behavior; promote enterprises to strengthen technological innovation; improve their product structure; and realize the upgrading of their industrial structure. In terms of increasing the capacity of the population to consume and promoting the upgrading of consumption, we will give full play to the fiscal and taxation system and policies in adjusting the distribution of income; improve the consumption ability of urban and rural residents; guide them to change to an intelligent, green, healthy, and safe direction; expedite the release of consumption potential; and form a virtuous circle of creating new demand with new supply that stimulates new consumption and pushes new consumption into new industry (business form). In terms of institutional supply, we will make reasonable division of the central and local powers and responsibilities for expenditure, improve the local tax system, strengthen the financial resources of the local government, continuously strengthen the supply of the financial system, reduce the dependence of the local government on the land finance, strengthen the ability of the local government to provide public services, and create the conditions for smoothly promoting the reform of the land, household registration, and social security system and promoting the free flow and optimal allocation of land, labor, and other factors of production between urban and rural areas and between regions.

II. Cruces for the Existing Fiscal and Tax Systems' Incompatibility With the Supply-Side Structural Reform

The supply-side structural reform is affected by the improper fiscal and taxation system reform and the unreasonable fiscal and taxation policies in the following aspects:

1. *The current fiscal and taxation system restricts the optimal allocation of factors and the improvement of total factor productivity*

One of the main tasks of the supply-side structural reform is to improve the total factor productivity by reforming and rectifying the distorted allocation of factors. However, the current fiscal and taxation system and policies restrict optimal allocation and technical innovation of production factors such as the talent, capital, and land and ultimately affect the continuous increase in total factor productivity.

(1) *Tax incentive is too weak to be conducive to the improvement of human capital quality and rational utilization*

The current tax policy design lacks the support for talent training, especially for the enterprise talent training, which is not conducive to improve the quality of human capital. At present, the staff training fees of high-tech enterprises and technologically advanced service enterprises are deducted before tax by less than 8% of the total wages, while the staff training fees of other enterprises can only be deducted by less than 2.5% of the total wages, which is not conducive to more enterprises developing staff training and improving the quality of the whole society's human capital. At the same time, the incentive effect of tax on technical innovation talents is too weak to be conducive to the rational use of high-end talents. Although research institutes and universities have introduced incentives for individuals to convert their scientific achievements into jobs, they are allowed to pay taxes on dividends or transfers. Individual income tax shall be paid in installments for the equity awards of the relevant personnel in the transformation of scientific and technological achievements. Taxes on the stock options, equity options, restricted stock, and equity incentives granted to eligible non-listed companies can be deferred. Selective tax preferential policy is carried out to encourage talents to invest in natural person's technological achievements. However, due to the limited scope of enjoyment and complicated examination and approval procedures, the effect of policy implementation is greatly discounted as a result of such tax preferential policies. In general, this is not conducive to arousing enthusiasm for innovation and entrepreneurship of technical personnel and the rational use of high-quality human capital.

(2) *The irrational direction and mode of financial investment and the existence of implicit financial guarantee are not conducive to the optimal allocation of capital*

Reasonable and efficient fiscal and taxation policies can give full play to the role of financial capital in guiding the optimal allocation of social capital. However, the current direction of financial investment in China is still unreasonable, e.g. more investment in mature industries and inadequate support for emerging industries such as offside, vacancy, and dislocation phenomenon. Other problems include the unreasonable way of financial investment, the decentralized investment of financial funds, and the excessive financial subsidies that lead to price distortion and disturb the normal operation of the market. Factors such as the dominant position of financial direct investment and the lagging multi-year rolling-budget reform lead to the limited popularization and application of public–private partnership. All the above problems not only affect the efficiency of financial capital allocation but also are not conducive to exerting the guiding function of financial capital to social capital. In addition, due to the existence of the government's implicit guarantee, more credit funds flow to the state-owned enterprises with less strong demand for capital and lower efficiency of capital utilization, while the private enterprises with a stronger demand for financing and higher efficiency of capital utilization have difficulty in obtaining funds. This mismatch of funds and loss of efficiency also affects the optimal allocation of social capital.

(3) *Dependence on land finance and unreasonable land use taxes and fees is not conducive to the efficient use of land resources*

The incomplete tax-sharing system reform has led to the fact that the division of power and expenditure responsibility is not symmetrical with the financial power; the financial power of governments at all levels, the transfer of land use rights (70 years for residential land, 50 years for industrial land, and 40 years for commercial land) in the coming decades, and the collection of land transfer income at one time have become important ways for local governments to solve the problem of insufficient financial resources. In the process of transferring land, local governments pay more attention to the income of transferring land than to the efficiency of land use. On the contrary, the increasing the scale of land sale, illegally selling land, occupying good cultivated land, and supplementing poor land in the balance of occupation and compensation occur from time to time.

In China, the land use tax is levied on land users; however, due to the imperfect tax policy, the land is not used reasonably to some extent, and a speculative behavior is generated, which affects the land use efficiency. Specifically, problems arising therefrom include the following: first, low cost of tax payment due to low tax amount of urban land use tax[1]; although the central government orders repeatedly, the issues of land enclosure,

[1]According to the size of the city, the land use tax is divided into four grades ranging from RMB0.6 to 30 per square meter, but it is 1.5 yuan per square meter for metropolitan cities.

land occupation, and land hoarding still exist; and then, the land use tax is exempted on newly cultivated land within 1 year from the date of approval, which leads to a large region of idle land and wasteland and reduces the efficiency of land use.

(4) *Fiscal and taxation policies are not prevalent enough to encourage technological innovation*

In recent years, China has issued a series of fiscal and taxation policies to encourage technological innovation. However, due to the lack of universality and compatibility of the policies and due to the fact that some of the policies have not yet been implemented, it is still unable to effectively play the role of encouraging technological innovation.

First, the special types of finance used for innovation are incomplete and inefficient. The category of special funds to support innovation in China is not complete. The *Outline of National Middle and Long-term Science and Technology Development Program (2006–2020)* issued in 2006 explicitly proposed to setting up the special fund to support introduction of technologies, but it has not been set up so far. Some of the special funds have been set up in the implementation of deviation from the original intention of the policy. The use of special funds differs significantly at all levels of government, resulting in the low efficiency of the use of funds in stimulating innovation. In addition, the S&T resources are possessed by several authorities including the Ministry of Science and Technology, the Development and Reform Commission, and the Ministry of Industry and Information Technology, so there are scattered resources, the duplication of scientific research projects, low efficiency of resource investment, and other issues affecting the efficiency of the use of science and technology funds.

Second, the investment of financial innovation funds is not very reasonable as the scope of support is limited and the way of support is singular. First of all, there is insufficient financial innovation fund in support of enterprises. The state financial funds for science and technology are mainly invested in universities and scientific research institutes, with little support for enterprises, especially for private enterprises. In 2014, only 5% of funds were allocated for science and technology from government departments and only 4.5% of funds were allocated for R&D. Second, the scope of support is limited. Although there are clear standards for the definition of SMEs, they are not followed in practice, so some SMEs have not yet been included in the scope of special funding support. Finally, the way of support is not reasonable. Most of the special financial funds support innovation by means of non-reimbursable subsidy and discount interest instead of equity investment, business subsidy, purchase of services, or market-oriented allocation of scientific and technological resources, such as scientific and technological innovation vouchers.

Third, the scope of application of tax policy to encourage innovation is limited and the way of support is not very reasonable. The current tax preferential policy to support innovation is more based on enterprise qualification rather than innovation activities. It is mainly applied to high-tech enterprises, which have innovative activities but have not yet been identified as high-tech enterprises and cannot enjoy preferential policies. Presently, new models and new business forms are emerging; although the evaluation standards have been adjusted, many newly established science and technology enterprises still cannot be identified as national high-tech enterprises, so they cannot enjoy preferential tax. Even for enterprises allowed to deduct the technological development expenses in the same year according to the current documents, due to the limited financial resources of the local government, ineffective propaganda, the threshold of private establishment, and so on, there are fewer enterprises that can really enjoy the preferential policies due to inconsistency between the confirmation standards of the financial and taxation departments and the enterprises on the technological development expenses. In order to encourage the connection between finance and innovation, China has issued a tax preferential policy to support the development of venture capital, but according to the current policy, venture capital institutions must invest in high-tech enterprises and will enjoy preferential tax. The tax incentives use more tax relief than tax deduction, pre-tax deduction, accelerated depreciation, and other indirect incentives; the latter is more conducive to mobilizing the enthusiasm of enterprises.

Finally, the preferential fiscal and tax policies supporting innovation have not covered the whole process of innovation. The current tax incentives to encourage innovation are mainly reflected in income tax. This "*ex post* favor" is applicable to the stage of industrialization and is limited to innovative activities that have already developed new products, new processes, and new technologies and achieved income from the transfer of results, while insufficient support has been given to innovative links such as research and development, pilot test, trial use, and promotion, as well as high-tech enterprises in their initial stages. In addition, China exercises less preferential tax for high-end laboratories and incubators. At present, only the eligible incubators for 2016–2018 are exempted from real estate, land tax, and urban land use tax, which are provided to the incubators for their own use, free of charge or through leasing. During the pilot period of the reform, the incubators are exempted from the value-added tax on the rental of sites, houses, and income from the provision of incubation services.

(5) *Resource and environmental tax is not perfect and unfavorable for the rational development and efficient use of resources*

The levy scope of resource tax in our country is small, and the resources such as water,[2] forest, grassland, and tidal flat have not been included in the levy scope. At present, there is no preferential tax policy to promote the recovery and utilization of resources, resulting in a great waste of resources. The following taxes are being levied in China: resource tax, consumption tax, city construction tax, and vehicle use tax related to the environmental protection. In addition, the low standard and narrow scope of environmental charge collection may cause the environmental resources to be possessed by enterprises without payment.

2. *The indirect tax structure and the mismatch of financial funds are not conducive to the optimization of the industrial structure*

The supply-side structural reform aims to adjust and optimize the industrial structure, expedite the elimination of excess capacity, develop emerging industries, promote the effective docking of supply and demand, and better meet the needs of the masses. Since the reform and opening up in 1978, a large number of factor resources have flowed into the middle and low-end

[2] In July 2016, Hebei carried out a pilot reform of water resources tax.

industries, resulting in repeated construction of the low-end industries, overcapacity, and insufficient development of the middle and high-end industries. The above phenomenon is the result of many factors such as inadequate reform of administration and finance and tax system and low level of technological innovation. The indirect tax structure and the mismatch of financial funds are important factors that affect the upgrading of industrial structure.

In China, value-added tax is mainly applied. The fiscal and taxation system in which consumption tax is levied from the production link is a fundamental change in the financial distribution system, and the enthusiasm for the development of industry has been high everywhere. In particular, the development of "high-priced and large-profit" industries is insufficient for investment in high-tech and emerging industries with long investment cycles and high investment risks and in service industries with "rich people and poor government". This is not only the cause of repeated industrial construction and excess capacity but also the cause for improvement of industrial technology, ultimately affecting the optimization and upgrading of industrial structure. China currently implements a tax system structure with commodity tax as the main body to promote optimization of industrial structure indirectly by influencing consumer behavior, while scientific and reasonable direct tax can directly affect the investment behavior of enterprises. It is more useful to change the business decision of enterprises, urge enterprises to strengthen technological innovation, improve product structure and so on. In the long run, it is more advantageous to promote the optimization of industrial structure. The preferential policy for foreign-related tax is weak in orientation. As there is irrationality in the foreign-related tax credit provisions, tax service cannot keep up with the pace of enterprises' "going global," which is not conducive to reducing the phenomenon of ineffective supply and overcapacity through international capacity cooperation and promoting the optimization and upgrading of industrial structure.

3. *The function of tax regulation is not conducive to the expansion of consumer demand*

Appropriate expansion of total demand is the main content of supply-side structural reform. The expansion of domestic demand, especially of consumer demand, is the top priority of the expansion of total demand in

China. At present, China's tax regulation function is not strong, which is not conducive to the increase of consumer demand and upgradation of the structure.

First, the current tax system is not conducive to improving the ability of residents to consume. Individual income tax cannot accurately reflect the taxpayer family population, support, employment, education, disability, and other basic conditions of the actual tax capacity, but increase the tax burden of the ordinary working class. The deduction of "insurance premiums and housing fund" for the working class also has obvious issues of robbing the poor and helping the rich, which has not yet brought the residential property into the levy scope of the real estate tax, so the inheritance tax and the gift tax are missing. This system of personal income tax and property tax directly leads to the widening of income distribution gap. The result is that the middle and low-income groups have the intention but no ability to consume, and the high-income groups have the ability but no intention to consume, which is not conducive to the expansion of consumer demand in general.

Second, the current tax system is not conducive to promoting the consumption of residents. Commodity tax occupies a large proportion in the current total tax revenue of China. Commodity tax attached directly onto the price of commodities has raised the consumer spending on purchasing commodities, and the tax transfer function on the inhabitants of consumption has an inhibitory effect.

Finally, the current consumption tax system is not conducive to the promotion of consumer upgrading. The scope of consumption tax collection in China cannot meet the needs of consumption upgrading and economic and social development. On the one hand, the consumption tax on cosmetics, high-grade watches, and other consumer goods is levied on the basis of a 17% value-added tax. It is not wrong to levy a consumption tax on these goods at the time of economic development and low living standards. With the upgrading of the consumption structure of the residents, these luxury goods will gradually become consumer goods for the masses, and they will continue to be heavily taxed, which is not conducive to the upgrading of the consumption of the residents. On the other hand, some high-energy-consuming, high-polluting, and other consumer goods have not been included in the scope of taxation, which is not conducive to guiding the green consumer behavior of the residents.

4. *The lagging reform on the division of powers and responsibilities for expenditure and financial rights is not conducive to the smooth advancement of reform in other fields*

The reasonableness of fiscal and taxation system not only affects the optimization of production factors, the upgrading of industrial structure, and the optimization of demand structure but also affects the smooth progress of land and household registration reform, which are closely related to the allocation of production factors. In order to solve the problem of insufficient financial resources, local governments take advantage of the two-way monopoly on the land market, collect the land at a lower price from the peasants, sell the land at a higher price in the land market, and take the income from the land sale as an important source of income. According to the data, the proportion of land transfer fee to local financial revenue reached 59.8% in 2013 and dropped to 56.2% in 2014. Although the fees in these 2 years have decreased, they are over 30%. The dependence of local governments on land finance is very high, including the developed provinces and the first- and second-tier cities. Since the Third Plenary Session of the 17th Central Committee, China has repeatedly emphasized the reform of the rural land expropriation system and the construction of a unified urban and rural land market, but the reform of the land system cannot be carried out smoothly under the circumstances that the central and local authorities as well as the responsibility of expenditure and the distribution of financial and financial resources are not greatly adjusted, and the income from land transfer is still the main source of local government income.

The same problem exists in the reform of the household registration system and the social security system. The reform of household registration system is to divest the welfare treatment attached to household registration and give the same welfare treatment to the settled peasants and urban residents. Under the circumstance that the main body of public service responsibility sinks and the local government's financial resources are insufficient, the reform of household registration system brings great pressure to the local government's public service expenditure. The reform of the household registration and social security system will not be carried out smoothly without expediting the straightening out of the relationship between the central and local authorities and the establishment of a system suited to the responsibilities of the central authorities and expenditure. However, if the reform in the above areas cannot be carried forward smoothly, it will directly affect the free flow and optimal allocation of land, labor, and other factors of production between the urban and rural areas and between regions and then affect the continuous increase of total factor productivity.

III. General Framework and Main Objectives of the Fiscal and Tax System Reform Under Supply-Side Structural Reform

1. *Basic ideas*

To give full play to the role of fiscal and taxation systems and policies in guiding the allocation of resources, technological innovation, adjustment of industrial structure, adjustment of income distribution, and upgrading of urban and rural residents' consumption and in safeguarding the reform of land, household registration, and social security systems. Under the prerequisite of the decisive function of the market in the allocation of resources, give full play to the functions of fiscal and taxation system in adjusting the cost of land, encouraging the human capital, guiding the flow of social capital, rectifying the distortion of the allocation of elements, and promoting the rational development and efficient utilization of production factors. Give full play to the functions of fiscal and taxation systems and policies in promoting technological innovation of enterprises, improving production and business environment, further stimulating market vitality and social creativity, guiding product supply innovation, and upgrading industrial structure. Give full play to the roles of fiscal and taxation systems and policies in regulating income distribution and guiding residents' consumption so as to improve the consumption ability and behavior of urban and rural residents, promote the expansion of consumption demand, upgrade the structure, and effectively connect the supply and demand at a higher level. Give full play to the roles of fiscal and taxation system reform in other areas of reform, focusing on the reasonable division of central and local powers and responsibilities for expenditure, improving the local tax system, strengthening the financial resources of local governments, strengthening the supply of financial system, and creating conditions for the reform of land, household registration, social security, and other areas.

2. *Main objectives*

Under the background of pushing forward the supply-side structural reform, deepen the reform of the fiscal and taxation system to achieve the following objectives (Figure 1):

(1) Substantially increase total factor productivity; compensate and encourage human capital; guide the social capital to optimize the allocation; promote the efficient utilization of land energy resources; encourage innovation and entrepreneurship; accelerate the improvement of the financial and taxation system and policies; greatly improve the allocation of labor, capital, land, energy resources, and output efficiency; stimulate the vitality of innovation and entrepreneurship; improve the level of technological innovation; and promote the total factor productivity to increase substantially.

(2) Promote the upgrading of the industrial structure; alleviate the burden of taxes and fees on enterprises; create a good environment for innovation and entrepreneurship; guide enterprises to increase R&D investment and industrialization; promote application of new products; encourage financial capital to support innovation and other key links; speed up the improvement of the fiscal and taxation systems and policies; foster and develop strategic emerging industries; promote the development of manufacturing industries towards high-end, intelligent, green service; extend producer services to specialization and high-end value chains; transform livelihood services to fine and

Figure 1. Logic Structure Diagram of the Fiscal and Tax System Reform Under Supply-side Structural Reform.

high-quality ones; and expand effective supply and medium and high-end supplies.

(3) Promote efficient docking of supply and demand; increase the income of urban and rural residents to promote the upgrading of their consumption; accelerate the improvement of the fiscal and tax system and policies; expand the consumption demand of urban and rural residents; guide them to change towards intelligent, green, healthy, and safe directions; expedite the release of consumption potential; form a benign cycle of creating new demand with new supply; promote new

consumption; invert new consumption into new industries; and realize the leap from low-level balance to high-level balance of supply and demand.

(4) Deepen the supply-side structural reform; straighten out the relationship between central and local financial power and administrative power to establish a system in which the central and local authorities are suited to the responsibility for expenditure; accelerate clarification of authority and reform of the tax system; regulate transfer payments; reduce the dependence of local governments on land finance; strengthen the local ability to provide public services and create conditions for smoothly advancing the reform of the land, household registration, and social security system and promoting the free flow of land, labor, and other factors of production between urban and rural areas and regions; and give full play to the basic functions and safeguard functions of the fiscal and taxation system in deepening the supply-side structural reform.

IV. Fiscal and Tax System and Policy Framework of Promoting the Supply-Side Structural Reform

The reform of fiscal and taxation system is the prerequisite for deepening the supply-side structural reform system, which not only guides the optimal allocation of resources, promotes the upgrading of industrial structure, and expands the consumption demand of residents but also creates conditions for deepening the reform of land and household registration; accelerates perfection of the financial and tax system and policy framework and lays a solid foundation for further promoting the supply-side structural reform in order to improve the efficiency of factor allocation and total factor productivity; promotes innovation of product supply and the upgrading of industrial structure; expands consumption demand and the upgrading of consumption structure of urban and rural residents; and promotes smooth progress of the reform of land, household registration, and social security system.

1. *Fiscal and taxation policies that promote optimal allocation of factors and increase total factor productivity*

(1) *Give full play to the functions of tax adjustment and distribution, accelerate perfection of tax preferential policies to encourage improvement of human capital, and promote rational utilization of human resources*

Establish and improve the compensation and effective incentive mechanism for human capital investment and promote the improvement and rational utilization of human resources quality, focusing on the reform of enterprise income tax and individual income tax. First, we will expedite expansion of the pilot reform of installment payment of individual income tax on equity earnings to the whole country. Second, exempt individual income tax on prizes awarded to the main R&D personnel for the transfer of scientific research achievements, the major technology achievement awards and technology progress awards granted by governments and enterprises below the provincial level, and the one-time allowances or subsidies and re-settlement allowances urgently needed by the high-tech enterprises for introduction of technological talents. Thirdly, impose half the individual income tax on dividends earned by middle and high-ranking talents in the enterprise of science and technology innovation and exempt individual income tax on the natural person shareholders of science and technology innovation start-up enterprises when they transfer undistributed profits into the company's capital so as to encourage high-tech talents to innovate and start a business. Fourth, appropriately increase the proportion of pre-tax deductions for staff and workers' education funds in science and technology entrepreneurial innovation enterprises, allow more than a portion to be carried forward in the following taxable years, and extend the policy of pre-tax deductions for staff and workers' education funds to strategic emerging industries so as to encourage enterprises to invest in human capital. Finally, deduct all or part of the individual income tax from the expenditures of family higher education and personal continuing education before payment of individual income tax, and encourage residents to invest in human capital.

(2) *Optimize the direction and mode of financial capital investment and guide the whole society to optimize allocation of funds*

Further optimize the investment direction of financial funds, invest more in emerging industries and public services, and give priority to projects that can guide social capital to enter the country under the same conditions so as to give full play to the role of government funds. Perfect the government investment mode and inspire social investment through expanding the franchise operation, promoting the government to purchase services, carrying out the cooperation between the government and social capital, perfecting the pricing mechanism in the public sphere, and perfecting the tax and fee preferential policies in project operation. Perfect the financial subsidy mechanism and support social capital to participate in the construction of key sectors through flexible investment subsidy, fund injection, guarantee subsidy, and loan interest discount.

(3) *Improve land use tax and fee policy and guide efficient allocation of land resources*

Change the one-time land leasehold system, which collects land use rights for the coming decades, to the annual leasehold system, which collects income from land transfers on an annual basis; improve the real estate tax as an opportunity to combine the annual rent with the retained link of the real estate tax not only to reduce the real estate developers' cost and urban residents' cost for land acquisition but also to improve the efficiency of land use. Simplify tax and fee in transfer transaction, abolish the land value-added tax, and use earnings from transfer of real estate and industrial land to pay individual income tax and enterprise income tax. Give full play to the role of tax in intensive and economical use of land; increase the amount of tax on land use in cities and towns; increase the cost of enclosing, occupying, and hoarding land; raise the tax and fee of the low-efficiency land use projects; force the low-efficiency land use project to quit; and increase tax and fee incentives for the secondary development of inefficient land so as to guide redevelopment and utilization of land.

(4) *Intensify the supporting role of the inclusive fiscal and taxation policies and encourage innovation of products and technology*

First, increase the support of finance to the innovation of science and technology and improve the efficiency of the allocation of science and technology resources. Expedite establishment of special funds to support digestion, absorption, and re-innovation of imported technologies and the application and promotion of major technological equipment and strengthen the performance evaluation of the use of special funds. Speed up integration of science and technology resources in the hands of government departments such as science and technology, development and reform, as well as the industry and information technology; further clarify the position and support priorities of various national science and technology plans, projects, and funds; and prevent duplication of deployment.

Second, increase financial funds to support enterprise innovation, expand the scope of support; and improve the way of support. Increase the support of national financial science and technology funds to enterprises, especially to private enterprises, and substantially increase the proportion of the use of science and technology funds from government departments in national financial allocations for science and technology and R&D expenditures of enterprises. Strictly implement the special fund support policy for small and medium-sized science and technology enterprises, expand the coverage of special funds, and guide more innovative resources towards enterprises. Provide support of enterprise innovation according to the stage of enterprise and product innovation and by means of subsidy, financial discount, equity investment, business subsidy or incentive, or purchase of services and products.

Finally, improve the preferential tax policies that support innovation. Based on international prevailing standards, continue to increase the intensity of pre-tax deduction of R&D investment tax. Further reduce income tax and value-added tax rates of the high-tech enterprises. Allow enterprises engaged in the research and development of specific cutting-edge technologies and products to draw reserves for risk of scientific and technological development, for trial production of new products, and for loss of funds so as to compensate for losses that may result from scientific research and development. Increase support of tax deductions and exemptions for losses caused by enterprise innovation, allow them to make up for losses from earnings of the first 3 years and refund of the income tax for the previous year. Revise and perfect the identification method of high-tech enterprises in time and bring more innovative enterprises into the scope of tax preference. Perfect the policy of tax credit for 70% of taxable income of corporate partners in venture capital enterprises and limited partnership enterprises and bring into the scope of tax preference those corporate venture capital institutions and limited partnership partners investing in small and medium-sized, small, and micro-technological innovation enterprises. Expand the proportion of indirect preferential measures such as pre-tax deduction, accelerated depreciation, and scientific research reserve to support innovation so as to combine preferential measures before the event with the preferential measures after the event, complement each other in advantages, and exert joint efforts.

Finally, formulate a tax policy that covers the whole process of innovation activities. Support enterprise innovation through preferential tax methods such as pre-tax deduction, tax deduction, tax reduction, return after levy of tax, and profit and loss offset. Change the current tax preferential policy system mainly based on income tax by increasing the preferential intensity of tax transfer to enterprises, especially high-tech enterprises in the seed stage and start-up stage and venture capital enterprises with more substantial benefits. Further increase the tax incentives for large innovative platforms.

(5) *Construct and improve the ecological tax system*

Carry out the resource tax reform in an all-round way; expand the taxation scope of tax on water, forest, grassland, beach, and other natural resources of merchandise attributes; and moderately raise the tax rate of major resource products. Carry out *ad valorem* collection of resource tax for all mineral products except those that are scattered in clay and sandstone and that are mostly cash traded and difficult to control, and set up the adjustment mechanism of resource tax income with the change of resource income. Further improve preferential tax policies that encourage recycling and utilization of resources, develop and utilize alternative resources, and improve the utilization of resources. Start collecting independent environmental tax to improve clean types of tax.

2. *Fiscal and tax policies for optimization of industrial structure*

Due to imperfect legal environment, credit environment, and tax collection and management system in China, it will take a long time for it to construct the tax system structure based on direct tax and adjust the tax system of value-added tax and consumption tax. In the short term, tax policy should be applied scientifically to promote the development of strategic emerging industries, service industry, and the upgrading of traditional industries. In the long run, it is necessary to adjust the proportion of direct tax and indirect tax in order to optimize the industrial structure.

(1) *Tax policies to promote development of strategic emerging industries*

We will focus on development direction and emphasis of strategic emerging industries by reducing tax burden on strategic emerging industries, encouraging popularization and application of new products, and encouraging financial capital to support innovation. We should also speed up perfection of tax policy to promote cultivation and development of strategic emerging industries. First, reduce or exempt corporate income tax on strategic emerging industries. Reduce enterprise income tax on qualified strategic emerging industries by 15%, exempt enterprise income tax on emerging industries that have a major economic security, exempt enterprise income tax on strategic emerging industries in the second year and levy half tax in the third year after the taxable year in which they have earned operational income, and appropriately raise the limit of reduction or exemption of tax on income from technology transfer. Second, enact new products to encourage promotion and application of tax incentives. If enterprises and public institutions purchase products produced by strategic emerging industrial enterprises that meet the conditions for recognition of fixed or intangible assets, the period of depreciation or amortization shall be appropriately shortened and the burden of enterprise income tax shall be reduced upon approval by a competent tax authority. Finally, formulate tax policies that encourage financial capital to support development of strategic emerging industries. Appropriately reduce or exempt the value-added tax on interest income of commercial banks that provide loans for strategic emerging industry projects. When a venture capital enterprise that invests in a strategic emerging industry loses money, it is allowed to make up for the loss in the current year with profits of the previous year and to refund the enterprise income tax that has been paid in the previous year.

(2) *Tax policies for development of the service industry*

Focusing on expansion of producer services to specialization and the high end of value chain and the transformation of living services to fine and high quality, we should speed up the improvement of tax policies. The preferential tax policy for high-tech enterprises should be extended to modern service industry, especially producer service industry. Improve the value-added tax system in line with the characteristics of the service industry, including appropriate reduction of the tax rates of the transport and other industries, take into full consideration the large proportion of human capital in service industry and the small proportion of fixed assets, and gradually improve the deduction range of value-added tax. Expand the scope of tax rebates on exports of services.

(3) *Fiscal and tax policies that promote the upgrading of traditional industries*

Focus on promoting the traditional manufacturing industry to high-end, intelligent, green service development and speed up the improvement of the fiscal and taxation system and policies. Increase the financial support for technological transformation of traditional industries and provide vocational education and quality training for traditional industries by means of government procurement education. The local government should play the role of financial investment and finance and set up the traditional industry transformation and upgrading fund. We will study the cancellation of provisional tariffs on exports of some products from traditional industries such as coal, steel, and non-ferrous metals and chemical industry; resume export tax rebates; and appropriately raise the rebate rates. We will make good use of the special restructuring award funds for industrial enterprises and provide reimbursement for the relocation of personnel in the process of resolving excess capacity in a coordinated manner.

(4) *Fiscal and tax policies to promote international capacity cooperation*

Expedite negotiations with the countries concerned for the avoidance of double taxation agreements to achieve full coverage of priority countries. In accordance with the needs of international production capacity and equipment manufacturing cooperation, financial discount is given to loans for enterprises to participate in the export of large-scale complete sets of equipment, project contracting and large-scale investment projects. We will improve the level of tax administration and tax services; establish and improve public information service platforms; collect and publish relevant state tax systems, collection and management systems, and law enforcement and services; and provide information support for "going global" enterprises.

3. *Fiscal and taxation policies to expand the consumption capacity of urban and rural residents and to promote consumption escalation*

Accelerate perfection of the fiscal and taxation systems and policies conducive to increasing the income of urban and rural residents and guiding the upgrading of the consumption structure, expand the consumption capacity of residents, promote the formation and expansion of the production and living consumption markets, stimulate innovation of the supply of products with the consumption demand, and promote the virtuous cycle of supply and demand as well as the structural optimization and upgrading.

(1) *Improve fiscal and taxation policies to enhance the consumption capacity of residents*

Speed up improvement of the fiscal and taxation system and strive to improve the consumption capacity of urban and rural residents, especially the low- and middle-income groups.

First, improve the individual income tax, real estate tax, inheritance tax, and other tax systems. Standardize and perfect the tax collection mechanism of individual income tax; appropriately adjust the tax rate structure of wage and salary income tax and other measures to further improve individual income tax; gradually establish a combination of comprehensive and classification of individual income tax and individual recurrent income[3] to carry out a comprehensive collection of tax; take into due consideration the family population, family support burden, education costs, and other factors to make a differential reduction of the tax base as well as other temporary and contingent income[4]; and continue to implement classification of tax collecting methods. Strengthen construction of the property tax system; combine the current urban land use tax and real estate tax into the real estate tax, timely levy real estate tax on residents, and accelerate the levy of inheritance tax and gift tax. Start levy of social security tax under the premise of accelerating the unification of urban and rural social security system.

Then, further reduce the goods tax and labor tax of individually owned businesses. Further increase the threshold of value-added tax for individually owned businesses, or change it to the zero-bracket amount. Lower the basic VAT rate and further lower the percentage charge of small-scale taxpayers in commercial sectors.

---

[3] Including the income from wages and salaries, the income from remuneration for labor services, the income from the production and operation of individual industrial and commercial households, the income from contractual lease of enterprises and institutions, the income from property lease, and the income from the author's remuneration.

[4] Including income from the transfer of property, interest, dividend, bonus, and royalties; accidental income; and other incomes.

(2) *Tax policies to adjust the consumption structure and behaviors of urban and rural residents*

Establish a dynamic adjustment mechanism for the scope of consumption tax collection; adjust the scope of the consumption tax and optimize the structure of the tax rate according to upgrading direction of the consumption structure of residents and the changes in the classification standards of high-energy consumption, high-pollution, resources-based, and high-grade consumer goods; and guide upgrading of the consumption and the improvement of the consumption behavior of the urban and rural residents according to the principle of increasing or decreasing the tax rate and the items to be charged. Bring the high-consumption, high-energy-consuming, and high-pollution products and services into the scope of consumption tax, especially the products that consume a high quantity of resources and seriously pollute the environment such as disposable goods, raw pulp paper, Freon products, plastic packaging products, and batteries in order to encourage consumers to use energy-saving and consumption-reducing products; and abolish consumption tax on out-of-date commodities including cosmetics to further release the consumption potential. Levy consumption tax in wholesale and retail processes instead of in production process, weaken the government's dependence on production tax, and focus on consumption and upgrading of consumption. Refund value-added tax or refund it proportionately as soon as it is imposed on general taxpayers who sell their own products or independently develop innovative products so as to guide producers not to pass on the value-added tax to consumers, reduce tax burden on consumers, and encourage urban and rural residents to expand consumer demand. Reduce the value-added tax rate on household consumer goods and gradually exempt VAT tax to create conditions for reducing the consumption cost of residents.

4. *Create a smooth fiscal and tax environment for reform of land, household registration, and social security*

We should further straighten out the relationship between central and local financial rights and administrative powers, improve the local tax system, strengthen the financial resources of local governments, focus on clarifying their powers and reforming the tax system, expedite the establishment of a modern financial system, create conditions for reforms in the fields of land, household registration and social security, and provide institutional safeguards for optimizing allocation of resources, safeguarding market unity, and promoting social equity.

(1) *Promoting division of powers and expenditure responsibilities between the central and local authorities*

Reasonably adjust the central and local powers to form a reasonable expenditure-sharing mechanism of various public services in accordance with the decision-making power and the principle of expenditure responsibility. Shift the focus of responsibility for decision-making, oversight, and expenditure in basic public services to the provincial and central governments, with the central and provincial governments being responsible for the expenditure of decision-makers; delegate the implementation and management responsibility to the provincial and subprovincial government, and give full play to the advantages of local government in the public service information. In the form of special transfer payment, the central government provides the fund guarantee for the central government to entrust the local administration authority, implement the central expenditure responsibility, and avoid the local government bearing the corresponding expenditure responsibility of the central administration authority excessively. We should also optimize and adjust the power and expenditure responsibility of governments at all levels according to the division of power, and as far as possible, make a detailed and clear division of all levels of government's expenditure responsibility. In the difficult division and the need for different levels of government to share the responsibility for expenditure, we should also refine the specific responsibility of governments at all levels as far as possible.

(2) *Improving the taxation system*

It is necessary to coordinate and push forward the major tax reform in the framework of perfecting the government revenue system to form a scientific, sound, and fully functional taxation system. On the basis of perfecting the tax system, we should further improve the tax-sharing system between the central and local governments to form a fiscal revenue system benefiting for scientific development, social fairness, and market unification and to form a fiscal revenue distribution system mainly based on the tax-sharing system.

First of all, strengthen the functions of the tax system. Standardize the commodity tax, optimize the income tax, improve the resource and environment tax and real estate tax to adjust and distribute taxes, and promote optimization of taxation structure to save energy resources and protect environment. Create a tax system with scientific, coordinated, and rationalized structure to adapt to the changes of the economic structure, tax source structure, tax collection and management ability, and development goal.

Then, improve the system of tax distribution based on the value-added tax and consumption tax sharing. We should implement the transitional plan for dividing the value-added tax revenues between the central and local governments, include all value-added taxes paid by enterprises in all trades and industries into the scope of the central and local sharing tax, where 50% of the value-added tax is shared by the central authorities and 50% by the local authorities according to the place where the tax is paid, and the income from the central authorities is refunded to the local authorities through tax reimbursement, thus ensuring that the existing financial resources of the local authorities remain unchanged and that the increment of the central revenue is distributed to the local authorities through a balanced transfer payment. Upon completion of changing the business tax into the value-added tax and rational division of the central and local revenues, reform the consumption tax into the shared tax and determine the central and local share ratios of the consumption tax, in which tax items pertaining to local authority will be collected by the local tax authority. Improve the local tax system with a focus on real estate tax, provide support for steady growth of local fiscal revenue, and make up for the influence of the adjustment of value-added tax on the reduction of local fiscal revenue.

(3) *Optimizing the transfer payment system*

Establish the transfer payment framework with definite functions, re-classify the items in the current financial transfer payment other than the general transfer payment, include part of the factors into the calculation of general transfer payment formula and include the rest of a special nature into the special transfer payment; integrate and standardize the existing special transfer payment items so that some of the actual equal effects of the special items are incorporated into the general transfer payment. Adjust and improve the transfer payment system to equalize basic public services. Regard equalization of basic public services as the responsibility of the central government and entrust local government with the implementation and management. Achieve the policy intention by introducing the designated expenditure direction, holding the distribution and management power independently, and distributing the whole block transfer payment according to the factor method. Regard all the value-added tax revenues as the source of funds transferred by the central government to local government so as to stabilize the growth mechanism.

Appendix: Tax System and Policy Framework Under the Supply-Side Structural Reform

	Types of tax	Adjustment of tax system/preferential tax policy	Purpose
Objectives of the tax system reform	Value-added tax	Improve the value-added tax system conforming to the characteristics of the service industry	Promote optimization of the industrial structure
		Reduce the basic VAT rate	Reduce the goods and labor tax on individually owned businesses and improve consumption capacity
		Further reduce the tax receipts for small-scale taxpayers	
		Further reduce the threshold of VAT for individually owned businesses or change it to the zero-bracket amount	
		Refund value-added tax or refund it proportionately as soon as it is imposed on general taxpayers who sell their own products or independently developed innovative products	Alleviate the tax burden on consumers and encourage urban and rural residents to expand consumption demand and adjust consumption structure

(*Continued*)

(*Continued*)

Types of tax	Adjustment of tax system/preferential tax policy	Purpose
	Reduce the value-added tax rate on consumer goods and gradually exempt them from tax or applying zero tax rate at the final stage	Reduce consumption cost and expand consumption demand
Consumption tax	Establish a dynamic adjustment mechanism for the scope of consumption tax collection; adjust the scope of the consumption tax; and optimize the structure of the tax rate according to upgrading direction of the consumption structure of residents and the changes in the classification standards of high energy consumption, high pollution, resources-based, and high-grade consumer goods; and bring the high-consumption, high-energy-consuming, and high-pollution products and services into the scope of consumption tax.	Adjust the consumption structure of residents and further release the consumption potential
	Optimize tax rate structure	

	Gradually levy the consumption tax from the current level of production (import) to the level of wholesale and retail consumption	Weaken the government's dependence on tax revenue in the production process and strengthen the consumption and upgrading of consumption.
Tariff	Abolish the provisional tariffs on exports of some products in traditional industries such as coal, steel, non-ferrous metals, and chemical industry to resume export tax rebates and appropriately raise the rebate rates	Promote upgrading of traditional industries
Individual income tax	Accelerate expansion of the pilot project of the reform of individual income tax to the whole country Individual income tax shall be exempted from incentives and subsidies for transfer of scientific research achievements, major technology achievement awards and technology progress awards from governments and enterprises below the provincial level, and one-off allowances or subsidies for settlement expenses urgently needed by high-tech enterprises	Establish and perfect compensation and effective incentive mechanism for human capital investment and promote the improvement and reasonable utilization of human resource quality

(Continued)

(*Continued*)

Types of tax	Adjustment of tax system/preferential tax policy	Purpose
	Individual income tax on dividend income from stock owned by senior talents in science and technology innovative enterprises by halving dividend income	
	Individual income tax shall not be levied on natural shareholders of scientific and technological innovation entrepreneurial enterprises to encourage high-tech talents to innovate and start their businesses while transferring undistributed profits into corporate capital	
	Allow family's higher education and personal continuing education expenditure to be fully or partially deducted before individual income tax and encourage residents to invest in human capital	
	Adjust the structure of salary and income tax rates	Give full play to the role of tax-regulating income distribution and improve consumption
	Establish the comprehensive and classified system of individual income tax	

Corporate income tax	Raise the pre-tax deduction proportion of staff and workers' education funds in scientific and technological innovation enterprises and allow the surplus part to be carried over in future tax years, extend the pre-tax deduction policy of staff and workers' education funds to strategic emerging industries, and encourage enterprises to invest in human capital	Promote the quality improvement and rational utilization of human resources
	Increase the pre-tax deduction of R&D investment	Support and encourage innovation
	Further reduce the tax rate of high-tech enterprises	
	Allow enterprises engaged in specific sophisticated technology and product research and development to withdraw scientific and technological development risk reserve, new product trial reserve, loss reserve, etc. to compensate for the losses that may result from scientific research and development	

(*Continued*)

(*Continued*)

Types of tax	Adjustment of tax system/preferential tax policy	Purpose
	Increase tax relief support for losses resulting from enterprise innovation and allow loss to be compensated with the profits of the first 3 years and provide income tax rebate for previous years	
	Revise and perfect the identification method of high-tech enterprises and bring more innovative enterprises into the scope of tax preference	
	Allow venture capital enterprises and limited partnership enterprises to enjoy 70% of income tax reduction or exemption and incorporate these enterprises into the scope of tax preference.	
	Reduce or exempt income tax on strategic emerging industries	Promote optimization of industrial structure and guide the innovation of product supply
	Issue tax incentives to encourage the promotion and application of new products	

		Issue tax policy that encourages financial capital to support the development of strategic emerging industries	
		Extend the tax preferential policies of high-tech enterprises to modern service industry, especially to the productive service industry	
	Value-added tax of land	Cancel land value-added tax and levy individual income tax and corporate income tax on earnings from transfer of real estate and industrial land	Guide efficient allocation of land resources
	Urban land use tax	Raise the tax rate of urban land use tax, raise tax rate of inefficient land use projects, and strengthen tax incentive for secondary development of low-efficiency land	
	House property tax	Consolidate the urban land use tax and the current real estate tax into the real estate tax and impose real estate tax on residents at the appropriate time	Give full play to the role of taxation in adjusting income distribution
	Inheritance tax and gift tax	To be levied as soon as possible	

(*Continued*)

(*Continued*)

Types of tax	Adjustment of tax system/preferential tax policy	Purpose
Resource tax	Gradually widen the taxation scope of resources, including natural resources with commodity attributes such as water, forest, grassland, and tidal flat and appropriately raise the tax rate of main resource products	Utilize resources efficiently and protect ecological environment by increasing the amount of resource tax
	Further improve tax preferential policies that encourage resource recycling, develop and utilize alternative resources, and improve resource utilization	
Environmental tax	To be levied at the appropriate time	

Chapter 3

Financial System Reform Under Promotion of the Supply-Side Structural Reform

Wang Yuan and Cao Yujin

Academy of Macroeconomic Research

Abstract

Promoting the supply-side structural reform needs support of the financial system in many aspects, so the reform of the financial system should be accelerated as a content of the supply-side structural reform to meet the overall needs of the supply-side structural reform. At present, there are still a series of problems in China's financial system. Banking and capital markets are constrained by institutional factors, resulting in low efficiency in allocation of financial resources. The mismatch of supply and demand structure of financial services, the insufficiency of financial support innovation, the transformation and upgrading of traditional industries, and the imperfection of monetary policy transmission and the financial supervision system have led to imperfection of the mechanism to prevent accumulation of financial risks, which is not conducive to the support of finance for the supply-side structural reform. According to the overall requirements of the supply-side structural reform and focusing on the problems mentioned above, we put forward the ideas of financial system reform under the supply-side structural reform as follows: exerting a decisive role of the market mechanism in allocation of financial resources, strengthening the ability of the financial service entity economy, promoting the reform of the banking system, relaxing access, strengthening competition and improving the efficiency of the allocation of credit resources, perfecting the capital market system, relaxing restriction, expanding the capacity and improving the efficiency, and increasing the proportion of direct financing. By developing diversified financing instruments, especially the direct financing instruments, the supply of financial services can be better adapted to the financing needs of the real economy. By perfecting the framework of monetary policy and the financial supervision system and maintaining the bottom line of non-systemic financial risk, the reform of the financial system can help remove excessive capacity and inventory, deleverage, reduce cost, promote adjustment of economic structure and cultivation of new impetus of economic growth, and provide strong support for the structural reform on the supply side. On this basis, specific policy recommendations are proposed as follows:

The supply-side structural reform is mainly to solve the five major problem in the current economic development (the slowing growth rate, the falling price of industrial products, the declining profit of entity enterprises, the falling growth rate of fiscal revenue, and the rising probability of economic risks) by increasing effective supply, reducing mismatch of supply structure, raising total factor productivity, and cultivating new power for medium- and long-term economic development. To solve the problem of mismatched supply structure, we need to promote transition of production factors from ineffective supply to effective supply. The financial system is the platform and channel of financial resources allocation, so its reform and improvement will be very necessary to promote optimization of capital elements' allocation and form a system and policy environment supporting innovation. Therefore, we should focus on the problem of the current financial system not adapting to the demand of the supply-side structural reform, perfect its functions, improve the efficiency of financial resources allocation, strengthen its ability to serve the real economy, and provide support for advancing the structural reform of the supply side.

I. Relationship Between Financial System Reform and Supply-Side Structural Reform

Promoting the structural reform of supply side is an important innovation to lead the new normal state of economic development and an inevitable choice to maintain the sustained and healthy development of China's economy for a period of time and to achieve a well-off society in an all-round way by 2020. Finance plays an important role in supporting many aspects of the supply-side structural reform, so it is necessary to take the financial system reform as an important content of the supply-side structural reform.

1. *Finance has different effects on demand and supply*

The financial system plays an important role in allocation of financial resources and is thus regarded as the core of modern economy. All sectors of the modern economy need the support of the financial system, and enterprises need financial support to maintain normal capital turnover and operations. As well as increasing investment and expanding business scale, residents need financial support to solve the problem of mismatch between income and consumption at different stages of the life cycle. The government also needs to use the financial system to play the role of counter-cyclical adjustment, to suppress economic fluctuations, and to apportion public expenditure more reasonably.

The increase or decrease of financial resources will influence both the demand and the supply. Finance influences demand and supply in the same direction. For example, sufficient fund supply in the market and lower interest rate will stimulate enterprises to increase investment and encourage residents to increase consumption; as a result, the total demand will be expanded and enterprises will generate new production capacity to expand supply. The increase of investment changes both supply and demand. When the increase of consumption only changes the demand and does not directly affect the supply, the influence of finance on the demand and supply is related to the proportion of investment and consumption. In the long run, the incompatibility between investment and consumption may result in an imbalance between demand and supply. From the perspective of time, the impact of finance on demand will appear in the short term, supply changes will gradually appear in the medium and long term, and the adjustment of supply changes will have a profound impact on the long-term economic growth in both the total amount and the economic structure.

Because of the influence of finance on demand and supply, monetary policy is usually regarded as the control policy for short-term economic aggregate, which aims to influence the total demand by expansion or contraction of monetary aggregate, promote the balance of short-term total supply and demand, and suppress the cyclical economic fluctuation. To influence the supply, the financial system needs to improve the efficient allocation of financial resources by means of its own reform and structural adjustment so as to better meet the demand for financial services from the real economy.

2. *To promote the supply-side structural reform, finance needs to play a key role*

After China's economy enters the new normal, new changes have appeared in the relative superiority of production factors, the resource allocation pattern, the production capacity and the industrial organization methods, the market competition characteristics, the resources environment restriction, the economic risk, and three big demand aspects. At the same time, the global competition of comprehensive national strength also presents a new situation after the international financial crisis, which leads to obvious changes in the external environment of China's economic development. In this situation, the CPC Central Committee has made a plan to adapt to and lead the new normal state of economic development and promote the supply-side structural reform.

To promote the supply-side structural reform, we should first improve the quality of supply and then promote the structural adjustment through reform, rectify distorted allocation of product factors, expand effective supply, improve the adaptability and flexibility of the supply structure to the changing demand, raise total factor productivity, and better meet the needs of the masses so as to promote sustained and healthy economic and social development. The five key tasks of the supply-side structural reform include de-capacity, de-stocking, de-leveraging, reducing cost, and improving weak points.

The supply-side structural reform needs financial support in many aspects. For example, in order to foster and strengthen the impetus of innovation-driven development, we need to solve the financing bottleneck problem of innovative enterprises by developing a financing mode adapted to innovation, especially the equity financing mode, and by changing the traditional loan mode which banks rely on for physical collateral. Another example, "improving weak points", needs financial services to extend further to the weak points such as "agriculture, countryside and farmers" and small and micro-enterprises to meet their financing needs. If we do not have financial resources allocation efficiency improvement, financial services supply and diversification of the main content and effective prevention of financial risks and other support, the supply-side structural reform will face severe challenges. Therefore, the reform of the financial system should be a part of the supply-side structural reform and be better coordinated with the structural reform in other sectors, adjustment of the economic structure, and the "de-capacity, de-stocking, de-leveraging, reducing cost and improving weak points" so as to form a driving force for smooth implementation of the supply-side structural reform.

II. Cruces for the Financial System's Incompatibility With the Supply-Side Structural Reform

Since the economic reform and opening up to the outside world in 1978, the reform in the financial field of China has been pushed forward gradually, and the financial system has developed rapidly, which has played an important role in supporting the economic development on the whole. However, there are still some structural and institutional problems in the current financial system that cannot meet the requirements of the supply-side structural reform.

1. *Inefficient allocation of financial resources*

With the reform and development of finance, the stock of financial assets in China has been enlarged, which has changed from the former shortage of capital to the abundance of capital. However, because of the unreasonable structure and system of the financial system, the scale of the financial assets is huge; the rapid growth of the financial assets cannot meet the financing needs of real economy, especially the SMEs, which shows that the efficiency of capital allocation is not high.

(1) *Structural and institutional issues in the banking industry are affecting the full functioning of market mechanism*

Although the proportion of banking assets in the total amount of financial assets in China is declining, the current financial resources held by banking institutions are large in scale and relatively high and remain the main suppliers of financial resources in China. The efficiency of resource allocation in the banking system has a significant impact on the overall efficiency of financial resources allocation. However, China's banking industry is significantly restricted by the structure, system, and other factors; the market mechanism plays an inadequate role in allocation of resources, and banks still depend on scale expansion as their profiting model to a certain extent, leading to the fact that the efficiency of financial resources allocation cannot be effectively improved.

First, the efficiency is hard to improve because of large banks occupying the main position in the banking industry. Negative effects include the following: (1) As large banks can use monopoly power to obtain higher returns, they are inadequately equipped to adapt to the changes in market demand, improve financial services, and increase the operational efficiency. In some large banks, the deposit–loan ratio is much lower. At the end of the first quarter of 2016, the ratio of ICBC and Agricultural Bank of China, which ranked top two in deposit among listed banks, was less than 70%. The low ratio of capital utilization, especially of loans to the real economy, indicated that there was a waste of financial resources. The monopoly power also makes large banks tend to pass more cost to the demander side; for example, with regard to bank service charges, the four state-owned commercial banks charge more items at higher rates than the small- and medium-sized banks. With regard to the rate adjustment, the action of the four big banks is basically the same, which makes it more difficult for the bank users to evade service charges. (2) Unlike the small- and medium-sized banks with obvious local characteristics, such as city commercial banks, large banks deal with business nationwide. Under the general branch system, the dispatch of financial resources at the head office is basically transferred from the underdeveloped regions to the developed regions, and the siphon effect is formed to aggravate the imbalance of financial development among different regions. In addition, influenced by the state-owned nature, development history, the impact of financial stability, and other factors, the large banks in the policy level of the voice are significantly higher than the small- and medium-sized banks, which leads to the formulation and implementation of financial policy that is more conducive to the large banks.

Then, private capital holders find it hard to play a role in allocation of banking resources. The vigor of non-governmental capital and the strong support of market mechanism for allocation of resources have been fully embodied in the course of reform in China. To improve the role of market mechanism in allocation of financial resources, we also need the non-governmental capital to play its role. According to the top 10 common shareholders of listed banks, there are some domestic non-state-owned corporate institutions, but the number of such shareholders is still relatively small, and the proportion of domestic non-state-owned corporate shareholders is also very small, so the influence of private capital on the decision-making and operation of the institutions is very limited. With regard to establishment of private banks initiated by private capital, the China Banking Regulatory Commission (CBRC) started pilot private banks, but only five of them were approved in the first batch. CBRC also put forward special requirements different from the general provisions of the *Commercial Banking Law*. For example, each pilot private bank must have at least two promoters and operate in four modes: (1) "small deposit and small loan", which sets the deposit limit and lower limit of wealth; (2) "large deposit and small loan", which sets the lower limit of deposits and the loan ceiling; (3) "public deposit and public loan", which means both deposit and loan are specific only to legal persons rather than individuals; and (4) "deposit and loan in specific areas", which limits the business and regional scope. These "rules and regulations" determine that private banks and existing commercial banks are in an unequal position in competition, thus restricting impact of private capital on allocation of financial resources.

(2) *Inadequate supply of capital market is due to institutional constraints*

In China, the development of capital market has long been falling behind the development of economy and the banking industry. The supply of direct financing cannot meet the demand, and especially the support to improve the weak links of economic development is far from enough.

The rate of securitization (the total market value/GDP of listed companies) in China is only about 60%, far lower than the United States (170%) and other countries. From the perspective of financing scale and proportion, by the end of July 2016, the stock of social financing was RMB2.188 billion, with a proportion less than 15%. The supply of capital market is insufficient and the function of investment and financing cannot be brought into full play, which results in the imbalance of the financial system structure and the uneven allocation of financial resources among enterprises. This is also an important reason why Chinese enterprises rely excessively on indirect financing based on bank credit and resort to informal finance such as private lending.

Institutional factors are the root cause for above-mentioned problems. The first is the stock issuance system. Due to the approval system in the stock issuance process, the enterprise issuing stock has to receive a certain degree of administrative intervention, and the market mechanism cannot fully play its role, which restricts the full play of the stock market fund-raising function. The approval system also affects the establishment and perfection of the delisting system in the stock market. The listed index of the companies that should be delisted has become "shell resources", which can be used to make profit and is even sought after by the market because of its scarcity.

Then come the stock market transactions and the corresponding regulatory system. Imperfect market transaction mechanism, inadequate supervision, and inadequate punishment imposed on illegal behaviors, together with the problems in the stock issuance system, have led to the speculative nature of the stock market. Speculative trading interferes with effective display of capital pricing function, weakens the ability of market to guide allocation of resources, and causes the market risk to be more easily accumulated and erupt.

2. *Mismatched supply-demand structure of the financial services*

With the transformation and diversification of China's economic system, private enterprises and SMEs play increasingly important roles in promoting economic growth, increasing employment, and accelerating innovation. However, the financial system has not adapted to this situation and effectively transformed the supply structure of the financial services, which leads to the mismatch between the supply and demand of the financial services. The mismatch between different ownerships and sizes of enterprises in enjoyment of financial services has restricted improvement of the supply efficiency and the adjustment and optimization of the economic structure.

(1) *Ownership discrimination still exists in delivery of bank credit loans*

Ownership discrimination in credit investment in China has existed for a long time and has made state-owned enterprises and private enterprises face unequal treatment in obtaining bank loans. Insufficiency of the decisive role of market mechanism in allocation of credit resources has resulted in distorted allocation of resources in the realm of real economy, specifically including the following:

- First, banks prefer to issue loans to state-owned enterprises. This is mainly due to the government's implicit guarantee to reduce the loan risk of state-owned enterprises; what's more, as the more stringent credit responsibility investigation system has led to a stronger risk-averse mentality of credit personnel in recent years, state-owned enterprises become the preferred choice for banks to issue loans. The differentiated threshold of bank loans to different enterprises makes the credit market artificially segmented. For state-owned enterprises, the supply of credit is relatively abundant and the price is relatively low; however, for private enterprises, the supply of credit is relatively short, the availability of credit is poor, and the price is relatively high. The problem of mismatch between demand and supply structure that appears on the credit market has added much to the difficulty for private enterprises to get loans due to higher cost.
- Then, banks analyze and judge the default risk of state-owned enterprises based on the government's rescue policy or action instead of the management and financial situation of these enterprises themselves, thus leading to their failure to deal with the default risk in time.

At present, some industries have excess capacity and some enterprises have too high a leverage ratio, which is the key problem to be solved in the supply-side structural reform. State-owned enterprises occupy a large proportion of the de-capacity and deleveraging tasks. Ownership discrimination in credit lending has contributed much to problems in these enterprises. For example, the production capacity is increased in state-owned enterprises that have already had excess capacity as a result of financial support; loans are released to some "zombie" state-owned enterprises that have already had an extremely high leverage ratio so that these enterprises will not go bankrupt and wait for government bailout.

(2) *Financing instruments for SMEs on the capital market are underdeveloped*

At present, there are over 10 million SMEs in China promoting economic development. However, the high threshold to the capital market and poor financing instruments for SMEs have led to the fact that a majority of SMEs find it hard to get loans from the capital market.

The stock market has expanded rapidly with development of NEEQ and the regional equity market in recent years. By August 2016, the total number of NEEQ-listed companies exceeded 8,500, with a total market value of more than RMB 3 trillion, but SMEs took up only a small percentage and the "inverted pyramid" structure of the stock market has not reversed so far.

In the bond market, despite significant expansion of the market size in recent years that provided stronger support for direct financing of enterprises, RMB 22.3 trillion of all kinds of bonds were issued in 2015, an increase of 87.5% over the same period of the previous year, and the custodian balance of the bond market amounted to RMB 47.9 trillion. Based on the type of bonds, however, we find that financial debts occupy as high as around 25% and that the SMEs set bonds, set bills, and private placement bonds occupy a small proportion. For SMEs, the market is short of high-risk bonds and has raised the financing cost. In 2015, private placement bonds issued by the SMEs were less than RMB 150 billion at a higher rate. Among them, the interest rate of private equity issuance listed on Shanghai Stock Exchange ranged between 4.7% and 15%, averaging at 8.76% with a median value of 9.0%. The interest rate on Shenzhen Stock Exchange ranged from 5.5% to 12%, averaging at 8.88% with a median value of 8.99%. In addition to guarantee fee, underwriting fee, audit fee, attorney fee, and rating fee in the process of issuing, the actual financing service cost amounted to about 13–15%.

3. *Inadequate financial support for economic restructuring*

The word "structural" in the supply-side structural reform indicates adjusting and optimizing the economic structure. To push forward the structural reform of the supply side, we should increase the effective supply, cultivate the new development power, and remove the ineffective production capacity, so that the traditional industries can adapt to the new situation and new demand through transformation. Finance that supports innovation has achieved good development and results in some countries. China has also made some progress in venture capital and science and technology finance. However, there are still some problems and difficulties. In addition, the financial support for transformation and upgrading of traditional industries is obviously insufficient, and there is still a gap as compared with the demand for supply-side structural reform. This kind of problem has been there for a long time; from the system factor, the main reason is that the access threshold to finance and especially to the banking industry has led to less diversity, inadequate market competition, and insufficient internal impetus for diversified services.

(1) *Financial services that support innovation are underdeveloped*

In recent years, venture capital and other financial instruments have developed rapidly in China. Traditional financial institutions have also begun to explore the service of technological innovation. There have also emerged special branches and related businesses such as "science and technology branch". However, the financial support for innovation is still obviously insufficient, and there is still a considerable gap between the implementation of innovation-driven development strategy and the requirement that innovation becomes the main driving force of economic development.

First, the venture capital fund and other equity investment tools provide insufficient support for innovation in real sense as they move toward pre-IPO fund at the stage of investment. According to international practice, in order to promote the development of venture capital and effectively guide its investment in the early and middle stages, we should give special support to policy, including adoption of more favorable tax policies for long-term investment and establishment of exemption conditions for supervision of small-scale equity investment. In China, however, as the capital gains tax is not levied, it is difficult to implement tax incentives for long-term investment and make a comprehensive statement of individual income tax. For venture capital fund, the investors are deprived of preferential tax policy. About quit channels for investment, the high threshold to the stock market, the restriction of capacity expansion, and the lagging development of the merger and acquisition market, especially the policy obstacle of the merger and acquisition transaction involving the state-owned enterprises, make the investment at the early and middle period face the difficulty to quit, thus restraining the enthusiasm of investors.

Then, the technological financial services carried out by banks do not meet the practical needs of innovative enterprises. Innovative enterprises, especially those in the initial stage, are usually short of physical collaterals such as land, real estate, machinery, and equipment, so it is difficult for them to obtain traditional mortgage loans. However, the intellectual property rights of new technologies owned by these enterprises have the same capacity as land, real estate, machinery, and equipment, which enables enterprises to obtain income and cash flow. In this sense, intellectual property rights should also be used as collateral for bank loans. At present, although some banks in China have released intellectual property mortgage loans, the effect is not satisfactory. For example, as early as in October 2006, the Beijing Branch of the Bank of Communications launched an SME intellectual property pledge loan financing product called “Shan Ye Tong”, and issued the first intellectual property pledge loan on the 30th of the same month. However, in nearly 3 years since the launch of product, more than 1,000 technology-based SMEs have applied for evaluation, and only about 50 have successfully obtained the loan. The bank sets a low proportion of financing, stating that the amount of credit granted by the patent for invention does not exceed 25% of the assessed value, the patent for utility model does not exceed 15%, the exclusive right of trademark does not exceed 30%, and that the maximum amount of loans in principle does not exceed $10 million. Besides the loan interest, enterprises must bear 1.25% appraisal fee, 1.25% attorney fee, and 1.5% guarantee fee, so the loan cost accounts for about 10% of a loan. In fact, enterprises finally receive inadequate financing support at a higher cost.

(2) *There is inadequate financial support for transformation and upgrading of traditional industries*

Under the demand of the supply-side structural reform, different industries and enterprises should take different measures according to the actual situation. On the one hand, by disposing of the "zombie" enterprises and removing invalid production capacity, we should reduce the invalid and low-end supply. On the other hand, by accelerating the transformation and upgrading, we should expand effective and high-end supply to improve total factor productivity. In this process, finance should play its role to guide the flow and reallocation of resources. In China, however, the financial system plays a weak role in guiding reallocation of resources to promote transformation and upgrading of traditional industries, and to a certain extent it constitutes an obstacle to the departure of ineffective capacity and the transformation and upgrading of traditional industries.

First, banks and capital markets have failed to play their due roles in the "de-capacity" process. Resolving excess capacity requires banks to play their role based on the operating and financial conditions of loan enterprises, objectively assess the risk status of loan, and in a timely manner dispose of loans issued as non-performing loans to enterprises that are already insolvent, such as "zombie enterprises", in order to enable such enterprises to withdraw from the market. In reality, however, loans are not cut off in timely manner due to banks' non-objective assessment and stated-owned enterprises' hope of obtaining government bailout. Companies that should quit from the market are not required to exit because of continued bank loan support. Resolving excess capacity also needs the capital market to play its role so that enterprise mergers and acquisitions and restructuring can be driven by market forces smoothly. Realizing enterprise merger and acquisition on the platform of the capital market will help integrate and utilize capacity, bring advanced technology and management into play, promote efficiency of the existing capacity utilization, and play the role of invigorating the stock. In the process of enterprise mergers and acquisitions, the capital market needs to find a reasonable price, and the relevant intermediaries need to provide necessary services. However, the capital market in China, especially the M&A market, is not well developed, and the service system supporting M&A is not perfect, thus leading to the difficulty and high cost of M&A among enterprises.

Then, the financial support in the process of traditional industry transformation and upgrading still needs to be strengthened. By updating technology, production model, and business model, the traditional industry can upgrade and form an effective supply to meet new demand. The process of upgrading usually requires more centralized and large-scale investment, such as upgrading machinery and equipment and building a new management system. Therefore, it requires external financing support. At present, however, the financial system of China provides insufficient support for upgrading of the traditional industries primarily because banks are less enthusiastic for intangible assets such as intellectual property rights, which affects the ability and incentive of traditional industrial enterprises to invest in technology for upgrading.

4. *Imperfect mechanism preventing accumulation of financial risks*

Preventing financial risk is of great significance to stable economic development. Once the outbreak of systemic financial risk triggers a crisis, it will not only bring about large fluctuations of economic growth in a short term, but also jeopardize the long-term economic development. In the past 2 years, there were some problems in China, such as sharp fluctuations in the stock market and exposure to risks in the field of Internet lending, which indicates that the financial risk prevention mechanism is not adaptable to the new situation and needs to be perfected urgently.

(1) *Poor monetary policy effect on the real economy brings about such risks as asset bubbles*

The appearance of monetary policy effect should be based on good policy transmission mechanism. The problem of the monetary policy transmission channel not being smooth has existed for a long time in China, which leads to insufficient transmission of policy effect to the real economy.

First, the targeted policy of increasing liquidity has not effectively alleviated the financing difficulties in corresponding areas. In recent years, the central bank has innovated policy operation methods such as directional reduction of standards, providing liquidity to financial institutions according to loan ratio, and so on, aiming to guide capital flow into the real economy, especially SMEs and some key industries. However, due to the influence of financial institutions and corporate behaviors, the policy failed to achieve the desired results. Financial institutions that are partly supported by the policy in practice use this part of low-cost funds to repay matured debt, or carry trade in the money market. No fund flows into the real economy but circulates within the financial system. Enterprises that have received some low-cost loans have benefited from diverting funds into security investment or transferring them to enterprises that are short of funds in areas such as real estate rather than expanding their own investment. Money that does not flow into the real economy but stays in the financial system or flows into the real estate and other fields has led to bubbles in the stock market, bond market, and real estate market.

Then, the decreasing capital cost has not been effectively transmitted to the real economy. It is also an important goal of structural monetary policy to reduce interest rate on the credit market and reduce the financing cost for the whole society. Judging from the actual situation, we find that the effect of the policy still stays at the money market level and has not entered the credit market.

There are defects in the financial supervision system and risks in the internet finance and other fields, which shows that the current framework of financial supervision in China still maintains the framework of segregated supervision that formed since the 1990s. It is the responsibility of three committees of the financial institutions to divide the responsibility of supervision according to the type of licenses obtained by the financial institutions, and to carry out institutional supervision. Affected by the trend of mixed operation in the world, China's financial institutions have realized mixed operation through establishment of subsidiaries and acquisition of equity of other financial institutions. Under the circumstance of the changing financial industry, the financial supervision system has not adapted to the reform and readjustment, which leads to blind, long, and arbitrage supervision. Some financial risks are separated from supervision, and the effectiveness of financial risk prevention and control is insufficient.

First, with the rapid development of new-type finance, the blind area of supervision under the mode of institutional supervision is becoming increasingly larger. In recent years, along with continuous expansion of the scale of financial assets in China, the strengthening of the concept of financial management, and rapid development of the Internet economy, many new institutions engaged in financial activities, such as the P2P network loan platform. However, under the mode of institutional supervision, regulators only supervise the financial licensed institutions, so that new institutions that engaged in financial activities dissociate from the unified supervision and form the blind area of financial risk supervision. Moreover, after the local risk exposure has aroused social concern, the regulatory department still failed to assume its responsibility but transferred the responsibility to the local regulatory authority. For P2P services, the *Guidance on Promoting the Healthy Development of Internet Finance* issued by the People's Bank of China has clearly been supervised by the CBRC; however, in the *Interim Measures on the Management of Business Activities of Network Borrowing and Lending Information Intermediaries*, the CBRC only retains the responsibility of formulating unified development policies, measures, and the supervision and management system, while the responsibility for supervision and risk disposal is entrusted to the local financial regulatory authorities. Due to the vertical management by financial regulatory departments, local financial supervision bodies face insufficient personnel, lack of regulatory means, and difficult administrative law enforcement, supervision, and risk management responsibilities.

Then, similar businesses also face fragmented regulators, resulting in the problem of regulator's arbitrage. This problem is particularly serious in the asset management business that has grown rapidly in recent years. Driven by the large debt size of various financial institutions and the process of interest rate marketization as well as residents' higher requirements for asset returns, asset management industries, including financing, entrusted with loans and investment have emerged in banks, insurance companies, securities companies, and fund companies. With the same nature of business, the regulatory rules are quite different because these rules are formulated by different regulators. In reality, when there are conditions for mixed operation, more funds are flowing into sectors under loose supervision for arbitrage.

Finally, the lack of monitoring and identification of macro-level cross-industry financial risk is not conducive to prevention of systemic risks. Under the trend of mixed operation, the deepening of business connection, convergence between different types of financial institutions, and the widening risk gap have led to faster transmission and diffusion of financial risks to a larger coverage. The international financial crisis triggered by the subprime mortgage crisis in the United States in 2008 has exposed the role of cross-industry risk transmission and diffusion in the transformation from local risk exposure to systemic risk and even crisis outbreak. Under the separation supervision system of our country, regulatory authorities are responsible for micro-prudential supervision of the financial institutions. Ensuring robustness of operation of each institution and the controllability of risk, the monitoring and early warning and prevention mechanism for cross-industry risk transmission in the macro-level are difficult to implement due to lack of effective supervision and coordination and full sharing of information, which is very disadvantageous to prevention of systemic financial risk.

III. General Framework for Financial System Reform Under the Promotion of Supply-Side Structural Reform

In December 2015, the Central Economic Work Conference proposed deepening the structural reform of the supply side under the new normal of economic development. This is a targeted solution to the prominent contradictions faced by China's economic development and the main line of economic and social development during the "13th Five-Year Plan" period. The supply-side structural reform puts forward new requirements for the reform and development of the financial system. To meet these requirements, we propose the following general framework for the reform of the financial system.

1. *Basic framework*

Give full pay to the decisive role of market mechanism in allocation of financial resources: strengthen ability of the finance to serve the real economy; promote the banking system reform, relax market access, strengthen competition, and improve the efficiency of credit resources allocation; perfect the capital market system, relax restrictions, expand capacity, and improve efficiency, and increase proportion of direct financing; promote development of diversified financing instruments, especially the direct financing instruments to make the supply of financial services better adapt to the financing needs of real economy; perfect the framework of monetary policy and financial supervision system and maintain the bottom line of non-systemic financial risk so that the reform of financial system can help eliminate excess production capacity and inventory, deleverage, reduce cost, and improve weak points; promote adjustment of economic structure, foster new impetus for economic growth, and provide strong support for the supply-side structural reform.

2. *Major objectives*

(1) *Improving the efficiency of financial resource allocation*

Relax the banking access, develop private banks, enhance competition, and improve the efficiency of bank credit resource allocation: improve the system of capital market; strengthen the function of multilevel capital market; give play to the role of direct financing to match diversified capital supply and demand; raise the proportion of direct financing to promote the overall efficiency of financial resources allocation.

(2) *Enhancing the adaptability and flexibility of the supply structure of financial services*

Accelerate improvement of the financial system mechanism: promote the market mechanism to play its due role; improve the ability of financial services supply to flexibly adapt to the financing needs of the real economy; stimulate development of the feeble sectors; alleviate the financing bottleneck restriction of entrepreneurial innovation, transformation, and upgrading; mobilize financial institutions to follow up on the new demand of real economy; increase the effective supply of financial services and reduce the contradiction of supply and demand structure.

(3) *Prevent and defuse financial risks and hold the bottom line of systemic financial risks*

Improve the monetary policy framework: strengthen the role of price-based tools, reasonably mix and use policy tools, and focus on dredging policy transmission channels to improve the effectiveness of monetary policy; reform the financial supervision system; change the concept of supervision; strengthen supervision and coordination; improve the macro-prudential supervision mechanism; achieve full coverage of financial risks and effectively prevent systemic financial risks.

3. *Key points of the reform*

(1) *Accelerate the diversified development of the banking system*

Promote full competition and relaxation of market access; allow more social capital to fund establishment of small- and medium-sized private banks; increase the number of small- and medium-sized banks, increase the supply of financial services for small- and medium-sized enterprises and private enterprises; alleviate the problem of financing; promote the coordinated development of small- and medium-sized banks, state-owned banks, and private banks to compete equally; speed up the efficiency of the banking industry; stimulate banks to increase effective supply to meet the demand for diversified financial services.

(2) *Perfect the functions of capital market to accelerate direct financing*

We must adhere to the market-oriented reform direction, expand the depth and breadth of the capital market, and improve efficiency and stability on the basis of serving the real economy. Focusing on the key tasks of the supply-side structural reform, we should increase the proportion of direct financing, especially equity financing, reduce the leverage of enterprises, and bring into play the positive role of financial resource market allocation in the process of removing excess capacity and inventory.

(3) *Develop financial services that support entrepreneurship and innovation*

Widen direct financing channels for entrepreneurial innovation: encourage venture capital funds to invest in early- and mid-term enterprises; develop institutional investors and encourage high-net-worth people to participate in venture capital and angel investment; establish the rotary board mechanism between NEEQ and the main board market to enhance the continuity of financing; guide banks to provide intangible assets, such as intellectual property and pledge loans; expand financial services in line with the characteristics of financial demand for entrepreneurial innovation; effectively change the situation that entrepreneurial innovation is constrained by financing bottlenecks.

(4) *Reform and improve the monetary policy framework and the financial regulatory system*

Further reform and improve the monetary policy system: promote the monetary policy framework from quantitative control to price-based control; establish and improve the macro-prudential management system; promote the transition from institutional supervision to functional supervision; reduce regulatory blind spots and regulatory arbitrage; achieve effective balance between innovation and risk; effectively prevent financial risks; firmly hold the bottom line and maintain financial stability.

IV. Suggestions for Financial System Reform Under Promotion of the Supply-Side Structural Reform

1. *Clearly define the conditions for access to the banking sector and allow qualified private capital to set up commercial banks*

Relax the restrictions on private capital entering the banking industry: Enrich the type and number of banking institutions, especially the small- and medium-sized ones; promote the competition of banking industry; encourage banks to adapt to the market demand and increase effective supply of financial services and improve the efficiency of financial services. At present, there are a small number of private banks invested by private capital in China. The scope of business is limited, and it is thus difficult to give play to the role of the structural reform on the financial supply side. It is suggested that on the basis of the pilot projects carried out by the private banks, we should clearly relax restrictions on private capital entering the banking industry: abolish restrictions on the number of shareholders, the specific market orientation, and the mode of operation of the private banks; allow the private capital to set up real commercial banks in accordance with conditions stipulated in the *Commercial Banking Law* so as to compete fairly with the existing commercial banks of other natures under the unified regulatory rules.

2. *Reform the issuance, trading, and delisting system of the stock market*

Meet the demand of supply-side structural reform: Further deepen the capital market reform; effectively expand the effective supply scale of capital market; optimize the supply structure and rationally dredge demand so as to develop multilevel capital market and expand the scale and proportion of direct equity financing to support deleveraging; improve the issuing mechanism of new shares, the refinancing system, and the mechanism of mergers and acquisitions; standardize development of the NEEQ and regional stock market; study and explore establishment of the over-the-counter market under the unified supervision;

enhance the ability of the capital market to serve the small- and medium-sized enterprises; strengthen the legal basis of safeguarding the healthy development of the stock market; strengthen the supervision and warning of the risks of various kinds of trading behaviors; suppress market speculation and promote the flow of market resources to the real economy; combine strict supervision with active guidance to eliminate redundant supply and optimize supply structure; improve the delisting system; clean up "zombie enterprises"; strictly control the restructuring of the listing; support "de-capacity"; further facilitate the use of capital market financing by enterprises; comprehensively reduce financing costs. We will deepen the reform of the GEM and NEEQ markets: vigorously support the listing of innovative start-ups such as the Internet, high-end manufacturing, and modern service industries; support the development of listed companies to the high-end sectors of the industrial chain through refinancing and mergers and acquisitions at home and abroad, thus facilitating the cultivation of a new momentum for economic development.

3. *Further widen the type of bond market financing instruments*

Accelerate the establishment of a unified national bond issuance and trading system, including unified access conditions, information disclosure standards, credit rating requirements, investor market system, and investor protection system: Improve the market mechanism; guide adjustment of the bond market structure and focus on expanding the size of corporate bonds; expand the issuance and over-the-counter trading of private securities of small- and medium-sized enterprises; increase the number of high-yielding bonds and asset secularization products; strengthen support for small- and medium-sized enterprises; continue to relax restrictions on the access of investors to the bond market; open the market to domestic and foreign commercial banks, insurance companies, asset management agencies, securities companies, trust companies, government investment management companies, fund management companies, pension funds, and other institutional investors.

4. *Standardize development of venture capital and equity investment funds*

The development of all kinds of investment funds is not only an important way to expand direct financing but also a necessary means to make up for the lack of support for innovation in bank credit and securities markets: It is suggested that the tax support policy should be adjusted and perfected, the scope of application of the current tax credit policy should be expanded, and the preferential tax policy for individual investment in the early- and mid-term start-up and innovation enterprises should be studied: further improve the model of government guidance; encourage venture capital guidance funds to participate in equity funds, joint investment, risk compensation, financing guarantees, and other ways to better play leading roles; relax the restrictions on banks, insurance companies, social security funds, commercial pensions, and other institutions participating in venture capital, equity investment funds through development of institutional investors and formation of a relatively stable long-term source of funds; develop the potential of high-net-worth people to support innovation, and promote angel investment; establish regulatory rules that are different from those of public issuance and trading securities; speed up the construction of an industry management system that combines moderate supervision with industry self-discipline; promote the development of venture capital and equity investment norms.

5. *Reform and improve the monetary policy framework*

After the interest rate marketization is basically completed, the operating environment of monetary policy changes and the framework of monetary policy will be adjusted and perfected as soon as possible: It is suggested that the monetary policy committee system should be improved and the independence and scientificity of monetary policy decision should be enhanced by extending the term of office of experts and absorbing officials from regional branches of the central bank: establish interest rate corridor to guide the market short-term interest based on the relatively stable 7-day Shibor interest rate; establish the floating corridor to guide the short-term interest rate to run reasonably in the corridor and to strengthen the role of interest rate instruments; establish the mechanism of periodical publicity of monetary policy decision information and multi-channel published information; enhance policy transparency; strengthen effective communication between the central bank and the market, form benign interactions, and gradually improve the guiding role of public expectations.

6. *Promote the transformation of financial supervision from institutional supervision to functional supervision, and strengthen regulatory coordination and macro-prudential supervision*

Change the concept of supervision from the current institutional supervision to functional supervision according to the nature of the business division of regulatory responsibility: After clarifying the scope of the financial business supervised by the supervisory departments, we should clarify the ownership of the supervisory responsibility as soon as possible for the financial business that is not under the unified supervision, and apply the supervisory rules to the same kind of business or formulate reasonable supervisory rules. For new financial business forms, it is necessary to clarify the responsibility of supervision in time, bring it into the unified scope of supervision, and eliminate the blind area of supervision dynamically: further improve the macro-prudential supervision system; implement the macro-prudential supervision responsibility of the People's Bank of China; improve the decision-making coordination and information-sharing mechanism of the three committees; achieve effective monitoring and evaluation of cross-industry, cross-market, and cross-border financial risks; form a monitoring and early-warning mechanism for financial risks to adapt to the trend of mixed operation; keep the financial system running steadily; enhance the effect of counter-cyclical adjustment; strengthen the capital buffer and the ability to resist risks on the basis of the steady operation of the single financial institution.

Chapter 4

Research on Building Innovation System to Support Supply-Side Structural Reform

Huang Hanquan and Sheng Chaoxun

Academy of Macroeconomic Research

Abstract

Constructing an open and efficient innovation system is an important part of the supply-side structural reform and plays an important role in de-capacity, de-stocking, de-leveraging, reducing cost, and improving weak points. To deepen the supply-side structural reform, we must speed up construction of the open and efficient innovation system. At present, China has created an innovation support system integrating government, enterprises, scientific research institutes, and universities, but there are still some problems such as underdeveloped core technologies, insufficient impetus for enterprise innovation, incompetent teams of the scientific and technological talents, and imperfect institutional mechanism; therefore, it is imperative to promote construction of the open and efficient innovation systems. For this purpose, we should perfect the incentive system, stimulate the vitality of all kinds of innovation subjects, promote innovation infrastructure, enhance the support of talent elements, and cultivate the social environment to encourage innovation and create a system arrangement which is favorable for innovation.

I. Creating an Open and High-Efficiency Innovation System — the Key to Promoting Supply-Side Structural Reform

Deeply understanding the significance of the innovation system and the supply-side structural reform is a logical starting point for us to analyze the relationship between constructing the open and efficient innovation system and promoting the supply-side structural reform. The OECD defines innovation system as an interrelated ecosystem composed of innovation subjects, innovation infrastructure, innovation resources, innovation environment, and external interaction. Among them, the system design and connection mechanism are the key to improving the innovation ability and efficiency. The purpose of the supply-side structural reform is to reduce production cost and transaction cost, rectify market distortion, promote innovation, and improve the quality and efficiency of the supply system. According to us, supply not only means provision of products or services but also includes more intensive allocation of production factors and effective new institutional supply. The five main tasks of "de-capacity, de-stocking, de-leveraging, reducing cost and improve weak points" proposed by the State Council of the CPC Central Committee in 2016 are specific contents of the supply-side structural reform. Thus, construction of an open and efficient innovation system is essentially an important part of the supply-side structural reform, which can provide support for the supply-side structural reform in multiple dimensions (see Figure 1), especially in fulfilling the main tasks of "de-capacity, de-stocking, de-leveraging, reducing cost and improve weak points".

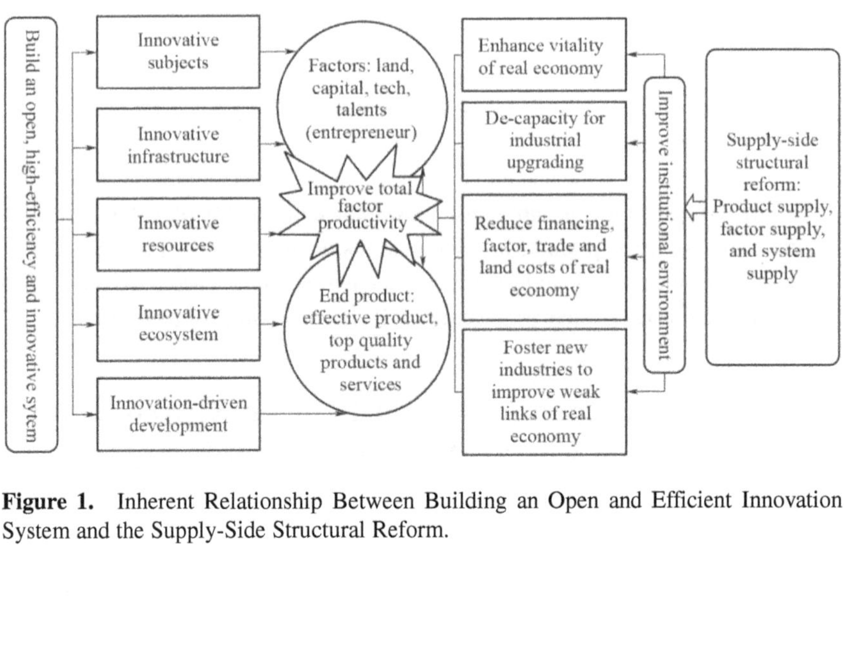

Figure 1. Inherent Relationship Between Building an Open and Efficient Innovation System and the Supply-Side Structural Reform.

1. *Constructing an open and efficient innovation system by "de-capacity"*

"De-capacity" is an important issue in the current economic development of China. It is also the primary task of the supply-side structural reform proposed by the Central Economic Work Conference in 2016. However, "de-capacity" does not mean "cutting industries". When excess capacity is cut off, we should actively develop new products through innovation and enhance industrial competitiveness. When the United States responded to excess capacity brought about by the financial crisis, it implemented the supply-side structural reform to enhance innovation and industrial competitiveness by making breakthroughs in clean energy, information, biology, and space technology to cut excess capacity. We should borrow its experience in this regard. The process of "de-capacity" aims to improve the ability of innovation and development of industry, speed up construction of an open and efficient innovation system, and encourage enterprises to achieve the purpose of "de-capacity" by developing new technology and new products and extending the industrial chain and line of products.

2. *Reducing cost by improving supply-side efficiency through innovation*

In China, under the influence of changing supply and demand, intensifying resource environment restrictions, inability of finance to serve real economy, and an imperfect market system in recent years, the rising manufacturing cost has denied China advantages over the leading industrialized countries and regions, which produces significant restrictions on the transformation and upgrading of the manufacturing industry in China. The fastest rise of cost occurred in labor and land. From 2011 to 2014, the average annual wage of urban manufacturing workers rose from RMB 36,700 to 514,000, an average annual increase of 13.5%, about 1 percentage point higher than the growth rate of the main manufacturing business in the same period, and about 7 percentage points higher than the growth rate of total profit. But from the perspective of future development trends, as the rising labor cost is difficult to reverse, we will improve labor productivity by means of innovation to hedge the rising cost. It is thus clear that cost can be reduced by improving the supply-side efficiency through innovation. Therefore, it is necessary to insist on a combination of cost reduction and efficiency improvement, encourage enterprises to increase R&D investment, promote transformation from "demographic bonus" to "talent bonus", improve the efficiency of factor output, reduce the relative cost by efficiency promotion, and promote the transformation and upgrading of the manufacturing industry.

3. *"Improving weak points" by enhancing the ability of innovation and development*

After years of development, China's industry has made remarkable achievements. Of the 500 major industrial products in the world, China has more than 200 products, with their output ranking first in the world. The production of iron and steel, cement, electrolytic aluminum, and shipbuilding accounts for more than 45% of the world's total. However, the problem of the large but not strong manufacturing industry in China is relatively prominent. Most of the 100 enterprises entering the world's top 500 are resource-based industries and financial and real estate companies, while the number of innovative enterprises is relatively small. According to the World Intellectual Property Commission's latest Global Innovation Index 2015, the scale of knowledge output, the innovative infrastructure, and the human capital status in China are leading the world, but the ranking of business environment and other aspects is relatively low. For example, with regard to protection of investor rights and interests among 141 sample countries, China only ranked 114th; for measures of production, learning and research, innovation clusters, government and private sector cooperation, and other indicators, China's ranking remained low. These are precisely the areas that the supply-side structural reform needs to strengthen in industry, and are also the focus of the next step to improve the innovation system and enhance the ability of innovation and development.

4. *Improving the institutional arrangement of innovation-driven development by emphasizing construction of the innovation system*

Future competition is to a great extent the institutional competition. Whether there are achievements of scientific and technological innovation will, to a large extent, depend on whether there is a good ecology of industrial innovation. However, China's economic development has long been driven by factors and investment, which leads to large but not strong economic development and to many institutional barriers which are not conducive to innovation. Through supply-side structural reforms, we should solve such deep-seated contradictions and problems as "worship of growth rate" and "dependence on factors and investment drivers" that have restricted the transformation of China's economic development pattern; we should also perfect the institutional arrangement of innovation-driven development, construct an efficient innovation system that is conducive to the emergence of innovation achievements, stimulate the innovation vitality of the whole society, implement the innovation-driven development strategy, and promote innovation-driven development.

II. Evaluation of the Status Quo and Bottleneck Obstacles of China's Innovation System

Though there is an innovative system that integrates government, enterprises, scientific research institutes, colleges and universities, and technological innovation in China, the overall efficiency remains low in the following aspects:

1. *The position of the enterprise innovation subjects is gradually determined, but the impetus and ability of enterprise innovation still need to be strengthened*

In recent years, China has increased support for technical R&D in enterprises to arouse enterprise enthusiasm for technical development; in addition, positive progress has been made in construction of the innovation system. But, China is short of core technologies with independent intellectual property rights, and enterprises need to strengthen their role in the innovation decision-making, investment in R&D, scientific research organization, and achievement application. For example, chips and integrated circuits, known as the "heart" of the electronic and information industry, need to be imported in large quantities, making them the largest imported commodity in China for three consecutive years from 2013, which amounted to $229.9 billion in 2015. High dependence of technology and core products has hampered industrial development. In March 2016, the United States imposed sanctions on ZTE, which banned ZTE from purchasing US chips, causing severe damage to the development of ZTE and related industries. In addition, the R&D investment of Chinese enterprises is obviously low. At present, the average R&D investment of large- and medium-sized industrial enterprises accounts for only 0.9% of the income of the main business, which is a big gap as compared with the average level of 2–3% in major developed countries, and directly restricts improvement of the innovation ability of enterprises.

2. *The team of innovative talents expands but is less competent*

In recent years, under the guidance of the strategy of rejuvenating the country by science and technology, investment in education and research and development has been constantly increasing, and talents of scientific and technological innovation are also growing rapidly. At present, China has become a country with the largest number of scientific and technological human resources in the world, according to *China Science and Technology Talent Report (2014)* issued by the Ministry of Science and Technology. In 2013, the total number of science and technology human resources reached 71.05 million people, of which the total number of R&D personnel as the core of science and technology activities increased rapidly to 5.018 million in 2013. According to the full-time equivalent statistics, the total number of R&D personnel reached 353.5 million people a year, exceeding that of the United States and ranking first in the world. In 2014, China's full-time equivalent of R&D personnel reached 3.94 million people a year, accounting for 28% of the world's total. According to the *China Science and Technology Human Resources Development Report 2014* issued by China Science and Technology Association, by the end of 2014, China's science and technology human resources totaled about 81.14 million people, ranking first in the world. However, there are three problems: low output efficiency per capita, scarcity of high-end innovative talents, and brain drain. According to the *Report on Human Resources 2016* published by the World Economic Forum (WEF), China's human capital index ranks 71st among 132 sample countries, but there is still much room for improvement. China has 38 R&D personal per 10,000 people, far lower than Japan (133/10,000), Korea (135/10,000), and Germany (132/10,000). According to the statistics of the Ministry of Science and Technology, the total number of real high-end talents in China is about 10,000 people, while the number of academicians in the United States is more than ten times that of China. In China, there are few academicians in the fields of aviation and cutting-edge automobiles, and there are a small number of winners of international science and technology awards such as the Nobel Prize, Ruska Prize, Gairdner Prize, Wolf Prize, Fields Prize, and Turing Prize. Of the top 250 scientists in the 22 disciplines of SCI statistics, there are more than 6,000 people in the world and fewer than 100 in China. According to a survey by the Ministry of Science and Technology, the proportion of PhD students willing to work in enterprises in China is less than 15%, while the same for the United States is as high as 80%. In addition, the brain drain phenomenon is also more prominent. Take international students as an example. In recent years, the return rate of Chinese international students has been 30–40%, lower than the international average of 40–50%; most of the students who returned are those with master's degrees, and only 5% of PhD students came back to China after graduation.

3. *Infrastructure of innovation is becoming increasingly complete, but the construction of technical innovation service system remains backward*

China has been increasing investment since the economic reform and opening up to the outside world in 1978, especially in recent years. The scale of innovation infrastructure, including major science and technology infrastructure, science and technology infrastructure platform, and industry innovation infrastructure platform, has continued to increase; the coverage area has been expanded, the technical level has been improved obviously, and the comprehensive benefits have become increasingly apparent. At present, China's major scientific and technological infrastructure in nuclear physics, life science, manned spaceflight, resource exploration, and other fields can provide strong support for upgrading the technical level of related industries. The co-construction and sharing of large-scale scientific instruments and facilities can also provide strong support for the promotion of innovation ability. At present, the construction of scientific and technological infrastructures such as national germplasm resources, national experimental materials, and reference materials' resources has steadily advanced, and the pace of construction of international scientific data centers and scientific and technological literature resources has been accelerated, thus gradually forming a national shared network. The construction of high-level scientific research institutes and research-oriented universities has been accelerated, and the role of scientific research institutes and universities as sources of innovation has been strengthened. In addition, a number of scientific research bases with international influence have been initially established. The state vigorously promotes construction of new R&D platforms such as the Industrial Innovation Center, and encourages construction of centers such as the State Engineering Laboratory and the State Engineering Research Center which are a combination of manufacturer, university, and research facilities. However, due to poor technical innovation service support ability, there are still some problems such as imperfect innovation supporting service organization, insufficient service contents, and a shortage of network efficient service systems, which restricts promotion of the industrial technological innovation ability. In particular, China's innovation system has been a long-standing problem impeding construction of related service support systems. For example, the backward reform of institutional systems in China makes the personnel and salary system of Chinese universities and scientific research institutes lag far behind the requirements of the era of innovation and development, hinders the flow and effective allocation of scientific and technological human resources, and suppresses the tremendous potential of scientific and technological innovation. Unreasonable restrictions from scientific research projects and fund management have seriously dampened the enthusiasm of scientific and technological personnel for innovation and development.

4. *Innovation environment continues to be optimized but needs further improvement*

The innovation environment is the sum of relations formed by a combination of various elements within the space of innovation subjects, including protection of legal environment of innovation, cultivation of an open and competitive market environment, and a strong social atmosphere. In recent years, with the implementation of a series of national and local policies aimed at optimization, the innovation environment in China has been continuously improved, showing a better development trend. For example, an increasing number of policies focus on encouraging market-oriented innovation, and the positive incentive effect of the market on innovation is increasing. But generally speaking, there are still many problems that seriously restrict the improvement of innovation ability, and the market environment and social atmosphere that encourage innovation need to be further cultivated and optimized. First, protection of intellectual property is insufficient. Poor awareness of intellectual property protection, cases of infringement on intellectual property from time to time, and loose punishment on infringers of intellectual property have led to "low cost of infringement but high cost of safeguarding rights", which is not conducive to stimulating innovation passion of enterprises. Second, the education system restrains innovation. The current education system of China attaches more importance to the inheritance of knowledge than to scientific and technological innovation, and more to standardized education than to individualized education. Under this kind of education system, the students' innovative thinking and ability are obliterated to a certain extent, which cannot meet the needs of the society for professional and innovative talents in an all-round way. Finally, collaborative innovation of knowledge and technology is not sufficient. The research of scientists and the computational innovation of entrepreneurs are not closely connected: the market demand cannot be immediately fed back to knowledge innovation, knowledge innovation cannot provide good service for technological innovation, and the market conversion rate of scientific research results remains low.

5. *The reform of scientific research system is deepened, but the market-oriented institutional mechanism still needs to be improved*

Since Comrade Deng Xiaoping put forward that science and technology were productive forces at the National Science Conference in 1978, great progress and remarkable achievements have been made in the reform of China's science and technology system, and the cause of science and technology has developed rapidly; in addition, a large number of major scientific and technological achievements have been made. In September 2015, the General Office of the CPC Central Committee and the General Office of the State Council issued the *Implementation Plan for Deepening the Reform of Scientific and Technological System*, stating the direction for better implementation of the reform decision of the CPC Central Committee and opening up channels for scientific and technological innovation and economic and social development. At the same time, however, there are still some drawbacks in the science and technology system. The market-oriented system of science and technology still needs to be perfected, since loose connection between technology and economy; imperfect cooperative innovation mechanism among industry, university, and research; asymmetric scientific and technological input and output; scattered, duplicated, closed, inefficient, and unreasonable research projects and funding arrangements; unreasonable technology evaluation mechanism; and underdevelopment of scientific research honesty and innovation culture all still exist. These problems have restricted the development of scientific and technological productive forces and hindered independent innovation and science and technology support for promotion of economic and social development capacity.

III. General Framework of Creating the Innovation System to Support the Supply-Side Structural Reform

1. *General framework: "One system and five pillars"*

At present, the general framework for constructing the supply-side structural innovation system can be summed up as "one system and five pillars". "One system" refers to the innovation system led by market, enterprises, talented people, and institutional systems and coordinated by all kinds of innovation actors, which combines government, manufacturers, universities, research institutes, and users. The "five pillars" include enterprises, talented people, and new scientific research institutions, intermediary organizations, alliances, and service agencies that provide good innovation environment and institutional guarantee, which can be explained as follows:

(1) **Treat enterprises as key actors:** Enterprises are key actors of innovation and the main building force of the innovation system. We should build an enterprise-based, market-oriented national technological innovation system that combines manufacturers, universities, and research institutes; reform the management system of scientific research projects to promote transformation of science and technology innovation from technology that is supply oriented to market that is demand oriented; establish an industrial technology research and development system with enterprises as key players; strive to create a group of innovative leading enterprises with strong R&D strength and international competitiveness; promote the healthy development of a large number of small- and medium-sized scientific and technological enterprises (see Figure 2).

(2) **Treat talents as the supporting force:** Talents are the first cause for innovation. To build an open and efficient innovation system, it is necessary to strengthen the innovative vitality of talents and promote emergence of a large number of innovative and entrepreneurial talents. We should attach great importance to introduction, cultivation, development, and employment of interdisciplinary, versatile, and

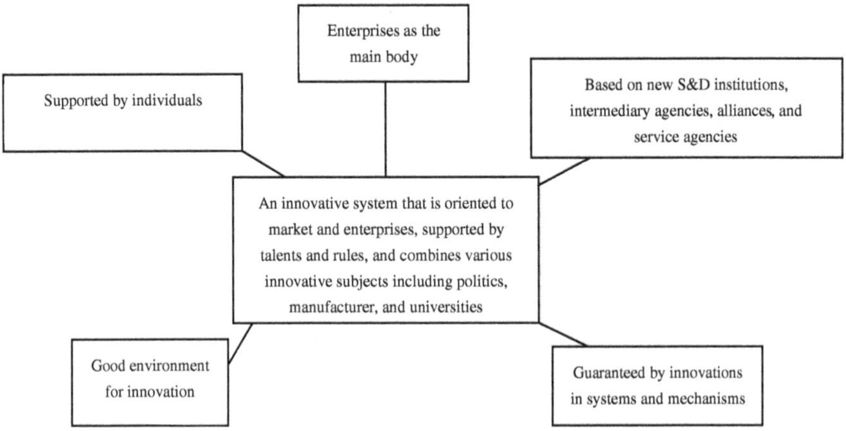

Figure 2. Sketch of the Innovation System.

professional talents in order to meet personnel demands of the economic social development and give full play to talented persons according to innovative policies for education, training, and immigration; deepen the reform of education system and personnel evaluation system; implement national strategy for priority development of education; accelerate growth of occupational, entrepreneurial, and lifelong education.

(3) **Base personnel development on new scientific research institutions, intermediary organizations, alliances, and service providers:** The innovation service support system is a weak point in construction of the supply-side structural innovation system in China. Create an innovative service platform that integrates creation, employment, and operation in enterprises; focus on integration of industrial base, personnel training, technological market, patent maintenance, redevelopment of overdue patents, financial support for venture capital, introduction of innovative methods, and market development; accelerate reform of specialization and marketization of new business incubation, intellectual property services, third-party inspection, and certification; build a platform for socialization, specialization, and networking of technological innovation services for development of enterprise innovation.

(4) **Rely on a good environment for innovation:** The competitiveness of the innovation system depends not only on the investment of resources such as capital and talent but also on the innovation environment. Among them, a good market environment is the fundamental support of innovation, so we should form a market mechanism of survival of the fittest. Let the market be the referee of innovation; stimulate the motivation for innovation; smoothen the cooperative environment as the prerequisite of innovation; create a smooth cooperative environment of industry–university–research to support innovation and to promote integration of various resources based on market orientation; make an effective investment and financing environment the "catalyst" of innovation and an important way to solve problems in innovation system; focus on construction of an efficient and convenient investment and financing system; strive to form a social consensus and atmosphere of "daring to innovate, daring to be the first, encouraging competition, advocating cooperation, pursuing success and tolerating failure"; create an open and fair environment for innovation and entrepreneurship.

(5) **Focus on innovation in institutional mechanism:** Institutional mechanism innovation is an important guarantee for construction of an open and efficient innovation system. Target science and technology toward economic and social development; give full play to the market's guiding role in the direction of technological research and development, route selection, factor price, and the allocation of innovative elements; deploy innovative chains around the industrial chain; further explore cooperative innovation mechanisms between industry, university, and research; eliminate the "isolated island phenomenon" in scientific and technological innovation; improve the overall efficiency of the national innovation system; strengthen application and protection of intellectual property rights; break down barriers restricting the spread of scientific and technological achievements; improve mechanism for technological transfer; promote capitalization and industrialization of scientific and technological achievements; strengthen the reform of scientific research management system; establish a mechanism in which the market determines the technical innovation projects, the allocation of funds, and the evaluation of results.

2. *Major objectives*

By 2020, a national innovation system with Chinese characteristics will be basically established to provide strong support for the supply-side structural reform. The role of enterprises and entrepreneurs in the decision-making of national innovation has been enhanced, and the investment in research and development has been greatly increased, so the ratio of the expenditure on research and development to the income of the main business has reached 1.1%. The number and quality of innovative talents have improved steadily. A team of innovative scientific and technological talents with broad scope, reasonable structure, and excellent quality has been formed, and the structure of human resources and employment has been improved markedly, with R&D personnel reaching up to 60 per 10,000 employed persons per year. Major science and technology infrastructure, science and technology infrastructure platforms, universities and research institutes, industrial innovation infrastructure platforms, and other innovative infrastructures have been created in Shanghai, Beijing, and Hefei to form a central framework for national science. Service organizations including intellectual property, technology intermediary, and innovation alliance have been further improved, and innovation and entrepreneurship services have become more efficient and convenient. The innovation environment is more optimized; the policies and regulations to encourage innovation are close to perfect, and the protection of intellectual property rights is stricter, which is conducive to the value orientation of innovation and the formation of cultural atmosphere. With the further deepening of the reform of the scientific research system, the flow of innovative elements such as talents, technology, and capital is smoother; the innovation chain is organically linked, and the synergy effect of the innovation system is more significant. The role of innovation system in the structural reform of supply-side is greatly enhanced to accelerate integration of traditional industries and growth of emerging industries, which plays a more prominent role in expanding effective supply and high-end supply and improving the quality and efficiency of the supply system.

By 2025, the innovation system will be more complete, and the synergy of all innovation players will be brought into full play, which will strongly support fundamental transformation of the development power. Enterprises become real players in innovation research and development, in basic realization of market-oriented clear science and technology projects led by enterprises, and in the government-led joint institutions of higher learning and research institutions to implement the linkage mechanism of production, learning, and research. There have emerged a large number of strategic scientific and technological talents, innovative entrepreneurs, and high-skilled workers, focusing on young scientific and technological talents, talent evaluation mechanisms, mobility, and motivation. The construction and layout of innovation infrastructure are constantly being optimized to form a pattern of cooperation and common support among national laboratories, national engineering technology centers, national enterprise technology centers, and industrial innovation centers, which plays a vital role in construction of interdisciplinary collaborative innovation networks and systems. The innovative service system is more synergistic and efficient, and integration of science and technology economy becomes smoother. With a good innovative culture atmosphere and strong rule of law, innovation is more productive than ever before. Institutional mechanisms conducive to innovative drive and innovation system construction are more mature and stereotyped after the basic policy system of scientific and technological innovation was formed; the technological innovation system is close to perfect after the overall efficiency of the national innovation system was remarkably improved. A large number of scientific and technological achievements were transformed into real productive forces to foster development of new kinetic energy sources.

IV. Recommended Policy Measures

We think it vital to perfect the incentive mechanism, stimulate all players' vitality in innovation, promote construction of innovation infrastructure, increase talent factor support, cultivate social environment to encourage innovation, and form a system arrangement favorable to innovation.

1. *Stimulate players' vitality in innovation*

Stimulate enterprises, universities, and scientific research institutions, new research and development institutions, and various types of specialized service institutions to enhance their innovation capacity and supply of innovation sources.

- **Strengthen the main position and leading role of enterprises in innovation:** Encourage enterprises to carry out basic innovative research; increase their participation in making decisions on national science and technology planning and application-oriented major science and technology projects; establish a key industry technology tackling system in demand-oriented, enterprise-led, enterprise-procured universities and scientific research institutions; focus on enterprise innovation capacity building through typical demonstration and other means; implement the top 100 projects for innovative enterprises; expedite cultivation of a number of innovative leading enterprises with independent intellectual property rights and well-known brands and international influence; strive to enable backbone enterprises to truly possess technological innovation capabilities of producing, researching, and developing in 5–10 years; cultivate a group of innovative enterprises and a large number of innovative and vibrant SMEs.
- **Promote integration of science and education:** Encourage institutions of higher learning, vocational colleges, and scientific research institutes to participate in construction of the national innovation system; support a number of high-level universities and scientific research institutes to form interdisciplinary, comprehensive, and crosscutting scientific research teams; speed up construction of a number of industrial innovation centers and innovative networks that are led by enterprises, academically collaborative, pluralistic investments and military–civilian convergence; develop new market-oriented research and development institutions; promote cross-industry collaborative innovation; build a number of high-level national laboratories to upgrade China's ability to innovate in science and technology in the field of national strategy.
- **Strengthen integration of information resources:** Encourage construction of technology transfer and service platforms; develop new forms of technology services, such as public support, crowdfunding, and public creation so as to provide technical support and relevant innovative services for transformation of new technologies, for development of new products, and for creation of new models; improve innovative service support systems at all levels, including financial

institutions, trade associations, industrial alliances, industrial parks, professional service organizations, etc. to gather innovative elements and resources so as to enhance the support capacity of innovative services.

2. *Promote construction of various types of innovative infrastructure*

Speed up construction of major national science and technology infrastructures: improve infrastructures in multidisciplinary fields such as energy, life, earth system and environment, materials, particle physics and nuclear physics, space, astronomy, engineering and technology; actively promote construction of three major comprehensive national science centers in Beijing, Shanghai; and Hefei; strive to build new facilities and platforms for scientific and technological innovation; upgrade the integration capability and level of national major science and technology infrastructure systems; establish a perfect and efficient input mechanism, an open and shared operation mechanism, a cooperative and innovative mechanism for production, learning, and research, and a scientific and coordinated management system; promote the opening up of scientific and technological infrastructure and innovative resources in universities and scientific research institutes; improve scientific and technological benefits of the construction and operation of the facilities.

To adapt to characteristics of innovative activities in the age of big science, we should speed up construction of scientific and technological basic conditions platforms, such as large-scale shared experimental devices, data resources, biological resources, knowledge and patent information services, and develop high-end scientific research instruments and equipment to improve the level of self-sufficiency of scientific research equipment; build infrastructures such as super-computing centers, national gene banks, and cloud computing platforms to form advanced information network support systems based on big data; promote co-construction and sharing of innovation infrastructure; integrate the cross-regional innovation resources; promote interconnection and coordination of innovation elements with new mechanisms and models.

3. *Strengthen talent support for innovation*

Talents are the most precious resources in the construction of innovation systems. High-level talent resources support enterprise innovation, scientific research and development, construction of major scientific and technological infrastructure, production–study–research service agencies, and the environment for innovation.

Therefore, it is important to improve the incentive mechanism of talent evaluation and service guarantee mechanism and promote the vitality of talent development. We should insist on value orientation, solve problems such as weak policies and imperfect distribution incentive mechanisms, which will have long-term effects on equity incentives, and make clear the direction of distribution and perfect the mechanism of distribution so that the income of scientific researchers and their creative work are closely related to their scientific value, economic value, and social value; implement flexible and efficient personnel selection in accordance with the laws of innovation to cultivate and attract talents, and provide them with competitive pay and environment support; promote the distribution of income from scientific research achievements, the incentive of stock rights, and the disposal of property rights among outstanding talents; establish the distribution policy that fully embodies the value of intellectual labor and service labor; make the intellectual work of scientific and technological personnel get a reasonable return, and endow them with greater autonomy in scientific research; encourage scientific research personnel to start businesses, and allow them to work part-time according to laws and regulations; implement a more active, open, and effective talent introduction policy; improve the system of permanent residence for foreigners; streamline procedures for skilled personnel to obtain permanent residence.

Further consolidate the foundations of basic education, higher education, vocational education, and innovation education: cultivate and bring up a large number of talents in scientific and technological innovation; implement major talent projects such as those aiming to advance innovative talents, to develop young talents, to upgrade the quality of business and management talents, to renew knowledge of professional and technical talents, and to revitalize high-skilled personnel in China.

4. *Create a social environment that encourages innovation*

An advantageous social and cultural environment is fertile soil for innovation, and the strength of the innovation ability is inseparable from the social and cultural environments such as social value concept, thinking habits, and behavior modes. First, perfect the legal environment for protection of innovation: speed up the legislative process of innovation; revise laws and regulations that do not conform to innovation-oriented documents; abolish the institutional provisions that restrict innovation; build a comprehensive and elaborate guarantee system. Second, cultivate an open and fair market environment: strengthen and perfect the market environment; form a survival of the fittest market mechanism; stimulate the original impetus of innovation. Finally, create a cultural environment that advocates innovation: promote the spirit of innovation; strengthen scientific education; inspire young people's interest in science and technology; strive to cultivate innovators with innovative consciousness and practical spirit; publicize the outstanding examples of scientific and technological workers and form a culture of innovation that encourages creativity and pursues excellence throughout the society; advocate contention of different thoughts; respect the individual character of scientists; strengthen confidence in innovation; promote formation of a social and cultural atmosphere that encourages competition, advocates cooperation, pursues success and tolerates failure, and strives to create an open and fair environment for innovation and entrepreneurship.

5. *Form institutional arrangements conducive to innovation*

We will deepen the reform of institutional mechanisms, break down the institutional barriers that are not conducive to construction of the innovation system, and promote the formation of institutional arrangements that are conducive to the burst of innovation achievements and perfection of the innovation system. First, strengthen protection of intellectual property rights: implement a stricter system for protection and enforcement of intellectual property rights; raise the winning rate and the amount of compensation awarded by obligees; fundamentally change the current situation of "infringement and protection of rights"; create an atmosphere and environment for respecting intellectual property rights throughout society. Second, implement an action plan for technology transfer: promote transfer and industrialization of technological achievements supported by financial funds; substantially increase the conversion rate of scientific and technological achievements through improving the licensing and management of intellectual property rights. Finally, improve the innovation-oriented evaluation system: promote classification and evaluation of universities and scientific research institutes; incorporate the influence of technology transfer and scientific research achievements on economic society into evaluation indexes; form a performance-oriented scientific evaluation system; perfect the talent evaluation system; further reform and perfect the professional title evaluation system; increase employers' evaluation autonomy; form a talent evaluation system conducive to innovative development.

Chapter 5

Research on Deepening the Reform of State-Owned Enterprises and Certain Industries of Monopolistic Nature From Supply Side

Wang Chenwei

Academy of Macroeconomic Research

Abstract

Deepening the reform of the state-owned enterprises (SOEs) and certain industries of a monopolistic nature is one of the key areas of the supply-side structural reform in China. Currently, there are a large number of problems to be resolved during development of the SOEs, such as the distribution of state-owned economy that needs to be optimized, the system of state-owned asset management that needs to be improved, the system of state-owned capital operation budget that remains imperfect, the system of modern enterprises that needs to be constructed, the industrial monopoly that obviously exists in SOEs including electricity, petroleum, and railways, and the fair play market environment that has not yet formed. Problems facing SOEs have originated from their institutional mechanisms while those facing certain industries of a monopolistic nature have arisen from administrative monopoly of SOEs, especially of the central enterprises (under direct control of the Central Government). Reforms of the SOEs and certain industries of a monopolistic nature in the future will focus on the following: (i) speeding up optimization of the state-owned economy distribution, perfecting regulatory systems of SOEs, and improving operating efficiency of the state-owned economy; (ii) deepening the reform of the state-owned property rights system, accelerating formulation of modern enterprise systems, facilitating de-administration of SOEs, removing administrative intervention in independent management of enterprises, separating public service institutions from government agencies, and isolating government social management functions from its state-owned asset owner's functions to enhance the operating efficiency and innovative capacities of SOEs; (iii) reasonably defining the boundary between government and market, addressing such problems as "lopsided, absent and misplaced" government functions, removing inappropriate intervention of administrative privileges in certain industries of a monopolistic nature to break the interest pattern established by administrative privileges; (iv) conducting design of individual market reform schemes based on characteristics of certain industries with a monopolistic nature, perfecting the price-forming mechanism, optimizing the resource allocation mechanism through deregulating and strengthening supervision, and creating an open, fair, uniform, and high-efficiency modern regulatory system; and (v) opening market, breaking up monopoly, and bringing a competitive mechanism into market to form a market structure with workable competition and improve overall operating efficiency on the supply side.

As a backbone force in China's socialist market economy, the state-owned economy plays a decisive role in the national economic system. The SOEs, especially the central enterprises, act as lifelines of China's economy entitled to national preferential policy and favorable resource conditions, which therefore enables SOEs to dominate and monopolize the market more easily than private enterprises. While some private enterprises monopolize such areas as fuel gas, heat supply, and water supply, they seem far less dominant than the SOEs, especially the central enterprises, in acquiring administratively monopolized resources due to their institutional deficiencies. For this reason, the key areas of supply-side structural reform in China include deepening the reform of the SOEs, weakening direct government intervention in all industries, creating a fair play market environment, and enabling the market to play a decisive role in resources allocation. Chinese President Xi Jinping once pointed out clearly that we would unswervingly deepen the reform of SOEs and allow them to play leading roles in supply-side structural reform.

I. Analysis of Problems and Causes of Reform in SOEs and Certain Industries of Monopolistic Nature

The state-owned enterprises (SOEs), especially the state-owned monopolistic enterprises, usually have advantageous positions and roles in China's economy. These enterprises, on the one hand, hold the lifelines of national economy and partly undertake public services and macro-control functions, and on the other hand operate as main-market participants to seek maximal profit. As a result, the state-owned monopolistic enterprises tend to trade off the national public goals for their profit goals, hence giving rise to many problems, such as mixed government and enterprise functions, poor innovative capability, and repetitive corruption, which have seriously impaired the operational efficiency and functionality of these enterprises. Over the three decades since implementation of the economic system reform and opening up to the outside world in 1978, reforms of SOEs have been further advanced, remarkable achievements have been made in reform of state-owned asset management systems, and great changes have taken place in the management mode of SOEs, the results of which include a significant increase of enterprises' profits, taxes, and competitive power. As of the end of 2014, the number of listed central enterprises and their subsidiaries increased to 385 companies after the shareholding reform, with their total assets accounting for 57%, total net assets for 75.6%, operating revenue for 60.6%, and total profit for 80% of all central enterprises; the number of the listed central companies ranking among the Fortune Global 500 increased from six in 2003 to 47 companies in 2014. Currently, however, there exist many problems concerning development of the central enterprises, and reforms thereof need to be deepened; for instance, sectors such as electricity, petroleum, and railways are highly monopolized, and a fair play market environment has not yet been created.

1. *Problems facing SOEs*

(1) *Inadequate reform of SOEs and state-owned asset management systems*

Despite remarkable results and tremendous benefits achieved in reform of SOEs and state-owned asset management systems, there still exist some deep-seated problems:

- First, the distribution and the structure of the state-owned economy need to be further optimized. On the one hand, no specific catalogs and standards are provided for the scope of key industries and areas essential to state security and lifelines of the national economy, which has resulted in overly extensive and dispersed distribution of national economy, difficulty in integration of industries, and unlikely optimization of resource allocation. In all 96 divisions of 20 categories of China's economic sectors, there are 94 sectors involving national economy and 90 divisions of 19 categories involving businesses operated by all subsidiaries of the central enterprises; there are 44 central enterprises involved in over 40 categories, accounting for 37.3% of all central enterprises. Nearly all of the local SOEs have taken part in all categories of economic sectors, but a majority of them are involved in unimportant sectors or key areas due to their small scale, weak capacity for technical innovation, as well as limited influence and less stimulatory effect on the sector. On the other hand, the pace of reforming the monopolistic industry and adjusting industrial distribution has lagged behind. Today, some industries such as electricity, petroleum, petrochemicals, telecommunications, railways, and finance are highly monopolized by the national economy, and the adjustment of industrial distribution remains under the control of administrative privileges and industrial monopoly.

- Second, the state-owned asset management systems need to be improved. The existing systems are designed for management of all personnel, specific affairs, and various assets, which imposes excessive administrative intervention in SOEs and hinders them from acting as main-market participants as a result of mixed functions of government and enterprises. On the one hand, the state-owned asset supervision system remains imperfect due to the fact that the government's public management functions are not totally separated from the state-owned asset provider's functions. There are still such problems as undefined responsibilities, inadequate supervision, and irrational allocation of various state-owned assets due to imperfect institutional mechanisms, laws, and regulations. The state-owned assets need to be supervised in a more effective and scientific manner as the state-owned assets of many enterprises are not yet incorporated into new regulatory systems. On the other hand, state-owned asset management is overly fragmented. From a transverse perspective, there are some large enterprise groups under supervision of the State-owned Asset Supervision and Administration Commission (SASAC), or the providers' responsibility is fulfilled by the Ministry of Finance, and there are nearly ten thousand enterprises under direct administration of the Central Authority. From a vertical perspective, the SOEs are usually administrated by governments at the central, provincial, local, and county levels, resulting in such disabilities as to implement unified management and effective liquidity of state-owned assets and to make overall planning of the distribution and structure of state-owned economy.

- Third, the state-owned capital operation budget systems need to be perfected. According to the *Constitution of the People's Republic of China*, the Ministry of Finance reserves the right to prepare a budget. In case of the Ministry of Finance's preparation of a state-owned capital budget, it either contradicts the SASAC provider's functions or means direct intervention of the government in enterprises. However, the truth is that the SASAC has not yet prepared a complete set of normative regulations for performance of the state-owned capital provider's functions and for collection, distribution, and use of capital gains because it remains unclear about who reserves the right to prepare the state-owned capital budget. In addition, the SASAC's preparation of such a budget may easily lead to further intervention in investment and operation activities of the SOEs. Practice shows that the regulatory authority of state-owned assets needs to lay down institutional norms for such problems as how to collect enterprise earnings, what is the percentage of collection, how to supervise, distribute, and use earnings collected, and how to conduct a scientific and quantitative assessment of each enterprise's performance.
- Finally, modern enterprise systems need to be improved. Currently, the deep-seated fundamental problems concerning the SOE governance structure remain unsolved due to mixed functions of government and enterprises and slow reform of the property rights system. Some SOEs, especially some large and super SOEs, have not undergone corporate system reform or shareholding reform. For those SOEs already subjected to shareholding reform, their majority shares are held by the state, especially in the northeastern region and Shanxi Province. For instance, the state-owned assets have occupied 45.8%,

54.1%, and 64.7% of all industrial enterprises' shares in Liaoning, Jilin, and Heilongjiang provinces, respectively; in some cities in Shanxi Province, this figure has reached up to 70%, far higher than those in the southeastern coastal provinces, i.e. 23.6% in Fujian, 23.4% in Guangdong, 18.0% in Jiangsu, and 14.9% in Zhejiang.[1]

(2) *Obviously slow reform of certain industries with monopolistic nature*

Over the three decades since implementation of the economic system reform and opening up to the outside world in 1978, the SOEs represented by the central enterprises have earned considerable gains, notwithstanding significant improvement of China's market system and substantial reform of competitive industries. This has become the shortest board of the Cask Effect Theory. Problems arising from buyer's monopoly and seller's monopoly are prominent and listed as follows:

- First, administrative interventions resulted in an imperfect operating environment of enterprises. Over the years, the mixed functions of government and enterprises have always been the toughest problem for SOEs, especially state-owned industries.

  The intertwined relationship between government and enterprises has led to the fact that the government acts as both the athlete and the referee in economic activities and thus intervenes excessively in microeconomic behaviors of the SOEs. In addition, the industrial monopoly of SOEs has also distorted the market environment, leading typically to bidirectional price distortion. Some prices that were forced down by intentional manipulation led to declining profits. For instance, prior to implementation of a differential water price, water suppliers suffered considerable losses when supplying water at a price lower than cost, and these losses were usually billed to the government. This situation did not start reversing until the differential water price was put into force in 2014. There were also some prices forced

[1] *Source*: *Statistical Yearbook* available on government websites of Liaoning, Jilin, and Heilongjiang provinces; provided by Shanxi Provincial People's Government website.

up by intentional manipulation, thus implanting a considerable quantity of unreasonable factors into business cost and allowing unnecessary expenses to be listed into business cost, including high salaries. For instance, according to the human resources market of Taiyuan, Shanxi province, in summer of 2015, employees engaged in the petrochemical industry earned a monthly salary of up to RMB 8,400,[2] far higher than the average of all sectors. Higher cost was one of the primary reasons for higher prices of petrochemical products, and also resulted in distorted market environment.

- Second, excessively high barriers for market access led to failure in forming workable competition among enterprises. First, difficult access to the market for private enterprises accounted for the limited number of competitive participants in most sectors. Then, it seems unlikely to realize workable competition on an unequal competition market because a monopolistic enterprise is overwhelmingly more dominant than one who is granted access later and it usually takes anti-competitive strategic actions in some key areas of the sector by virtue of its advantageous strengths. Finally, the competitive market was generally dominated by SOEs rather than by private enterprises, where competition merely occurred among individual SOEs or state-controlled enterprises; the state-owned asset owner was the sole stakeholder of all competitors, and losing in such competition meant a big loss of the state-owned assets.
- Third, regulatory systems should be established and the monopolistic situation should be broken. Currently, the regulatory authority adopts a combined system of administration and supervision for certain industries with a monopolistic nature, whose regulatory functions are fulfilled by government agencies in charge of such sectors as telecommunications (by the Ministry of Industry and Information Technology), civil aviation (by the Civil Aviation Administration of the Ministry of Transportation), postal services (by the State Postal Bureau of China), and municipal public utilities (by the Ministry of Housing and Urban–Rural Development and by Ministry of Construction at all levels).

[2] Statistical data on remunerations of all sectors in the summer of 2015 available at Taiyuan Human Resources Market.

Under such regulatory systems, the regulator and enterprises under supervision that are naturally correlated by mutual interests may easily result in an alliance of interests and "soft supervision", which will foster rather than curb monopolistic behaviors. Few regulatory restrictions on monopolistic enterprises will certainly lead to unfailing infringement on consumers' rights and interests.

- Finally, the dominance of state-owned assets disqualified private enterprises from making investment in certain industries with a monopolistic nature. Currently in China, the fixed asset investment in certain industries with a monopolistic nature is generally embodied by a limited quantity of private capital. By percentage, private capital has accounted for less than 1% of production and supply of fuel gas, less than 2% of telecommunications and other information transmission services, and less than 1% of railway transportation. Despite a slightly higher percentage of private capital in municipal public utilities such as gas and water supply, it almost seems impossible for private enterprises to put capital into industries directly controlled by the Central Government. Some main enterprises of the telecom industry are successfully listed after shareholding reform, but they are largely controlled by state-owned capital. An overwhelming majority of shares of listed companies are under indirect control of the state-owned asset management authority, and as soon as the authority has seized the whole ownership of the parent group, along with a certain quantity of shares being possessed by other state-owned shareholders, it will lead to a limited quantity of negotiable shares of public shareholders in total assets.

2. *Analysis of causes*

Currently, the fundamental problem facing SOEs arises from institutional mechanism while the root cause of problems in certain industries with a monopolistic nature lies in administrative monopoly of SOEs, especially of the central enterprises. As far as SOEs are concerned, the "proxy agent" problems appear particularly serious, including mixed functions and unequal rights and responsibilities of government and enterprises as well as lack of effective mechanism for state-owned asset supervision, which results in low efficiency of SOEs management and in severe loss of state-owned assets when enterprises are carrying out activities such as investment, operation, acquisition, and restructuring. As far as the external environment of an SOE's survival is concerned, China's current market economy system remains imperfect and the government management system adaptable to the market economy system also remains unsound, thus giving rise to frequent occurrences of the government's "lopsided, absent and misplaced" functions and excessive interventions in microeconomic entities' market activities, which further incurs frequent losses of corporate profits. The causes of these problems are specified as follows:

- First, SOEs are not reformed thoroughly and SOEs' functions are not totally isolated from the government's functions. By nature, the state-owned assets are owned by the "whole people". Nevertheless, the "whole people" is merely an abstract conceptual noun disabled from directly exercising the property right over state-owned assets, but a government entity is justified and legalized to do so. For this reason, the ownership by the whole people means nothing but the government ownership. In exercising the property rights of state-owned assets, the government usually fulfills both of the asset provider's and regulator's functions, and in many cases it "in person" intervenes in an SOE's investment and management activities or "in person" appoints the chairman and general manager of an SOE. This is where the "proxy agent" problem has arisen and why an SOE head is only responsible for a government authority and becomes less motivated to make timely adjustments of corporate production and operation activities in response to the fluctuating market. In addition, the government tends to impose multiple business objectives on SOEs, of which the political object often precedes the efficiency objective; as a result, SOEs become less motivated to reduce cost and improve efficiency. Irrespective of their low efficiency and high cost, the SOEs' monopolistic position enables them to reap colossal profits; what's worse, some SOEs impair consumer rights and interests by enforcing unfair clauses while providing highly priced but inferior products.

- Second, the market is dominated by SOEs using administrative monopoly. First of all, some profit-driven enterprises often reserve the exclusive rights to provide products and leave no space for consumers to make choices, which consequently results in monopolized prices and profits. Then, some administrative officers abuse their administrative rights to pursue personal interests, or lay down local policy and regulations to protect regional and sectoral interests, or implement a series of differential prices to impose discriminatory charges on enterprises at monopolized prices, which, on the one hand, has impaired healthy economic development, distorted the orderly market, broken the free competitive pattern, reduced the efficiency of resource allocation, and cut down total social wealth, and on the other hand, led to additional uncertainties in expected inflation and economic development. In effect, price monopoly means redistribution of social wealth, where monopolized profits are flowing into the monopolists' rather than the consumers' pocket.
- Third, industrial regulatory systems remain imperfect due to the absence and lopsidedness of effective supervision. Imperfect supervisory systems and mechanisms of monopolized industries are attributed largely to the ambiguous relationship between government and SOEs and the government's unclearly positioned functions in the development of SOEs. Currently, a combined administration supervision and administrative control system is adopted in most monopolistic industries such as telecommunications, civil aviation, railways, and postal services. In a deep sense, the regulatory system of combined administration and supervision reflects conflicting roles of such functions as performed by the government's asset provider, regulator, and public service institutions, consequently resulting in weak, excessive, absent, and lopsided supervision of monopolized industries and in less authoritative and effective administrative supervision. In addition to competent authorities, other administrative authorities also possess great regulatory powers that may lead to repetitive or multiple supervisions in some sectors but to omission of supervision in some other sectors.
- Finally, laws and rules of monopolized industries remain imperfect. China's legal and regulatory system has been under continuous

improvements since implementation of the policy of economic reform and opening up to the outside world in 1978. Despite considerable amendments to the *Electricity Law*, *Railway Law*, and *Civil Aviation Law* of the People's Republic of China in 2015, these laws need to be further improved in response to the advancing marketization process. Effective implementation of these laws in practice remains a particular concern, though there are legal provisions addressing administrative monopoly that arises from government interventions. Legislative deletion is the primary cause of problems hindering reform and development of monopolized industries. On the one hand, legally absent or unauthorized business management and supervision may result in regulatory failure due to unfair clauses imposed by monopolists, which may further lead to impairment of consumer interests, difficulty in legal supervision of monopolized industries, and ineffectiveness of supervision. On the other hand, some regulatory authority's overly discretionary power results in low transparency of the regulatory process so much so that many government behaviors are crossing the line to lopsidedness, absence, and misplacement of supervision. These behaviors contrary to rules of market economy have provided favorable conditions for administrative monopoly and increased risks in rent-seeking activities.

II. General Framework and Focal Points for Deepening the Reform of SOEs and Monopolized Industries

Currently, China's economic development has entered a new normal stage where there are numerous challenges facing economic transformation and development as required in such proposals as "deepening reform comprehensively", "allowing market to play its decisive roles in resources allocation", "implementing the 'Belt and Road' initiative", and "promoting law-based governance". There is also a bottleneck hindering China from moving toward a medium- and high-income nation from a medium-income nation; besides, China's economy is facing intensifying economic downturn pressure, declining corporate profitability, and weakening growth rate of fiscal revenue resulting from unprecedented resistance, challenges, and hardships. Irrespective of periodical factors, these problems are essentially related to some pending structural problems on the supply side, which erupted due to external stimuli during economic transformation, and are terribly detrimental to sustainable economic development, social harmony, and stability. In the new period of economic new normal, therefore, deepening the reform of SOEs and monopolized industries to facilitate supply-side structural reform will be of far-reaching strategic importance for long-term and sustainable development of China's economy.

1. *General framework*

Deepening the reform of SOEs and monopolized industries aims to seek qualified market participants, normalize and strengthen market competition, inspire market entities' vitality, impetus, and creativity, substantially optimize supply structure, and improve supply efficiency. The reform of SOEs and monopolized industries was explicitly stressed in the *Decision of the Central Committee of the Communist Party of China on Some Major Issues Concerning Comprehensively Deepening the Reform* adopted at the 3rd Plenary Session of the 18th Central Committee of the Communist Party of China (the CCCPC). For this reason, the reform of SOEs and monopolized industries was generally designed to do the following: (i) adhere to precedent legislation, law-based advancement, all-round consideration, and staged implementation, and press ahead with the principle that "allows both entry and exit, observes dos and don'ts" and "ensures reasonable entry and orderly exit" in accelerating optimization of state-owned economy distribution, improving regulatory system of state-owned assets, ensuring preservation and appreciation of state-owned assets, and making state-owned economy serve the economic strategy of China; (ii) deepen the reform of SOEs' property rights, accelerate establishment of modern corporate systems, promote de-administration of SOEs, facilitate separation of government's functions from those of enterprises, state-owned asset owners, and public service institutions, improve operational efficiency and enhance innovative capabilities of SOEs; (iii) reasonably define the boundary between government roles and market roles, speed up transformation of government functions, solve problems concerning "lopsided, absent and misplaced" government functions, eliminate improper intervention of administrative privileges in monopolized industries, and break the interest pattern established by administrative monopoly; (iv) lay down market-oriented reform schemes based on characteristics of monopolized industries, improve pricing mechanism, optimize resource allocation mechanism, ease administrative control but strengthen supervision, and create a just, open, uniform, and high-efficiency modern regulatory system; (v) open the market, break up monopoly, and introduce competition in all competitive areas to form a market structure for workable competition; and (vi) reduce enterprises' operational cost and eliminate inefficient production capacity by reform of SOEs and monopolized industries to improve the operating efficiency on the supply side.

2. *Focal points*

(1) *Deepen the reform of SOEs to seek microeconomic entities adaptable to the market economy system*

We should first promote the reform of SOEs' property rights in monopolized industries and ensure diversified sources of investment; second, create a modern corporate system that features "clearly-established ownership, well-defined rights and obligations, independent functions of government and enterprises, and scientific management", and build SOEs into legal entities and market entities featuring independent operation, self-financing, self-discipline, and self-management; third, deepen all internal reforms and improve internal management systems of personnel, labor, and distribution to form a mechanism that allows reasonable entry and orderly exit of employees and managers as well as differential remunerations; and finally, eliminate enterprises' social functions to ease their burdens.

(2) *Accelerate transformation of government functions to separate government functions from enterprises and state-owned asset management*

We should first reasonably define the state-owned asset owner's functions of government, the regulatory functions of market, and the operational activities of enterprises to completely solve "lopsided, absent and misplaced" functions of the government; second, accelerate isolation of SOE's operational management functions from functions of the competent administrative authority of the industry to cut off the competent authority's direct interventions in enterprises and promote separation of government functions from enterprises' and state-owned asset owner's functions; and finally, carry out reform in the system and mode of government administration, strengthen the government's functions to make policy and regulations and supervise the market, normalize and direct enterprises' behaviors by means of marketization, and strive to create a market environment for fair competition.

(3) *Direct and implement classified reforms of monopolized industries*

First, we should focus on the reform of administrative monopoly industries, break up monopoly, introduce market competition, and form a competitive market structure. Second, for natural monopoly industries, we should remove administrative monopoly factors, enhance technical innovation, break market barriers established by technological monopoly, and gradually strengthen market competition in all areas into which competitive mechanism can be introduced. Third, for special monopoly industries that may make a difference to national security, we should strengthen industrial control, supervision, and guidance, and gradually introduce competition to achieve healthy development of these industries. Finally, we need to distinguish between monopolistic and non-monopolistic sectors; monopolistic sectors should be opened to the market, but for non-monopolistic sectors, we should ease control, strengthen supervision, lay down criteria, and create an industrial benchmark.

(4) *Open the market and introduce competition to form a market environment for workable competition*

We should first vertically split monopolistic manufacturers and push non-monopolistic business onto the market after separation; second, transversely split monopolistic manufacturers and break regional market segmentation and market monopoly to promote interregional connectivity of market; third, carry out restructuring and integration of monopolized industries and make use of market operations to optimize a combination of all factors such as effective mechanism, reasonable property rights, and advanced technologies, and to prevent the government from making arbitrary arrangements and administrative interventions; and finally, introduce new competitors, lower barriers for access to monopolized industries, and encourage social funds to get access to monopolized industries in many different forms.

(5) *Speed up construction of legal system to reduce external constraints on development of monopolized industries*

On the one hand, we should make further amendments and improvements of laws and regulations on monopolized industries, make explicit provisions for setup of regulatory authorities and the right–responsibility–interest relationship, price, and quality of products and services and the market access conditions of the regulated enterprises according to their technical and economic features, and provide legally normative guidance to maintain orderly competition on market. On the other hand, we need to change the situation where industrial laws and regulations were formulated under the leadership of competent authority of the industry, and subject these laws and regulations to revision and improvement under the leadership of legislative authority.

(6) *Establish modern control and regulatory framework of monopolized industries*

We should first transform our concept of enterprise management and control, and change the government's management mode from direct control of enterprises' production and management to market-oriented supervision that is performed by a legally authorized special regulatory agency; second, set up an independent regulatory authority, ensure it operates in an independent, authoritative, and professional manner, define its functions and implement specialized supervision over monopolized enterprises; third, establish coordinated and uniform regulatory systems, gradually cancel non-administrative license approval, and introduce market regulating modes such as license management and operating concessions; and finally, make scientific and reasonable regulatory procedures and ensure they are open to all participants.

III. Proposed Strategies for Deepening the Reform of SOEs and Monopolized Industries

1. *Optimizing the pattern of state-owned economy*

It was clearly stated at the 3rd Plenary Session of the 18th CCCPC that state-owned capital "will be put primarily into the important sectors and key areas that make difference to national security and lifelines of the national economy, and will be focused on providing public services, fostering important, forward-looking and strategic industries, protect ecological environment, support technological progress and secure national security". This statement has indicated the direction of deepening structural adjustment of state-owned economic distribution. For this reason, we will press ahead with the principle that "allows both entry and exit, observes dos and don'ts" and "ensures reasonable entry and orderly exit" to accelerate classified reform of SOEs in both commercial and public service sectors and increase the pace of the distribution and structural adjustment of state-owned economy.

On the one hand, the state-owned economy will appropriately retreat or reduce its capital input to allow more market space for private capital and private economic development. Competitive SOEs that want to selectively retain some of their capital inputs should be well positioned in market, concentrate on their core businesses, enhance their R&D capability of core proprietary technologies, improve competitiveness of their core businesses, and become a leading force to stimulate development of the whole industry. Commercial SOEs should focus on fostering true competitive entities on market, improve their competitiveness, and give priority to assessment of their business performance targets, preservation and appreciation of state-owned assets and their competitive power on market. We should also promote transfer of state-owned property rights and eliminate enterprises that are less competitive and suffer long-term losses according to returns on capital investment, and should accelerate disposal of inefficient, invalid, and non-performing assets.

On the other hand, as to important public service industries and key sectors, we should ease employment access and introduce social and private capital while appropriately increasing input of state-owned capital so as to raise the degree of market competition of competitive businesses, improve quality and efficiency of industrial operations, and ensure social and private capital will play greater roles in service of national macro-control, state security, national economic operation, and fulfillment of tasks designated by the government. Public service SOEs should concentrate on improving quality and efficiency of their public services, give priority to their core businesses, optimize resource allocation of public services, and enhance their capability of sustainable management. We should also set up the industrial benchmark system, introduce market mechanism for all sectors that can be opened to market, and focus on assessment of enterprises' cost control, product and service quality, operational efficiency, and support capacity, with social evaluation introduced in such assessment.

2. *Deepening the reform of state-owned asset management system*

The key to state-owned asset management lies in how to handle the relationship between the government and the market and how to avoid lopsided, absent, and misplaced functions of the government. The key to deepening the reform of state-owned asset management system lies in how to implement the *Several Opinions about Reform and Improvement of State-owned Assets Management System* issued by the State Council, how to reasonably define the government's roles in state-owned assets management, how to strengthen supervision of state-owned assets and capitals, how to reform the authorized management system of state-owned assets, how to set up several companies to operate state-owned capitals, and how to support eligible SOEs to be restructured as state-owned capital investment corporations. The answers are as follows:

- First, accelerate transformation of the government's roles in state-owned assets management. No longer will the government excessively intervene in SOEs' micro-market behaviors, nor will it act as the manager of an SOE; instead, the government should change itself into a rule maker and an industrial regulator obligated to perform functions of macro-control, market supervision, public services, and social management and to create market environment for fair competition. Specifically, the government is obligated to do the following: (i) according to the percentage of its investment in the wholly owned, controlled, and shareholding enterprises, perform the contributor's legal responsibilities for preservation and appreciation of state-owned assets in enterprises it has invested in, is entitled to capital gains, major decisions, and election or appointment of managers, but will not interfere with the daily management activities of the enterprises; (ii) thoroughly reform the methods used to appoint and manage leaders of SOEs in monopolized sectors, develop new principal–agent relationships and shorten the principal–agent chain; (iii) strengthen supervision over income distribution of monopolized industries, reform the wage and income distribution system, and curb overly rapid growth of staff's income; (iv) help enterprises set up a reasonable incentive system, especially the price incentive mechanism, and actively explore equity incentive methods including the operator-owned shares and stock option; (v) strengthen supervision to prevent excessive competition or lack of workable competition; and (vi) strictly define and adjust in a timely manner the range of administrative monopoly; for some special products and sectors that require administrative monopoly, improve quality of products and services, and introduce market competition when conditions have matured.

- Second, improve the system of state-owned assets supervision. The key is how to achieve the transformation from "supervision of assets" to "supervision of capital". Answers include the following: (i) perfecting the mode of state-owned assets management, which will be achieved by normalizing the operation and management forms of state-owned assets that may change into state-owned capitals and by weakening the "state-owned" feature of SOEs, because the state-owned assets of an overwhelming majority of SOEs are possessed, operated, and managed in the form of state-owned capital, except very few of them that must be operated by wholly SOEs, so as to provide both state-owned and private enterprises with equal access to all production factors; (ii) innovating the mode of state-owned capital supervision, which will be achieved by properly handling the relationship between the state-owned asset supervisory authorities and the SOEs, by separating the government's public management functions and asset provider's functions in SOEs from operational management functions of SOEs, by establishing a state-owned asset regulatory authority independent of governments at all levels and responsible directly to the National People's Congress (NPC) to perform the asset provider's responsibilities on behalf of the state government so as to ensure separation of the government's social economic management functions from its state-owned asset owner functions and from enterprises' functions of independent operation and management; (iii) strengthening construction of all state-owned asset systems, which will be achieved by perfecting the system of state-owned financial assets, cultural assets, and natural resource asset management, by seeking a new system of state-owned asset management, and by promoting high-efficiency management and operation of all types of state-owned assets; and (iv) promoting centralized and unified supervision of state-owned operational assets, which will be achieved by incorporating state-owned assets of enterprises subordinate to the Party and government organs and public institutions into state-owned operational assets under centralized and unified supervision, by strengthening fundamental management of state-owned assets and formulating relevant regulations according to the principle of unified norms and unified work system, and by setting up a nationwide staged management system of state-owned capital operations.

- Finally, reform the authorized operation system of state-owned capital. This is one of the critical points for reforming and improving the state-owned asset management system. We need to restructure or set up the state-owned capital investment and operation company, and require the state-owned asset regulatory authority to authorize the state-owned capital investment and operation company to perform the capital provider's responsibilities for state-owned capital within the authorized scope, which aims to build an "isolation belt" between the government and the market so that the state-owned assets regulatory authority will focus on "supervision", the state-owned capital investment and operation companies will focus on "management", and the company itself will focus on business operation. This has changed the previous mode, by which the state-owned assets regulatory authority directly performed the asset provider's rights and responsibilities in the enterprises under its supervision, into a new mode, by which the state-owned capital investment and operation company will perform the asset provider's rights and responsibilities in the enterprises it has authorized. As a result, according to the standard corporate governance structure, the state-owned assets regulatory authority's directives will be passed via the platform of the state-owned capital investment and operation company down to all lower levels in the form of marketization so as to avoid the government's direct interventions in the market and realize true separation of the government's supervisory functions from the enterprises' management functions.

3. *Deepening the reform of modern enterprise system in SOEs*

The key to deepening reform of SOEs lies in adapting to the new situation of marketization, modernization, and globalization by perfecting the modern corporate governance structure to improve efficiency of state-owned capital and invigorate SOEs, establishing a modern corporate system that features clear ownership, well-defined rights and responsibilities, and separation of administration from management and scientific management based on reform of the mixed ownership and property rights system, comprehensively promoting law-based governance, and constantly enhancing the vitality, control, influence, and risk resistance capacities of national economy so as to allow SOEs to play leading roles in China's economic development.

- First, deepen reform of the SOEs' mixed ownership. Reform of property rights, as the key to deepening the SOEs reform, aims to address the problem of wholly state-owned "single shareholder". This round of reforms of mixed ownership will not aim at formal shareholding reform of SOEs but at introducing private and social capitals into

SOEs, changing the property structure, assisting SOEs in setting up modern corporate systems as required by market economy, facilitating holistic listing of the entire large-size SOEs, promoting manager and employee stock ownership, inspiring staff's initiative and creativity, and making SOEs change their operational mechanism. Specific measures are as follows: (i) the reform of mixed ownership of the fully competitive commercial SOEs is aimed to invigorate national economy, enlarge functions of state-owned capital, ensure preservation and appreciation of state-owned assets, improve economic benefits, and develop new business modes and diversify stock ownership by introducing other state-owned capital or all types of non-state-owned capital; (ii) for important industries and key sectors essential to national security and economy, the reform of mixed ownership is aimed to ensure the holding position of state-owned capital and encourage non-state-owned capital to participate. Especially for SOEs in natural monopoly industries, the mixed ownership reform aims at separating network from operation and opening the competitive business so as to facilitate marketized allocation of public resources, strengthen law-based classified supervision, and normalize the profit-making mode; (iii) for public service SOEs including water, electricity, gas, heating, public transport, and utilities, the mixed ownership reform is aimed to strengthen classified guidance, promote eligible enterprises to diversify their investors, and encourage non-SOEs' participation in management through purchase of services, franchising, and proxy agents. The government should strengthen supervision of price level, cost control, service quality, safety standards, information disclosure, operational efficiency, and support capacity, and conduct differentiated assessment of enterprises according to their features on performance indicators and preservation and appreciation of state-owned assets, where social evaluation should be referenced; and (iv) all types of capital are encouraged to participate in reform of SOEs' mixed ownership, including non-public capital, collective capital, contributions of foreign investors, share acquisition, subscription of convertible debts, and equity replacement, by means of public–private partnership (PPP) mode. State-owned capital is also encouraged to participate in non-SOEs in multiple manners.

- Second, improve the modern corporate governance structure of SOEs, with a focus on construction of the Board of Directors and perfection of the decision execution and supervision mechanism that features equal rights and responsibilities, coordinated operation, and effective balancing functions. Specific measures are as follows: (i) normalize the acts of Chairman and General Manager to exercise power; ensure decisions made by the Board of Directors, supervision by the Board of Supervisors, and operation by the Management are acted upon; allow the Party group to play its core political roles; avoid nominal existence of the Board of Directors and the final say of the "top leader"; and standardize corporate governance; (ii) maintain the Board's legal rights to make major decisions, elect, or employ staff and distribute remunerations, and ensure managers' autonomy in management as authorized by law; (iii) strengthen mutual restraints inside the Board of Directors, make sure that external directors occupy a majority of on the Board, including employee representatives, especially in the wholly state-owned and wholly owned SOEs, implement the voting system of "one person one vote", and ensure the Board of Directors is responsible for its decisions; (iv) improve the Board of Directors and the director evaluation methods, strengthen appraisal and management of directors, adjust the post of, dismiss, or conduct legal investigation into the director who is responsible directly for major decision-making errors; and (v) further strengthen construction of the external director's team and expand source channels.
- Finally, deepen internal reforms on personnel, labor, and distribution systems, aiming to formulate a mechanism that allows entry and exit of employees, promotion and demotion of managers, as well as rise and decline of incomes. Specific measures include the following: (i) deepen reform of the SOEs' leader management system to eliminate administrative ranks and similar treatment; set up a categorized and classified management system of SOEs' leaders; allow the Board of Directors to make direct appointment and conduct legal election, selection, appraisal, and management of business managers; empower business managers to promote or demote staff, define rights, and obligations of the Board of Shareholders, Board of Directors, Board of Supervisors, and the top management; and separate the decision-making rights from management rights; (ii) promote reform of SOEs' personnel management

system to set up a professional manager market; advance marketization reform of SOEs' management personnel; introduce competitive post mechanism, and create a staff mobility and allocation mechanism that allows entry and exit of personnel as well as promotion and demotion; (iii) explore formulation of the distribution system of state-owned capital gains, improve all state-owned asset operation budgets and gain-sharing systems, and ensure transfer of state-owned capital gains into reinvestment and social security funds rather than into fiscal revenue so as to reflect the public ownership of state-owned assets shared by all citizens; and (iv) strengthen internal supervision, improve internal supervisory system, fulfill supervisory duties of the Board of Supervisors, audit division, discipline inspection and supervision division, inspection tours, legal division, and financial division, perfect and enhance the executive power of the monitoring system, strengthen supervision over the power-centralized, capital-intensive, resource-intensive, and asset-intensive divisions and posts, and strengthen internal process control to avoid abuse of power.

4. *Breaking all administrative monopoly industries*

Reform of administrative monopoly industries is the key to reform of monopolized industries. The longstanding administrative monopoly has resulted in a fixed structure of benefits distribution, so breaking it will inevitably undermine some people's vested interests. To achieve this purpose, we must place reasonable restrictions on the power of government, decentralize power to the market and society, and make full use of existing anti-monopoly resources to regulate market rules for administrative monopoly industries, weaken the monopolistic position of existing administrative monopolists, allow non-public enterprises to participate in some competitive sectors, improve the supervisory system of monopoly industries, and create a good environment for fair competition among all types of enterprises.

- First, make reasonable restrictions on the power of government and define the boundary between government roles and market roles to prevent the government's lopsided and misplaced administration. Specific measures are as follows: (i) further decentralize government powers, reduce or cancel items subject to administrative approval, liberalize market access, ease administrative control and monopolized resources, cancel unreasonable administrative control, and promote reform of resource mechanism and market pricing mechanism; (ii) normalize the government's administrative behaviors, promote the power list system, define rights and obligations of each division and each job, lawfully cancel and strictly administrate a number of administrative powers contrary to requirements of comprehensively deep reform; (iii) comprehensively promote law-based administration, set up a legal examination system of major decisions, strengthen administrative law enforcement, ensure laws are enforced strictly and justly while law-breakers are prosecuted, set up and improve all-round supervisory mechanism of administrative behaviors, perfect legislative, judicial, and internal supervision, and strengthen surveillance by the masses and media; (iv) implement transparent supervision of powers; regularly publicize the size of government agencies, administrative expenditure budget, and civil servants' compensation and integrity; implement a public enquiry system of government affairs; strengthen restriction and supervision of key sectors and positions; and improve internal level supervision and special supervision of the government; and (v) normalize administrative control of market prices, ensure the power of price control in special sectors will not be established unless approved by legislative body, and ensure any administrative authority that has obtained the price control power will be subject to the *Price Law of the People's Republic of China* and the public hearing when exercising such power.

- Second, anti-monopoly activity according to the laws should be enforced. Despite inadequacy of the existing *Anti-unfair Competition Law* and the *Anti-trust Law*, some of their normative contents are strongly restrictive to administrative monopoly. Specific strategies include the following: (i) strengthening the fundamental position of the *Anti-trust Law* to ensure its applicable authoritativeness, and pressing ahead industrial anti-monopoly policy and measures to ensure there are laws and rules to follow; (ii) improving the inspection system of fair competition, and making timely adjustments and revisions to existing industrial normative documents contrary to the *Anti-trust Law* so as to ensure the role of the law in administrative monopoly industries; (iii) setting up "legislative challenge system" to ensure legislation or legislation draft of specific monopoly right is written by a neutral party delegated by a legislative body instead of an administrative agency related to the specific monopoly right, and to ensure that the monopoly right establishing proposal is subject to consultation by an expert committee organized by the legislative body and deemed to be established as a single power rather than one established in the unit of "category", e.g. "a monopoly right that makes difference to lifelines of the national economy"; and (iv) ensuring that the NPC Standing Committee, as a specially established supervisory organ of the *Constitution*, legally eliminates and examines any legislation suspected of violating the existing Constitution, and that it is canceled or declared invalid if such violation is proved.

- Third, set up a professional, transparent, and single-functioning anti-monopoly agency. Certain industries of a monopolistic nature usually do not depend totally on the market for resource allocation due to their technical and economic features. The anti-monopoly agency is essential to improving efficiency and normalizing behaviors of certain industries with a monopolistic nature. According to the *Anti-trust Law*, the law enforcement power is centralized in three divisions of the anti-trust committee, such as anti-trust division of the Ministry of Commerce, price supervision and inspection division of the National Development and Reform Commission (NDRC), and anti-trust and anti-unfair competition enforcement division of the State Administration of Industry and Commerce (SAIC). The "double-level and three-division anti-trust system" used in enforcement of the anti-trust law has led to inconsistent standards and low efficiency of law enforcement. According to requirements for anti-administrative monopoly, a professional supervisory agency should be established, consisting of transportation (including railways, highway, water transport, and civil aviation), energy sources (including electricity, natural gas, and coal gas) and telecommunications (Telecom, Radio & Television, etc.), so as to define government power and behavior style in supervision of certain industries with a monopolistic nature; cancel unnecessary administrative formalities and functions; centralize supervision functions dispersed among several functional divisions into one supervisory agency; set up and perfect a relatively independent supervisory agency of certain industries with a monopolistic nature; and separate the government's supervisory functions from its administrative functions.

- Finally, accelerate anti-monopoly reforms at both administrative and judicial levels. At the administrative level, the following are required: (i) encourage SOEs and private enterprises to participate in industrial fields where no monopoly rights are required by existing laws; (ii) by means of executive order, abolish or prohibit monopoly rights authorized by the administrative authority itself (including executive association under its control); (iii) require the Ministry of Finance and the Ministry of Land and Resources to set up a special agency responsible for verifying the quantities of public natural resources (land, mining right, etc.) occupied by enterprises and collect rents from resource occupiers at market prices; (iv) require the State-owned Assets Supervision and Administration Commission (SASAC) to specify the upper limit of SOEs' wages and salaries and impose penalty on those beyond the limit; and (v) require the Ministry of Finance to set up a special agency to supervise the financial conditions of SOEs, especially of the central SOEs; propose SOEs' profit-sharing plans to the State Council, and supervise delivery and reinvestment of SOEs' profits. At the judicial level, the following are required: (i) allow parties involved to lodge a lawsuit directly in the court against an enterprise suspected of administrative monopoly, which not only requests the monopolistic enterprise to assume civil liabilities but also requests the court to examine the legitimacy of the enterprise's monopoly position; (ii) revise relevant legislation so that the court is essentially entitled to check up administrative monopoly cases and dispose of the enterprise's monopolistic position; (iii) transform the existing anti-trust administrative law enforcement mechanism to consolidate the law enforcement agency and its functions, improve its authoritativeness, justify its procedures, ensure justice, transparency, and involvement, and eradicate black case work; and (iv) set up a public prosecution system for administrative monopoly.

5. *Creating workable competition market structure that gives consideration to both the scale economy and competitive efficiency*

The reform of monopoly industry is intended not only to break up monopoly but to create an effectively competitive market structure that gives consideration to both the scale economy and competitive efficiency, weakening direct government intervention and suppressing economic monopoly.

- First, set up a mechanism to split natural monopoly business from non-natural monopoly business. The network economy character of natural monopoly is one of the important reasons why it can produce scale economy. However, as technical changes lead to increasing changes in the boundary of national monopoly business, parts of businesses in traditional natural monopoly industries are no longer of the natural monopoly character; therefore, it is necessary to separate natural monopoly business from non-natural monopoly business in the following manners. On the one hand, we will set up a mechanism for separation of natural monopoly business from non-natural monopoly business to reasonably define the sectors and scope of non-natural monopoly businesses. In natural monopoly industries, the natural monopoly businesses are centralized in fixed network operation fields, such as line and pipeline transmission of electricity, urban heating, gas and running water supply as well as wire communication networking business in telecommunications and rail track networking business in railway transport. Other competitive businesses include generation and retail business of electric power, long-distance calls, mobile and value-added services in telecommunications as well as passenger and cargo transport of railway and civil aviation businesses. On the other hand, set up a mechanism to invert monopolistic businesses into non-monopolistic businesses by introducing market competition into some of the monopolistic businesses as technological level improves.
- Second, promote classified reforms of monopolistic and non-monopolistic businesses. Depending on various features of monopolistic and competitive businesses in natural monopoly industries, the government should implement differentiated reforms to ensure effective roles of market competition mechanism in natural monopoly industries while guaranteeing the scale economy benefits natural monopoly, achieve workable competition that gives consideration to both competitive vitality and scale economy, and improve operational efficiency of these industries. On the one hand, the reform of

monopolistic businesses will aim to change "big monopoly" to "small monopoly" so as to meet the regulatory needs of scale economy and establish an industrial benchmark and set up benchmark competitive mechanism. On the other hand, the reform of non-monopolistic businesses will focus more on establishing a fair and open market for full competition to let the fittest survive than on making arbitrary arrangements by administrative means so as to promote industrial integration and improve industrial competitiveness.

- Third, set up a classified management mechanism of SOEs' social responsibilities to clearly define obligations of the government and monopolistic enterprises in performance of social responsibilities and provision of universal services, under which the government is obligated to fulfill functions of public and universal services while the enterprises are responsible for performance of universal services. First, the core social responsibilities of public service SOEs include high-efficiency supply of public services and fulfillment of universal services, where the appraisal indicators include supply of public services, product standards and service quality, manufacturing cost, and price fairness. Second, the core social responsibilities of functional SOEs focus on special functions assigned by the state government and highlighted by public policy orientation, where the appraisal indicators include the realization degree of the state-assigned functions, social benefits of products and services provided, as well as the degree and performance of enterprises' involvement in addressing social problems. Third, the core social responsibilities of commercial SOEs are limited to quality of products and services, integrity and compliance in management, safety in production and operation, low-carbon, environment protection and conservation, as well as preservation and appreciation of state-owned assets, where the appraisal indicator is limited to appreciation level of state-owned assets. Finally, set up a cost compensation mechanism for universal services, including fiscal subsidy and universal services fund, to change cross-subsidies from "secret" to "open" subsidies for enterprises' businesses, clearly define responsibilities of the government and enterprises, and specify the boundary between policy-related businesses and operation-related businesses of enterprises.

- Finally, further improve regulatory system of monopolized industries. Promoting reform and development of monopolized industries requires further improvement of the regulatory system and mechanism, avoidance of lopsided and absent supervision, and prevention of overlapping management in regulatory functions. First, legally set up coordinated regulatory systems by defining the scope of powers of the government; formulate scientific and reasonable regulatory procedures, canceling unnecessary administrative licenses, changing old practices that focus more on licensing than on supervision, and strengthening in-process and after-event supervision. Second, improve the monopolistic cost constraint mechanism by setting up and improving the daily ongoing supervision mechanism for cost accounting, service quality, safety standards, and universal services in monopolized industries, and strengthening punitive measures for violations; establish the cost constraint mechanism in monopolized industries by supervision, checkup, and publicity of their cost and introduction of third-party assessment. Third, set up and improve new systems for price control to establish the ceiling prices of monopolistic industrial products by defining the upper limit or referencing international prices of a similar industry or domestic prices of the same industry so as to force monopolistic enterprises to take cost-reducing actions; improve price hearing systems, set up incentive and restrictive mechanisms for hearing representatives, broaden representatives' information acquisition channels, reduce the "public opinion proxy" cost, and grant a certain amount of cost compensation to hearing representatives so that they can represent public opinions in a true sense; encourage social groups to act as public opinion proxy, including guilds that are willing, capable, and constrained to do so; protect consumers' rights to supervise and participate in hearings, and make timely disclosure of hearing materials to consumers to ensure their right to information.

6. *Strongly supporting non-public economies to participate in reforms of SOEs and monopolized industries*

Reform of mixed SOEs' mixed ownership requires the involvement of non-public economies. Supporting measures need to be taken to foster non-public economies in terms of market access, property right protection, market supervision, fair competition, and financial innovation. It is of vital importance for non-public economies to participate in reforms of SOEs and monopolized industries.

- First, broaden the fields of non-public economic development by implementing the negative list market access system, encouraging and directing private enterprises to participate in SOEs' system transformation, restructuring, equity capital increase and corporate operation and management by means of contribution, shares acquisition, convertible debt subscription, and equity replacement so as to promote entry of private capital into monopolized industries and sectors, investment, construction, operation and management of resource energy, infrastructures and municipal public facilities, such as running water, gas, heat, public transport, and sewage and garbage treatment; encourage private enterprises' participation in social undertakings such as financial service, education, scientific research, healthcare, culture, sports, and social welfare; encourage private capital to participate in cultural creative enterprises transformed from operational cultural institutions; encourage private capital to host brand competitions, build and participate in operation of stadiums; encourage and support private capital to legally operate preschool education, primary and secondary schools, secondary vocational schools, junior and advanced technical colleges, universities, and vocational training institutions. By procurement of public services, the government will direct private capital's orderly entry into such public services as education, culture, and sports.
- Second, improve supportive policy systems for private economy; strengthen taxation supervision by expanding tax sources and reducing tax rates to alleviate burdens on private enterprises, especially on entrepreneurial and employment-, technology-, and service-oriented enterprises, to whom tax preference needs to be granted; standardize types of administrative charges to cancel recurring charge items, prohibit arbitrary charges, penalties, and donations imposed on private enterprises and alleviate their operating burdens; encourage financial authorities to annually withhold a proportion of private economy's

additional taxes as the development fund for private economies, which, along with other funds, will form the credit guarantee fund for private enterprises; increase policy support for innovative development of private economies to guide private enterprises into strategic new industries such as new energy, new materials, IT, and biotechnology; increase policy support and services for medium-, small-, and micro-sized enterprises (MSMEs) to reduce their burdens, expand financing channels, and support technical innovation and expansion of technology-oriented private enterprises and MSMEs.

- Third, create a favorable external environment for development of private enterprises and MSMEs by supporting them in expanding financing channels, such as "national treatment" and equal rights with SOEs; focus on loan guarantee of private enterprises by formulating government measures for the guarantee system; accelerate establishment of effective public service platform to create conditions, markets, more social resources, and production factors for private enterprises with vitality and prospects so that they may enjoy the same treatment as other enterprises in investment, financing, tax, land use, and foreign trade.
- Fourth, eliminate differentiated ownerships on factor market by accelerating reform of factor marketization, increasing efforts in market allocation of land, resources, information, technologies, and talented personnel, and creating an open and fair environment for factor market competition; try to solve restrictive factors such as land, finance, and technology that may affect economic development of private enterprises by building a policy support system to promote SMEs' development, and reducing their operating cost; broaden private capital's investment and financing channels, reduce market access threshold of various financial institutions, allow private capital to set up financial institutions, and encourage financial institutions such as small and medium banks, securities agencies, guarantee companies, trust companies, and assets management companies to provide a fair and open environment for capital market competition so as to improve these institutions' capabilities of professional services and market competitiveness, and to broaden private capital's financing channels.
- Finally, guide private economies to set up modern corporate systems by solving extensive management of family enterprises and

encouraging private enterprises to separate their ownership from management rights; encourage private enterprises to be listed or raise funds on overseas markets and promote manager and employee stock ownership; accelerate industrial transformation and upgrading of private enterprises to change their extensive operation mode and take active part in strategic new industries such as new energy, new materials, IT, and biotechnology so as to promote independent innovation, transformation of development mode, and create new competitive advantages for private enterprises; strengthen reasonable guidance and supervision of private enterprises and enhance construction of their social credit system and mechanism to direct them in conducting technical innovation, improving management level, ensuring production safety, and improving their comprehensive qualities and competitiveness.

Chapter 6

Thoughts and Strategies for Opening Wider to the Outside World Under Supply-Side Structural Reform

Wu Jiansheng, Ji Jianjun and Jin Ruiting

Academy of Macroeconomic Research

Abstract

China's opening up situation is currently facing great changes from both internal and external environments, such as the rising cost of domestic factors, gradual loss of traditional comparative advantages, weakening external demands, and increasingly severe trade frictions. Therefore, the supply-side structural reform is of great importance to China's opening wider and changing from a big trading nation to a strong trading nation. In addition, opening wider, correcting factor market distortion, and rebuilding comparative advantages are important supporting factors for the supply-side structural reform. Under the new normal, opening up, transformation, and upgrading will be prioritized in cultivation of the innovation-based environment, reform of the factor market, experimental reform of the Free Trade Zones, and construction of the "Belt and Road".

As China's economic development enters the new normal at the present stage and in response to the new situation, new tasks, and new requirements of the supply-side structural reform, we will further promote a new round of high-level and all-dimensional opening up to facilitate the process of reform, innovation, and development.

I. General Framework for Supply-Side Structural Reform and Opening Wider

1. *Connotations of China's supply-side structural reform*

The contents of supply-side structural reform can be decomposed into "supply-side + structural + reform", which essentially means that, taking "enterprise, industry, factors, resources and systems" on the supply side as the hitting points and acting points and centering on improvement of supply quality and benefits, use is made of reform to promote the structural adjustment, rectify the distorted allocation of factor resources, and strengthen the adaptability of the supply structure to changes in the demand structure so as to increase effective and high-end supplies, reduce ineffective and low-end supplies, improve total factor productivity as a new engine for economic development, and eventually create a new economic growth system that features a high-efficiency combination of supply and demand structures, full invigoration of market entities' vitality, and considerable enhancement of the level of productivity.

2. *Opening wider — Core connotation of the supply-side structural reform*

Like "a bird's two wings and a car's two wheels", the reform and opening up are a dialectical unity that accelerate each other. On the one hand, the supply-side structural reform is aimed and prioritized to realize economic structure adjustment and industrial transformation and upgrading, seek new kinetic energy for economic growth, and push industries toward a medium- and high-end level, which coincides with the objective and main tasks of opening wider to the outside world, such as enlarging foreign trade and investment, acquiring key resource factors, and enhancing new advantages for international cooperation and competition. On the other hand, the five main tasks of the supply-side structural reform, including capacity reduction, de-stocking, deleveraging, cost reduction, and improving weak areas, will not be fulfilled unless in an open environment. For example, overcapacity will only be reduced by external output of China's surplus and advantageous capacity and high-end equipment by means of foreign trade structure adjustment and international cooperation in production capacity; cost reduction will only be achieved by improving customs clearance efficiency and reducing import/export taxes and duties; and improving weak areas will require support from increasing import of advanced technologies and equipment, key components, and nationally scarcest energy sources and materials.

3. *Supply-side structural reform — A catalyst to opening wider*

Opening wider will not succeed without deepening reform, and the latter can provide important institutional support for the former. At the present stage, factors that impose constraints on China's optimization and upgrading of foreign trade and on its transition from a big trading nation into a strong trading nation are centralized on the supply side. Currently, China's industries remain at the medium- and small-end level around the globe, considering its foreign trade failing to demonstrate comprehensive advantages in technology, brands, standards, quality, and services, and its export product quality and grade failing to meet the changing demands on the international market. In this tough situation, increasing effective supply of products and institutions through supply-side structural reform will facilitate transformation of China's foreign trade into import of advanced technologies and equipment, key components and nationally scarcest energy sources and materials, and full-industry chain export of high-grade and high-value-added products, technologies, and services, and will also promote international cooperation on production capacity and construction of free trade zones.

4. *Opening wider — A reverse force to propel supply-side structural reform*

Deepening reform will not succeed either without opening wider to the outside world, because the latter acts as a reverse force to propel the supply-side structural reform. On the one hand, the supply-side structural reform is reversely propelled by optimizing the structure of foreign trade and investment. Currently, as the international economic situation is subject to considerable adjustments, industrial competition in all countries is getting increasingly fierce and the developed economies are carrying out the "re-industrialization" strategy in an attempt to take on the commanding heights of the global industry chain. This means that opening wider will raise demanding requirements for supply-side structural reform. On the other hand, the new round of international rules' reconstruction will lead to reform of institutional mechanisms in China. In recent years, some high-standard new international rules, including TPP and TTIP concerning intellectual property, labor, environment, SOEs, and government procurement, have been mostly associated with the supply-side structural reform, which plays a demonstrative and leading role in China's practice, regardless of various pressures and challenges arising therefrom.

II. Key Areas of Opening Wider Under Supply-Side Structural Reform

1. *Carrying out international cooperation on production capacity to promote China's industrial development toward a globally medium- and high-end level*

(1) *Promoting output of China's surplus and advantageous capacity and accelerating transition of China from a country with strong manufacturing power into one with strong institutional systems*

On the one hand, we will relieve overcapacity pressure, adjust and upgrade domestic industry structure, broaden and deepen China's participation in international division of labor by undertaking the following: (i) pushing China's competitive industrial capacity of technologies, standards, and services in capital-intensive and technology-intensive industries such as high-speed railways, nuclear power, telecommunications, and new energy sources toward global markets by means of key cooperative projects with countries along the "Belt and Road" to build up the "Made-in-China" brand; (ii) getting effective access to core technology, brands, international distribution channels, new commercial modes and business types, and internationally advanced management experiences of global high-end manufacturing industries by means of carrying out cross-border M&As and setting up joint ventures; and (iii) working with other countries in strategic cooperation on production capacity to build the international economic cooperation corridor and overseas industrial agglomerations. On the other hand, we will give full play to enterprises' subjective roles and accelerate cultivation of internationally competitive and influential transnational enterprises by undertaking the following: (i) streamlining administration and decentralizing powers to facilitate enterprises' overseas investment and help enterprises go global; (ii) establishing a bilateral and multilateral cooperative mechanism for customs clearance of goods, entry and exit of personnel, monetary settlement, judicial and tax cooperation; and (iii) ensuring effective implementation of cooperation in production capacity through various mechanisms and platforms.

(2) *Encouraging introduction of foreign advanced technologies to improve our weak areas*

On the one hand, we will ease investment access and deepen reform of the foreign capital management system by strengthening in-process and after-event supervision and innovating supervision and service methods of foreign capital management; shift focus from the size of foreign business and investment to quality of capital introduction to encourage foreign investors' participation in producer services, strategic emerging industries, and advanced manufacturing industries; improve supporting capacity and full-industry chain development of regional industries to attract more transnational companies into high-end service industry; and strengthen combined introduction of foreign capital, technology, and brainpower to improve comprehensive benefits of foreign capital. On the other hand, we will adjust and optimize the regional and industrial distribution of foreign capital, adhere to green, low-carbon, and cyclic development and promote gradient transfer of eastern coastal industries to the central and western regions so as to facilitate interregional coordinated development and opening wider to the outside world.

2. *Accelerating optimization and upgrading of China's foreign trade into import of advanced technologies and equipment, key components, and nationally scarcest energy sources and materials as well as full-industry chain export of high-grade and high-value-added products, technologies, and services*

(1) *Enhancing competitiveness of foreign trade products and exploiting potentialities of foreign trade export market*

We will increase investment in R&D activities, provide support for enterprises' independent innovation, and encourage enterprises to make use of advanced applicable technologies in transformation and upgrading of traditional industries so as to meet medium- and high-end demands on international market and foster new growth points of China's export. We will also create new competitive advantages of traditional industrial export to secure market shares of China's foreign trade export in accordance with requirements for quality and refinement.

(2) *Increasing import of scarcest materials and equipment to effectively make up for gaps of supply on domestic market*

This will be achieved by the following: (i) increasing import of advanced technologies and equipment, key components, and energy resource products to make up for gaps of supply on domestic market; (ii) promoting export by increasing import of key technologies and equipment to optimize domestic factor resource structure and raise value added of export products; and (iii) strengthening coordination between import policy and industrial policy to facilitate transformation and upgrading of manufacturing industries.

(3) *Innovating foreign trade development mode to develop new business types of services and foreign trade industries*

On the one hand, we will promote pilot projects of cross-border e-commerce, methods of market procurement, and foreign trade and integrated foreign trade service providers to facilitate innovation and applications of business modes. On the other hand, we will deepen reform of the service trade management system, lower the market access threshold, and select some experienced and operable service sectors as key sectors to undergo pilot innovative service trade modes so as to form replicable and transferable modes and experiences.

3. *Promoting transformation and upgrading of processing trade to enhance the overall level of China's processing trade industry*

(1) *Propelling transition from low-end to high-end product processing industry to increase technical content and value added of products*

We will focus on changing "processing" into "R&D and manufacturing", i.e. a transition from the traditional processing trade into independent development and manufacturing of products; promote upgrading of traditional labor-intensive processing trade industries such as textile, apparel, suitcases, bags, shoes, hats, and furniture toward capital- and technology-intensive industries such as IT and machinery manufacturing, or promote upgrading of manufacturing processes from traditional processing and assembling as well as low-end parts manufacturing toward high-end, key, or core components manufacturing. In addition, we will prolong the value-added section of processing trade behind the border to increase percentage of domestic enterprises.

(2) *Expanding the value-added chain of processing trade behind the border to direct processing enterprises upstream of the industrial chain*

We will focus on changing the traditional practices, where raw materials are provided by and finished products are delivered to foreign clients, into a new processing trade mode by which raw materials will be provided by and finished products will be delivered to both domestic and foreign clients, which means a transition from processing products under foreign orders to flexible and independent management of processing business according to market demands, or a transition from processing and assembling to high-value-added production. On the one hand, processing enterprises will be encouraged to move upstream of the industrial chain, including product development and design. On the other hand, we will change from "trading" into "global marketing", i.e. building a global marketing network, so as to extend processing trade chain toward logistics, brand, and marketing channels downstream.

(3) *Optimizing regional distribution of processing trade to maintain advantages of China's traditional processing trade*

By facilitating factor mobility and establishing industrial transfer parks, we will encourage gradient transfer of traditional labor-intensive and land-intensive processing trade to the central and western regions so as to make the inland region become a main undertaking place for coastal processing trade chains.

(4) *Integrating and optimizing customs special supervision areas to accelerate transformation of processing trade management mode*

We will focus on consolidating all special supervision platforms including the export processing zones, bonded areas, and bonded port areas to realize transfer of processing trade toward the international closed supervision parks; incorporate the previous processing businesses of investor's raw materials or imported raw materials into customs special supervision areas for uniform and normative management; and promote upgrading of customs special supervision areas toward free trade zones.

4. *Alleviating burdens on foreign trade enterprises to enhance their supply capability of high-quality and low-price products*

(1) *Reducing labor cost, financing cost, and tax burden of foreign trade enterprises to enhance their cooperative and competitive advantages*

At the present stage, the rising costs of foreign trade enterprises are largely caused by the following: (i) the rising labor cost in recent years in

China, which is obviously higher than most neighboring developing countries; (ii) the rising financing cost, including the rising credit cost, the lowering loan limit, the prolonged cycle of loan approval, the narrowing financing channels, and increasing difficulty in obtaining bank loans or credit; (iii) the wave-like rise of exchange rate cost, which weakens the competitive advantages of export enterprises; and (iv) tax burdens on foreign trade enterprises in China, which is obviously heavier than economies such as Brazil, Indonesia, Malaysia, Japan, and South Korea, excluding India and the Philippines.

(2) *Bringing down import/export expenses to facilitate customs clearance*

Currently, Chinese foreign trade enterprises have to pay three types of import/export expenses: (i) charges collected by such government agencies as customs, quality inspection and quarantine, environment protection bureau, and food administration in performance of their public duties; (ii) charges collected by the government, public institutions, and their designated organizations for provision of services; and (iii) charges collected by port operators, management and shipping agents for provision of services. According to incomplete statistics, there are about 93 items chargeable for import and export activities in China, including about 12 items of administration business charges and about 81 items of operating service charges. To facilitate customs clearance, China has promoted the integrated regional clearance and the fast customs clearance system based on information exchange, mutual recognition of supervision, and mutual assistance in law enforcement; however, China remains at a lower level than developed economies in transnational cooperation, document standardization, and appeal feasibility.

5. *Playing roles of financial support to effectively prevent against potential risks in financial openness*

(1) *Broadening enterprises' financing channels to reduce cost of foreign investment and external financing*

Problems currently facing China's foreign trade enterprises include narrower financing channels and a unitary financing mode. The medium- and long-term loan exchange rate of state-owned enterprises generally remains up to 4%, but that of private enterprises stays above 6%, obviously higher than 1–2% in European and American countries. At present, the integrated financing cost of China's foreign trade enterprises is as high as 10–15%, 3–5 times the cost in economies such as the United States and Singapore.

(2) *Strengthening important functions of financial service support in construction of the "Belt and Road", international cooperation in production capacity, and steady growth of foreign trade*

The existing financial mechanism arrangements make it difficult to meet the rigid demands of considerable capital in construction of the "Belt and Road", international cooperation in production capacity, and steady growth of foreign trade. According to estimates by Asian Development Bank (ADB), the infrastructure construction of Asian countries requires investment of more than US$800 billion per year, which will lead to a huge financing gap. Regarding international cooperation in production capacity, most key cooperative projects are capital intensive so much so that they will not be implemented without support from effective financing platforms. In facilitating growth of foreign trade, the main problems include inadequate financial product innovation, financing channel expansion, and financial service optimization, thus resulting in increasingly difficult and high cost of financing.

(3) *Improving Renminbi's exchange rate mechanism to steady its internationalization*

After restarting the exchange rate reform in July 2005, the central government established the floating rate system to adjust and manage the currency basket based on market supply and demand. On August 11, 2015, the Central Bank of China declared the newly reformed central parity rate forming mechanism consisting of "the closing rate + currency basket exchange rate changes". The key to maintaining steady operations of China's financial market lies in improving the Renminbi rate forming mechanism and in stabilizing the reasonable market expectation. Renminbi's successful entry into SDR is an important milestone marking its integration into the global monetary system. Currently, the Central Bank of China has arranged currency swaps with 36 national and regional central banks, totaling RMB 3.3 trillion. With perfect infrastructure for Renminbi internationalization, China has made Renminbi liquidation arrangements with 20 countries and regions. The clearing system of Renminbi cross-border and offshore business has formed since the release of the China International Payment System (CIPS, Phase I). Due to effectiveness of Renminbi's entry into SDR and deepening of the "Belt and Road" construction and international cooperation in production capacity, the sustainable demand of Renminbi on the global market has paved the way for the currency's internationalization.

6. *Taking active part in global economic governance to push the international economic order toward a fair and reasonable direction*

(1) *Promoting reform of global economic governance to continuously strengthen China's institutional discourse power in global economic governance*

Currently, a number of emerging economies led by China are playing increasingly important roles and effects in global economic governance; the G20 Forum has significantly consolidated and improved its position and roles in consultation and coordination of global macroeconomic policies; the BRICS nations and Shanghai Cooperation Organization (SCO) are increasingly influential in international and regional affairs; in addition, the IMF and the World Bank are undergoing reform of shares and voting rights. All this has provided new opportunities for China to lead the global economic agenda and enhance its discourse right in global economic governance.

(2) *Encouraging developing countries' equal participation in global economic governance and effectively promoting reform of international monetary system and international financial supervision*

Upon establishment and operation, the Asian Infrastructure Investment Bank (AIIB) and the BRICS Bank have become important new forces in the international development finance system. As Renminbi becomes an important regional currency in Asia, it seems highly likely that the East Asian finance stability mechanism will decouple itself from US dollars, and that Renminbi will be a global hard currency. IMF's transition from advocating deregulation of capital controls to recognizing the necessity and rationality of developing countries' control over capital movement helps emerging economies including China and developing countries to play greater roles in reform of the international finance system.

(3) *Promoting FTA negotiations to accelerate construction of a global high-standard FTZ network*

Currently, China has signed official bilateral investment treaties (BITs) with 56 nations along the "Belt and Road", and is actively negotiating with the United States and European nations about the Sino-US BIT and Sino-European BIT, respectively. After concluding 14 free trade agreements (FTAs) with 22 countries and regions, China is now creating the upgraded version of the Sino-ASEAN free trade zone so as to promote negotiations on the Regional Comprehensive Economic Partnership (RCEPA) agreement and a China–Japan–ROK free trade area.

III. General Framework and Strategies for Opening Wider to the Outside World Under Supply-Side Structural Reform

1. *General framework*

According to the four national strategic plans (i.e. comprehensively building a moderately prosperous society, deepening reform, ruling by law, and strengthening Party self-discipline) and five national general plans (for construction of economy, politics, culture, society, and ecological civilization), we will earnestly implement the innovative, coordinated, green, open, and sharing development ideas, actively adapt to the new normal of economic development, make overall plans for internal reform and opening up to the outside world, make full use of domestic and international resources, focus on open development under supply-side structural reform, adjust and optimize export-oriented economic structure, improve quality and benefits of export-oriented economy, implement more proactive, open, and win–win strategies, give priority to both import and export, combine introduction and output of advanced technologies, coordinate global and regional cooperation, comprehensively deepen reform of the foreign-related economic system, properly understand China's new position and advantages in global division of labor and industrial chain, take active part in global economic governance and reform, and comprehensively raise the level of China's open economy.

2. *Promoting institutional innovation to build new system of open economy*

(1) *Creating new mechanisms for sustainable development of foreign trade*

- First, we will improve the foreign trade promotion policy system by directing foreign trade enterprises in adjustment of import/export product structure and market structure, encouraging SMEs to expand the international market, giving play to the support functions of finance for foreign trade development, and encouraging financial institutions to develop more financial products in support of trade development.
- Second, we will raise the trade facilitation level by perfecting the quota and license management system and the processing trade management system, simplifying customs clearance procedures, improving regional clearance cooperation mechanisms, supporting extension of port functions toward inland regions, enhancing e-port functions, promoting sharing and coordination of government information and

business related to trade, improving classified management methods of customs enterprises as well as inspection and quarantine credit system of import and export enterprises, improving customs clearance efficiency, further simplifying entry–exit approval procedures of foreign trade personnel, and striving to conclude visa exemption agreement with more countries.

- Third, we will make use of the roles of intermediary agents by deepening reform of the management system and operating mechanism of industrial guilds and importers/exporters' chambers, improving and strengthening their functions and roles in other information services, industrial self-discipline, and maintaining enterprises' rights and interests, strengthening dialogs and communication with originations and enterprises relevant to bulk commodity exporting countries, and enhancing discourse rights and pricing rights on international bulk commodity market.
- Finally, we will build and improve the promotion system of trade in services by encouraging development of trade in producer services; based on new technologies such as big data, cloud computation, the Internet of Things, and the mobile Internet, promote transformation of service industry and foster new types of services; and innovate the financial service system for trade in services, promote upgrading of outsourcing service, and improve cross-border delivery capacity of services.

(2) *Innovating foreign capital management system*

- First, we will ease foreign capital market access by actively promoting service enterprises to open wider, such as enterprises engaging in finance, education, culture, and healthcare; relax restrictions on foreign capital access to services such as the nursery, old people's homes, architectural design, accounting and audit, commercial trade and logistics, and e-commerce.
- Second, we will create a market environment for fair competition; adopt the "pre-establishment national treatment" and "negative list" methods for foreign capital management, include into the list those areas to which foreign capital's access is prohibited or restricted and

grant access permits to those not included on the list, and give the same treatment to both domestic and foreign-funded enterprises; minimize and standardize administrative approval, promote transition of government management from prior approval to in-process and after-event supervision, and improve the investment facilitation level; and actively explore the national security review system to carry out national security review on foreign capital.

- Finally, we will promote FTZ construction, accelerate realization of FTZ strategies, create global high-standard FTZ networks based on peripheral regions, enlarge the scope of pilot FTZs, and promote institutional innovation in a broader region.

(3) *Deepening reform of overseas investment management system*

- First, we will establish the principal positions of foreign investment enterprises and individuals by relaxing restrictions on investment approval, exchange control, financial services, and factor mobility to promote the foreign investment facilitation level; following the principle that "anyone who invested, made decisions and benefited therefrom will assume risks", allow enterprises and individuals to carry out overseas investment and capacity cooperation activities on their own strengths.
- Second, we will improve the level of "going global" services by perfecting the policy system for fiscal tax and finance to coordinate and promote foreign investment, accelerating negotiations and conclusion of investment agreements with relevant countries and regions, and perfecting the consular protection system so as to provide overseas investment enterprises with such services as right protection, investment promotion, and early risk warning.
- Finally, we will accelerate construction of the overseas investment legal system by improving and perfecting the legal environment and management mechanism conducive to enterprises' overseas investment; direct overseas enterprises to operate in accordance with local laws and regulations and fulfill local social duties; and strengthen safety risk assessment of foreign investment to reduce investment risks.

(4) *Perfecting the long-term mechanism for "Belt and Road" and international cooperation in production capacity*

- First, we will set up a long-term win–win mechanism to promote construction of the "Belt and Road" and international cooperation in production capacity, which features government promotion, enterprises' independent management, and marketable operations; deepen marketization reform to establish enterprises' principal position on market, improve corresponding systems such as policy support, risk prevention, and information release, and facilitate the government, enterprises, and other principal parties to jointly participate in the "Belt and Road" construction and international cooperation in a production capacity.
- Second, we will create a high-standard FTZ network that is based on peripheral regions, radiates toward the "Belt and Road", and is geared toward the whole world; build and strengthen connective partnerships with countries along the Belt and Road; promote construction of international trunk channels, promote construction of overseas economic trade and cooperative zones at major traffic nodes and ports, and create the international economic and trade cooperation corridor.
- Finally, we will set up the capacity cooperation policy coordination mechanism with peripheral countries and those along the "Belt and Road", strengthen communication and coordination with all countries, enlarge information sharing, enhance policy coordination and consistency in foreign capital market access and supervision, and gradually build the regional financial cooperation and risk prevention early warning mechanism.

(5) *Building regional coordination and opening up system*

- First, we will popularize or replicate successful experiences of the pilot FTZ reform throughout China, make new supplements, and promote regionally collaborated opening up to the outside world based on local conditions.
- Second, we will accelerate creation of the open platform in inland regions, encourage construction of processing trade, export base, and

FTA parks in the central and western regions, provide support for development zones to carry out cross-border regional cooperation, innovate processing trade modes, and promote gradient transfer and industrial acceptance of processing trade in the central and western regions.

- Finally, we will foster new advantages in opening up along borders, and build key border development and open pilot zones as well as border economic cooperation zones into an important platform for China's cooperation with peripheral countries.

(6) *Strengthening institutional discourse rights in global economic governance*

On the one hand, we will create a new mechanism for international economic and trade negotiations by consolidating negotiation resources and bargaining chips, making scientific decisions on negotiation plans, and optimizing the negotiation process, and strengthen enforcement, supervision, and performance assessment of negotiation plans to increase efforts and validity of foreign negotiations. On the other hand, we will take active part in global economic governance by deepening reform of the global economic governance system, allowing the United Nations, G20 Forum, and BRICS nations to play their platform roles in global economic governance, and increase emerging market and developing countries' rights to speak and represent their interests in global economic governance, we will participate in reform and rule-making activities of global economic governance, put forward new propositions, initiatives, and solutions for global issues, and constantly enhance China's discourse rights and influence in making international rules and setting standards.

3. *Policy suggestions*

(1) *Promoting comprehensive construction of the "Belt and Road"*

- First, we will deal properly with the relationship between the short- and medium- and long-term main tasks of the "Belt and Road" construction. For the short-term tasks, we will follow the principles of "making breakthroughs at key points from easiness to difficulty" to construct some demonstration projects such as roads, railways, ports, and parks, and open one or two strategic channels for land–ocean transportation, with first priority given to the China–Pakistan Economic Corridor, second priority given to the China–Mongolia Economic Corridor, the New Eurasian Land Bridge Economic Corridor, and the China–Indochina Peninsular Economic Corridor, and third priority given to the Bangladesh–China–India–Myanmar Economic Corridor and the China–Central Asia–Western Asia Economic Corridor. For the medium- and long-term tasks, we will follow the principles of "overall planning, coordination and steady headway" to implement the important tasks and key projects consisting of "policy coordination, facilities connectivity, unimpeded trade, financial integration, and people-people bond", and promote transition of the "Belt and Road" construction from the initial stage to the comprehensive harvest stage.

- Second, we will address three major problems concerning construction of the "Belt and Road": (i) capital supply: the key is to allow Renminbi to participate in construction of the "Belt and Road", moderately increase reserve and use of foreign exchange, and create an environment for all types of capital to participate in construction of the "Belt and Road"; (ii) cooperation mode: the key is to define in a timely manner the division of labor and position of the central government, local government, and enterprises, encourage innovative cooperation mode (e.g. investment and trade mode, major strategic project transnational cooperation mode, assistance and commercial cooperation mode, and multinational enterprises' promoting commercial project mode), and let NGOs play their roles; and (iii) development concept: the key is to make up and tell the "Legend of China" and introduce China's development concepts and experiences at multiple levels, on multiple dimensions, and in multiple channels, for instance, telling the "Legend of China" by offering foreign assistance training programs, encouraging think tanks to carry out international exchange, or treating a part of industrial park construction and key project construction as output carriers of development concepts.

- Finally, we will do a good job in construction of all "Belt and Road" economic corridors. The first priority corridor will be led by the government through all-dimensional cooperation, and upon completion, it will play demonstrative roles to stimulate construction of other corridors. The second priority corridor will be based on the Far East region and closely combined with China's Northeast Revival Strategy and the Beijing–Tianjin–Hebei Co-development Strategy. Construction of the New Eurasian Land Bridge Economic Corridor will be carried out through capacity cooperation and deep resource processing cooperation to exhibit the supporting roles of the Xinjiang core region and to realize internal and external linkage. Construction of the China–Indo-china Peninsula Economic Corridor will focus on infrastructure connectivity to improve the level of trade and investment facilitation and create the regional transnational production network. The third priority China–Central Asia–Western Asia Economic Corridor will be constructed in combination with geo-situation, foreign economic relations, diplomatic, and foreign aids. Construction of the Bangladesh–China–India–Myanmar Economic Corridor will take into consideration all parties' interests, subregional cooperation, and local government roles. In addition, construction of the 21st Century Marine Silk Road will be carried out to achieve development of port and port-surrounding industries.

(2) *Actively carrying out international cooperation in production capacity*

- First, we will actively create the "China-centered" industrial eco-chain. As a large systematic engineering, promoting international cooperation in production capacity requires top-level design and overall planning as well as innovative experiences. In the new situation, international cooperation in production capacity will be implemented steadily in accordance with intrinsic operating mechanism of the market, i.e. delivering domestic products, standards, technologies, capital, and services onto international markets.

- Second, we will work out a medium- and long-term plan (2016–2030) for international cooperation in production capacity based on construction of the "Belt and Road" strategy, make quick adjustments in key cooperative areas, enrich the directory of cooperative countries, optimize the trade cooperation mode, innovate commercial cooperation mode, improve bilateral and multilateral cooperation mechanism, and standardize overseas management behaviors of enterprises so as to promote Chinese technologies, capitals, and brands on the global market and try to increase China's foreign industrial investment from US$120 billion in 2015 to US$320 billion in 2030.
- Third, we will set up a capacity cooperation promotion organization aimed to work out international capacity cooperation strategies and provide relevant services; under coordination by the Chinese economic counselor's office in foreign countries dispatch working groups into key countries to carry out extensive investigation and send back monthly reports to the relevant authority; and set up commercial assistance centers in key countries to provide support for foreign governments or agencies that will come to China for talks about international cooperation in production capacity.
- Fourth, we will deepen reform of the financing system and promote capital account convertibility, interest rate liberalization, and foreign exchange supervision methods to achieve overseas enterprises' free financing on the international market; seek new financing methods such as "project financing", "equity financing", and "bond financing" based on the existing "offshore loan against domestic guarantee" financing method, and allow policy financial institutions to play their comparative advantages in providing medium- and long-term loans. Currently, the "project financing" method can be used for international cooperation in production capacity to establish a project company by financial investors and strategic investors. We will encourage enterprises to adopt "equity financing" and "bond financing" methods; improve policy insurance mechanism for overseas financing or set up investment loss reserves in countries engaging in capacity cooperation; and accelerate negotiations about bilateral and multilateral capacity cooperation mortgage guarantee treaties for major projects. In addition, we will strengthen

financing support from multilateral development financial institutions, including AIIB for international cooperation in production capacity, and further improve governance structure and investment management.

- Fifth, we will set up "industrial alliance" of enterprises engaging capacity cooperation to support development of leading enterprises and enhance their competitiveness on the international market; make use of "grouping" advantages to accelerate establishment of the "industrial alliance"; promote integration and optimization of upstream and downstream enterprises in twelve major industries to build a comprehensive information platform based on cooperative projects. The industrial alliance of enterprises engaging capacity cooperation will be subject to dynamic management and weekly meeting systems; the number of enterprises is adjusted according to the market situation to ensure scientific and orderly arrangement of investment abroad; and strengthen policy guidance for overseas industries, accelerate existing tax policies, with priority given to simplifying import/export tax rebate procedures and optimizing types of taxes, and improve control and supervision of finance and foreign exchange.
- Finally, we will allow trade guilds to play active roles by fostering four types of intermediary agencies, building a comprehensive pubic platform consisting of information, standards, factors, personnel, and risk control, and setting up and improving credit assessment systems for intermediary agencies. Based on the *Guidelines for Foreign Investment Cooperation Countries (Regions)* issued by the Ministry of Commerce, we will give further details of the country trade investment information, provide a separate chapter of international capacity cooperation under each country, and build a "comprehensive service platform for international cooperation in production capacity" to provide a package of services for enterprises to expand overseas markets.

(3) *Accelerating optimization and upgrading of foreign trade*

- First, we will consolidate and improve comprehensive competitiveness of foreign trade products, and utilize advanced applicable technologies to transform traditional labor-intensive industries, foster new competitive strengths in international cooperation, exploit and meet medium- and high-end demands on the international market, and seek new growth points of export industry; strengthen traditional advantages and enhance traditional industries' competitive strengths in export; encourage enterprises to increase investment in R&D activities, enhance their independent innovative capabilities, grasp true demands on the international market, and provide effective product supply.

- Second, we will improve our weak areas in import activities and implement proactive import policies to enlarge import volumes, promote balanced development of foreign investment, and optimize import structure by means of the following: (i) supporting import of advanced technology and equipment, key components, energy resource products, energy-saving and environment-friendly products and other products that meet requirements of upgrading consumption so as to make up for gaps on the domestic market; (ii) strengthening coordination and interaction between import policy and industrial policy to promote transformation and upgrading of manufacturing industry, improve comprehensive import benefits, and promote industrial innovation, transformation, and upgrading based on import; and (iii) combining direct acquisition of technologies with independent innovation, paying much attention to secondary innovation and integrated innovation of imported technologies, realizing factor agglomeration at a higher level, providing more preferential policy for high-tech import, and allowing import/export collaboration to play its important roles in promoting domestic economic development.
- Finally, we will focus on innovation of the foreign trade development mode. On the one hand, we will press ahead with innovation of cross-border e-commerce, market procurement trade mode, comprehensive trade enterprises, and overseas warehousing. On the other hand, we will develop new types of business of trade in services, carry out pilot innovation of trade in services, improve supply quality and level of trade in services, increase efforts in reform of management system of trade in services, bring down market access threshold, and guide

orderly flow of resources into technology- and knowledge-intensive modern high-end services.

(4) *Accelerating transformation and upgrading of processing trade*

- First, we will improve the appreciation rate of processing trade according to types of business; list into the catalog of commodities permitted for processing trade all emerging industries such as new energy, new materials and biomedicine, all technology- and knowledge-intensive industries including electronic information and all capital-intensive industries including equipment manufacturing that contain higher value added, meet the change trends of China's resource factor endorsements, remain at a development stage in the domestic market and will stimulate economic growth; list into the catalog of commodities prohibited for processing trade all labor-intensive industries such as textile and apparel, suitcases, bags, shoes, hats, toys, and furniture that contain lower technical content and value added and may stimulate economic growth to some extent; and list into the catalog of commodities prohibited for processing trade all industries, including "industries manufacturing high energy consumption, high pollution and resource products", that contain lower value added, consume huge quantity of resources and energy sources, and fail to comply with the changing trends of China's resource factor endorsements. In addition, we will continue to implement differentiated supervision policies for sectors of different types and make reasonable adjustments in percentage and payment scope of security deposits.
- Second, we will optimize regional distribution of processing trade industry, and continue to adopt the policy difference in management modes of the catalog of commodities permitted for processing trade and bank deposit account that are currently effective in the eastern regions as well as in the central and western regions of China; encourage investment in industrial clusters in the central and western regions; encourage local authorities in the central and western regions to set up processing trade parks, strengthen cooperation with

government agencies in the eastern regions, and give preferential policy to leading processing trade enterprises, and encourage processing trade enterprises in the eastern regions to move into parks in the central and western regions and form supporting industrial clusters.

- Finally, we will improve the value chain of processing trade sectors; work out the *Catalogue of Key Equipment Purchased by Processing Trade Enterprises*; exercise idle account of 17% VAT for law-abiding processing trade enterprises to purchase key equipment within the catalog, and encourage these enterprises to utilize advanced equipment in deep processing; provide policy support for enterprises' expansion upstream and downstream of industrial chains, and allow enterprises to enjoy bonded policy for all equipment and materials necessary for R&D, design, and testing activities, and enjoy idle account of deposit as offered to commodities' permitted processing trade; provide fiscal and tax support for domestic enterprises that have established self-owned brands and marketing channels; simplify outward processing approval formalities to improve the efficiency of deep processing carryovers by means of centralized approval of outward processing so that enterprises will file with the customs several outward processing contracts after submitting an outward processing application to the customs; exempt law-abiding enterprises from payment of risk deposit in dealing with cross-customs carryovers; make adjustments in policy and measures detrimental to improving appreciation rate of processing trade; for instance, 17% VAT imposed on processing trade enterprises and general trade enterprises for their import or domestic purchase of equipment will be deducted from their output taxes; and appropriately set the policy adjustment period to ensure idle account of their VAT book so as to avoid a huge amount of funds being occupied.

(5) *Taking a combination of measures to reduce cost of foreign trade enterprises*

- First, we will take classified measures to reduce import/export taxes and dues of foreign trade enterprises. Type I charges for public services will be canceled on the basis of sufficient financial funds appropriated by the central government. Type II charges basically for public service will be reduced significantly and included into the scope of basic public finance. Type III charges collected by market entities as operating service charges will be reduced precisely. Charges with higher market competitiveness, such as handling charges and stowage charges, will be determined in a market bidding manner. Monopolistic charges, such as berthing and unmooring fees, will be reasonably adjusted through public hearing.

- Second, we will improve the customs clearance facilitation level of foreign trade enterprises by means of the following: (i) innovating customs clearance modes to simplify formalities and improve efficiency of customs clearance to the utmost extent; (ii) implementing guaranteed customs clearance for enterprises with good social reputation, improved internal governance, and sustainable profitability; (iii) improving efficiency of customs clearance through trial implementation of green channels and proactive implementation of electronic, intelligent, creditable, self-help, and paperless declarations; (iv) promoting transverse "customs–inspection collaborative platform" and vertical "customs–customs collaborative platform" and "inspection–inspection collaborative platform" on the basis of integrated regional customs clearance in five regions, such as Beijing–Tianjin–Hebei, the Yangtze River Economic Belt, Guangdong, the Northeast, and the Silk Road Economic Belt, so as to minimize the cost of customs clearance of foreign trade enterprises; and (v) strengthening international cooperation in customs clearance, with priority given to cooperation with the US, EU, Japan, and countries along the "Belt and Road" in terms of law enforcement management, mutual recognition of supervision, technical connectivity, integrated standards, risk prevention, capacity building, and risk control.
- Third, we will make better use of comprehensive competitive advantages of foreign trade. By way of controlling labor cost, we will reduce unemployment insurance rate, with the employer's percentage reduced to 0.8% at the current stage, the average rate of work-related injury insurance down to 0.5%, and the premium rate of maternity insurance down to 0.3%, and after consolidating the accounts, will

reduce the employer's payment of pension insurance to 19% and basic medical insurance rate to 4%. By way of controlling land cost, we will accelerate optimization of the land supply modes, such as medium- and long-term lease, lease instead of transfer, lease followed by transfer, combined lease and transfer, progressive supply and flexible transfer years, so as to reduce the cost of initial land use by foreign trade enterprises. In deepening reform of the fiscal and tax system, we will focus on adjustment of the central and local governments' financial rights and disposal rights; if conditions permit, appropriately increase the disposal rights of basic public services, and reduce urban land use tax and deed tax to the lowest level. All parties concerned are encouraged to share land development cost of foreign trade enterprises, and on the secondary market, joint ventures are encouraged in joint development and use of land so as to minimize transaction cost of primary development of land. In control of logistics cost, we will reduce and exempt taxes and dues, consolidate logistics tax items, and improve VAT tax deduction policy so as to facilitate integrated and large-scale management of logistics, deregulate logistics, improve efficiency of international logistic customs clearance, promote connectivity between logistic enterprises and cities, and raise the socialization level of logistics. In control of transaction cost, we will reduce the cost of foreign trade enterprises' access to market, set up the list of government rights and responsibilities and the negative market list, reduce exit cost, break the institutional path dependence, optimize administrative license and approval, allow online supervision platforms to play active roles, and promote online approval.

(6) *Allowing financial services to play their supporting roles*

- First, we will release more financing products and tools; create policy conditions and encourage financial institutions (banks, trust, securities, and funds) to implement preferential interest rates, maximize discount rate of mortgages for foreign trade enterprises; offer prior subsidized loans, compensation payment for risk loans, and subsidy for guaranteed rates to foreign trade enterprises with steady market performance, profit expectation, and with good social reputation; and transfer fiduciary loans to key sectors and projects of foreign trade under national policy guidance.

- Second, we will open in an orderly manner the domestic capital market on a legal and marketable basis; encourage development of multi-level capital markets to enhance enterprises' direct financing capacity on the capital market; break policy barriers and encourage development of the regional equity market in coastal regions where foreign trade has developed well, and accordingly standardize and direct healthy development of private equity sectors so as to pave the way for enterprises to expand financing channels.
- Third, we will promote signing of bilateral currency swap agreement with countries along the "Belt and Road", and encourage foreign trade enterprises to integrate with the international financial market and carry out a free foreign currency swap business so as to promote in-depth integration of both internal and external markets.
- Fourth, we will press ahead with cross-border use of Renminbi among foreign trade enterprises and individuals as a result of China's policy advantages in FTZs; strengthen policy innovation, allow foreign trade enterprises inside the FTZs to issue RMB bonds outside China and transfer in a timely manner all funds raised back to China; encourage financial institutions (banks) inside FTZs to carry out RMB lending business with overseas institutions and individuals under prudent and steady principles; research and promote issuance of SDR-denominated bonds and build a SDR-denominated bonds' platform in regions with mature conditions.
- Finally, we will allow pilot FTZs to play their institutional advantages. Pilot FTZs are granted incomparable institutional and policy advantages. Under the premise of the government's moderate intervention that is unlikely to incur systematic risks, enterprises may be encouraged to utilize overseas low-cost funds (including Hong Kong) in eleven major FTZs, such as Shanghai, Guangdong, Tianjin, Fujian, Liaoning, Zhejiang, and Chonqing.

(7) *Playing important roles in global economic governance*

- First, we will take active part in global economic governance to create new advantages in cooperation. On the one hand, we will strengthen coordination and consultation of the macroeconomic policy; make good use of the bilateral and multilateral cooperative mechanism to strengthen coordination with main economies in macroeconomic policy and rules; and increase the transparency and predictability of the respective policy so as to offset spillover risks due to adjusting variation in main economies' monetary policy and reduce negative external influences. In addition, we will advocate mutual exchange and reference to address asymmetric problems concerning institutions, policy, and standards. On the other hand, we will promote reform of the international financial system and optimization of its governance structure; based on platforms including G20 Hangzhou Summit, place all development issues at outstanding positions in the framework of the macroeconomic policy, emphasize combination of short-term and long-term policies, strengthen coordination and structural reform of the macroeconomic policy, and take comprehensive measures in economic governance; allow monetary, fiscal, and structural policy to play their roles, and promote economic growth and trade investment facilitation by deepening reform so as to push the world economy toward a robust, sustainable, balanced, and all-inclusive road to growth.
- Second, we will endeavor to obtain the institutional discourse rights compatible with China's economic strengths. First, under the currently existing international governance framework, we will constantly enhance China's discourse right and decision-making power. In the international rules for deep sea, polar region, and networks, China will enhance its ability and level of participation in decision-making and formulating standards and agenda. Second, we will promote innovation and adjustment in the international economic system, and actively promote coordination of regional financial cooperation mechanism including BRICS New Development Bank, AIIB, and the Silk Road Fund with the current international finance system. Finally, we will actively fulfill responsibilities and obligations of China as a

big power to demonstrate China's "soft strengths" by addressing climate change and providing foreign assistance.

- Finally, we will accelerate consulting and signing of bilateral investment treaties to create a high-standard globally oriented FTZ network. We will actively promote and conclude negotiations as soon as possible on Sino-US and Sino-Europe bilateral investment treaties (BIT), and without challenging TPP, create an upgraded version of Sino-ASEAN FTZ, promote negotiations on the Regional Comprehensive Economic Partnership (RCEPA) agreement, start negotiations on Asia–Pacific FTZ and Sino-Europe FTZ, and accelerate negotiations on bilateral investment treaty and FTZs with key countries along the "Belt and Road" and part of TPP member countries.

Chapter 7

Research on Innovation and Policy of Resource and Environment System in the Context of Supply-Side Structural Reform

Li Zhong

Academy of Macroeconomic Research

Abstract

This chapter clarifies the relationship between resource environment and supply-side reform from the theoretical basis of new economic growth theory, market failure, tragedy of the commons, externality theory, property right theory, and sustainable development, and makes clear that resource environment is the important content of factor supply, product supply, and system supply. At the same time, it analyzes the existing problems of resource environment from the supply-side perspective, and points out that institutional deficiency is currently the fundamental cause of the supply constraint problem of resource environment in China. On this basis, the chapter puts forward paths to optimize the allocation of resources, improve the efficiency of allocation of resources, increase the effective supply of eco-environmental products and services, and give full play to the constraint and backward action of resource environment supply-side reform. In addition, it puts forward some institutional innovation measures for the supply-side reform of resource environment, such as strengthening the state ownership of resource environment, perfecting the state management right of resource environment, and establishing the system of resource environment transaction.

In order to effectively solve the structural contradictions faced by the current economic operation of China, the Central Government has clearly put forward that it is necessary to strengthen the supply-side structural reform while moderately expanding the total demand. Resource environment, as the important content of factor supply, product supply, and system supply, plays an important role in the supply-side structural reform. Currently, the mechanism of marketization in China is not perfect, and the efficiency of resource allocation is not high. Economic development by sacrificing the ecological environment has become a weak point of economic and social development and constraints. In order to promote the supply-side reform, it is necessary to vigorously promote the innovation of resource environment system and bring the market into full play in the allocation of resources, increase the eco-environmental products and make up for the eco-environmental shortcomings, strengthen the hard constraints on environment, implement stricter access to environment, and promote industrial transformation and upgrading.

I. Theoretical Basis for Resource Environment Supply-Side Reform

The theory of the supply-side reform of resource environment is based on the theory of new economic growth and theories of market failure, tragedy of the commons, externality theory, property rights theory, and sustainable development theory.

1. *New economic growth theory*

According to this theory, the total supply capacity of the economic supply side is grouped into four elements: labor, capital, land (natural resources), and technology, and the production function is derived thereof:

$$Y = f(L, K, R, \ldots) + \text{TFP},$$

where L standards for labor, K for capital, and R for resource; TFP is total factor productivity derived from technological progress, improvement of efficiency, and scale effect.

On this basis, we further believe that supply includes product supply (goods and services), factor supply, and system supply.

2. *Market failure*

The so-called "market failure" refers to the fact that the market mechanism has many limitations or shortcomings in realizing the allocation of resources to the extent that it cannot achieve the Pareto Optimum and the expected socio-economic objectives. Manifestations of market failure include the following: public goods, incomplete information, asymmetric information, external effects, and unfair distribution. "Market failure" is the reason for government intervention and is often used to describe situations where market forces are unable to meet public interests. Resource environment has the characteristics of public goods or quasi-public goods, which is also the reason why resources have long been allocated by the government.

3. *Tragedy of the commons*

In 1968, G. Hardin, a famous scholar, proposed the Tragedy of the Commons in his article published in the journal *Science* (Hardin, 1968). To solve the tragedy of the commons, Hardin thought that the individual's pursuit of individual interests would not naturally be transformed into the pursuit of group interests through Adam Smith's "invisible hand". After pointing out the limitations of law and conscience, he suggested that the solution to the dilemma of society should be "mutual restriction and mutual identification". In fact, Hardin believes that there is no scientific solution, but only political means, including the state's efforts, to prevent the tragedy of the commons.

4. *Externality theory*

Externality, also called externality effect, refers to the situation in which an individual, while engaged in economic activities, has had a positive or negative effect on other individuals, but has not obtained the due remuneration or assumed the due responsibility. A.C. Pigou first analyzed environmental pollution as an external problem in 1932. His theory of externality not only reasonably explains the economic root of environmental problems but also provides a clear economic analysis of the solution to environmental problems, i.e. we must correct the market failure through government intervention. The government can internalize the externality and solve the market failure of environmental problems by taxing behaviors that cause the negative externality of the environment (Pigou tax) and subsidizing behaviors that produce the positive externality of the environment.

5. *Theory of property rights*

Coase believes that, as long as the property right is clear and the transaction cost is zero, the market itself can solve the market failure caused by externality through property right negotiation without government intervention. The prerequisite for Coase's theorem is private property, that is, the property right is explicit (explicitly stipulating penalties for rights, restriction, and destruction of property), exclusive (exclusivity, that is, all benefits and costs arising from the ownership of the property are given directly to the owner), transferable (transfer from the owner to another under the conditions of voluntary exchange between the parties), and mandatory or enforceable (guaranteed to protect from infringement and involuntary seizure). Resource environment belongs to public goods; with shortage of natural resources and destruction of ecological environment, the asset attribute of natural resources is becoming increasingly obvious and the market value is constantly rising; so, only by clarifying the property rights and trading through the market can the tragedy of the commons be solved.

6. *Theory of sustainable development*

In 1987, the United Nations Commission on World and Environmental Development, chaired by Norwegian Prime Minister Gro Harlem Brundtland, issued a report on *Our Common Future*, formally proposing the concept of sustainable development. *Agenda 21*, adopted at the United Nations Conference on Environment and Development in 1992, regarded economy, society, and resource environment as an inseparable whole that constructed a comprehensive, long-term, and progressive framework for sustainable development. In September 2015, the United Nations

Development Summit adopted the *Sustainable Development Agenda 2030*, which identified 17 sustainable development goals and 169 targets. The Sustainable Development Theory refers to a development that can meet the needs of contemporary people and will not impair future generations' ability to meet their needs, which recognizes the value of the natural environment and emphasizes that economic development should be based on natural resources, be coordinated with the carrying capacity of the environment, be aimed at improving the quality of life, be adapted to the progress of society, and be compatible with the economic, social, and resource environment.

II. Relationship Between Resource Environment and Supply-Side Structural Reform

We will focus on the theoretical basis and key tasks of supply-side reform to analyze the positioning and role of the resource environment in it. In the supply-side reform, the resource environment performs special positions and functions, serving not only as an important content of the supply-side reform but also as an important means to promote the supply-side reform.

1. *Resource environment: An important element of factor supply*

Whether from the perspective of production function or from the three levels of supply, the resource environment is an important content of factor supply. Factors of production refer to the most basic resources needed for social reproduction. Generally speaking, labor, land, and capital are the most important factors of production. With the development of economy and society, energy and mineral resources are also included in the category of production factors. Ecological environment plays an important role in the scale and quality of economic growth through environmental carrying capacity and its influence on labor force. With the economic growth of China approaching the upper limit of the carrying capacity of the natural environment, the aggregation of various pollution problems has a greater impact on the health and supply of the labor force, resulting in impact on the scale and quality of economic output. Therefore, the ecological environment is also an important content of factor supply.

2. *Resource environment: An important content of product supply*

Resource products are the essential content of product supply. However, the relationship between ecological environment and supply-side reform is not fully understood at present. The ecological environment is generally regarded as the external factor and constraint condition of the economic development, so it is not incorporated into the theoretical system and framework of the supply-side reform. From the *Guiding Opinions on the Environmental Roles in Promoting the Supply-side Structural Reform* (Document No. 45/2016) promulgated by the Ministry of Environmental Protection on April 14, 2016, it can be seen that these Opinions regard ecological environment as an external condition promoting the supply-side reform but fail to recognize that the ecological environment itself is an important content of the supply-side. President Xi Jinping's scientific assertions such as "lucid waters and lush mountains are invaluable assets" and "protecting ecological environment is to protect productive forces, and improving ecological environment is to develop productive forces" have profoundly revealed the important position of ecological environment as the intrinsic attribute of productive forces. Therefore, we believe that from the three levels of supply, ecological environment is an important content of product supply (goods and services). With the economic development and social progress as well as the increasing public demand for good ecological environment, ecological environmental products including fresh air, clean water, and pleasant climate have become scarce resources. Eco-environmental products include ecological products, environmental protection products and services, as well as agricultural products, industrial products, and service products, which are necessary for human survival and development. The eco-environmental products have economic attributes, including the following: (1) positive externality, which shows that the spillover of eco-environmental products can make the social benefits outweigh the private benefits, and the difference between them is the positive externality of the eco-environmental products; (2) attributes of public goods and quasi-public goods; and (3) commodity attribute and scarcity as they are also of the use value and value.

3. *Resource environment: An important means to promote the supply-side reform*

In the five major tasks of supply-side reform, resource environment plays an important role and occupies an important position, so it is an important means to promote supply-side reform.

- First, it can force enterprises to reduce overcapacity. Under the market economy system, the ways to cut overcapacity cannot merely include administrative orders but should be flexible in the use of tax, price, land, environmental protection, and other economic means. Resource environment is one of the most effective economic means to get rid of capacity. By straightening out the price mechanism of water, electricity, gas, and other resources, we can force the industries of high water consumption and high energy consumption to quit. The reform of resource and environment tax and fee aims at ad valorem imposition of the resource tax and the environmental tax at the appropriate time and at increasing the cost of utilizing resources and environment so that enterprises with high consumption, high pollution, and high emission can be forced to reduce overcapacity. Strengthening environmental supervision and moderately adjusting environmental standards and thresholds will promote the elimination of backward capacity and resolve the problem of excess capacity.
- Second, it is helpful in improving weak points. At present, the resource environment is a weak point in China's economic and social development. Since the reform and opening up to the outside world in 1978, the exploitation of resources and the destruction of ecological environment have caused serious ecological environmental problems. Resource environment has become a leading challenge impeding economic development and product supply. By promoting the economical and intensive utilization of resources, we can promote rational

exploitation and utilization of resources and guarantee the demand of sustainable development of economy and society; by strengthening the ecological environment management, we can improve the quality of the environment and the supply of ecological products so as to effectively make up for the shortcomings in the field of resource environment in China.

- Finally, it helps to reduce costs. The low efficiency of resource utilization in China leads to high cost of raw materials; at the same time, with the improvement of national environmental protection standards and the strengthening of supervision, the cost of environmental protection investment is also increasing, thus leading to a decline of enterprise competitiveness. Through innovation of energy-saving and environmental protection technology, we can reduce the input of resources and pollutants produced in unit production, and thus reduce the cost of raw materials and pollution treatment.

III. Analysis of Problems and Causes in China's Resource Environment From the Perspective of Supply-Side Reform

From the supply-side point of view, the effective supply of resource environment in China is insufficient, and the restraint to the economic and social development is strengthened, which is collectively referred to as problems concerning restrictions on supply. However, the performance of resource and ecological environment supply constraint is not identical, and resources are disposed unreasonably and utilized extensively, and the efficiency of resource utilization is low, which can also be attributed to structure imbalance; meanwhile, the ecological environment is manifested in the lack of total supply. The formation mechanism and the reason lie in the defective system arrangement.

1. *Inefficient allocation of resource elements*

At present, the phenomena of distorted, mismatched, or inefficient allocation of resource elements seem serious in China.

(1) *Mismatch of land resources and imbalance of supply and demand of construction land*

The supply side of land resources is more complex in three aspects. (1) The supply of construction land is insufficient to meet the rapid progress of urbanization and industrialization. Indicators of construction land use in China shall be managed as planned as they do not agree with the demand of construction land for economic and social development, which leads to the scarcity of land resources and the insufficiency of effective supply of land resources, further to the prominent contradiction of land supply and demand; especially in some big cities, with large populations gathering, land supply is in serious shortage. (2) The efficiency of land supply is low but the cost of land is high. In China, the division of urban and rural land market, together with strict examination and approval of construction land, has caused low efficiency of land supply; other reasons include a long period of examination and approval before land expropriation that often leads to a large increase in land cost. (3) The structure of land supply is out of balance. The urbanization rate of population in China reached up to 56.1% (2015), but the demand for rural construction land was bigger than that for urban construction land. From the perspective of land use structure, the proportion of industrial land is high, about 28%, far higher than that of developed countries, and eco-environmental land is decreasing, including wetland, green space, ecological corridors, and so on.

(2) *Inefficient allocation of water resources and serious waste of resources*

The serious shortage of water resources in China has become a bottleneck in economic and social development. On the one hand, the problem of supply-side water resources in our country arises from the fact that the distribution of productive forces is not suitable to the endowment of water resources; on the other hand, it is reflected in the extensive utilization and waste of resources and the low efficiency of water resources utilization. According to World Bank statistics, in 2013, the unit water resource productivity (GDP divided by freshwater consumption) in China was only 62% of the global average in 2013, compared with 0.09% in Singapore,

2.3% in Denmark, 4.5% in the United Kingdom, and 9 % in Germany. The water consumption per 10,000 industrial value added was 67 cubic meters, 6.5 times that of the UK and Japan, and 1.5 times that of the United States. The effective utilization coefficient of irrigation water is 0.52 while the international advanced level is 0.8. The leakage rate of urban pipe network is above 15%, as against the international advanced level below 6%. The amount of unconventional water use is about 5 billion cubic meters, accounting for only 0.8% of the total water supply in China.

(3) *Dislocation of supply and demand of mineral resources and extensive utilization of resources*

Without regard for the imbalance between the supply and demand of mineral resources under the downward trend of the economy, the supply-side problems of mineral resources in China are mainly as follows: First, the marginal environmental cost of mining enterprises is partly or wholly absent, which makes the marginal cost of mining enterprises less than the social marginal cost, leading to the deviation of the actual exploitation amount and market price of mineral resources from its optimal exploitation amount and optimal price. Second, some important resources are monopolized by state-owned enterprises, and the market-oriented pricing mechanism is not perfect. Oil and gas resources, for example, have been monopolized by large state-owned enterprises such as PetroChina, Sinopec, and CNOOC for a long time; private enterprises have been discriminated against, market access has been blocked, and oil and gas prices are still priced by the government rather than by market competition. Finally, scientific and technological innovation is insufficient and the utilization efficiency of mineral resources is low. The total recovery rate of mineral resources and the total utilization rate of co-associated mineral resources in China are about 35% and 40%, respectively, which is about 20 percentage points lower than that in developed countries.

2. *Insufficient supply of eco-environmental products*

(1) *Inadequate supply of ecological products*

With the rapid development of industrialization and urbanization, farmland, green space, and water systems are reduced; pollutant and garbage emissions are increased, and air, water, and soil pollution is aggravated. Because of ecological destruction and environmental pollution, ecological products are in serious shortage; clean water, clean air, and non-polluted land become scarce products, especially in the urban agglomeration area.

(2) *Inadequate supply of environmental products*

The development of China's environmental protection industry is lagging behind, and the supply of environmental protection enterprises, technology and equipment, products, and services is insufficient. Take the hazardous waste treatment as an example: Due to serious shortage of qualified waste disposal enterprises in China, it is difficult to meet the increasing production volume of hazardous wastes, coupled with the lax supervision and the interest movement, leading to a large number of hazardous wastes being handed over to non-qualified enterprises at a low price, and these enterprises have not done any treatment at all before directly dumping the wastes in landfills or abandoned mines, causing serious harm to the ecological environment.

(3) *Inadequate supply of environmental public services*

Government investment is insufficient; environmental governance capacity is limited; the overall level of environmental quality improvement is not obvious; and environmental public services cannot meet people's increasing demand for environmental protection. In particular, the rural environmental protection public service facilities are seriously inadequate; as a result, most of the rural sewage is not treated before being discharged.

3. *Poor function of eco-environment restrictions*

It is common to attach importance to development but not to protection. In some areas, there is a lack of environmental bottom-line thinking and respect for nature. Mountains, rivers, wetlands, forests, and pastures are wantonly occupied. Pollutants are discharged without restriction, leading to environmental degradation or even loss of function. China has relatively systematic laws and regulations on environmental protection. In recent years, several laws and rules have been enacted to protect environment, but they are less binding on some local governmental authorities who, in order to attract investment, chose to reduce environmental protection standards and thresholds, with local resource environment endowments not being taken into account and the intensity of development exceeding the upper limit of the carrying capacity of environmental resources.

4. *Analysis of the forming mechanism and reasons of the resource environment supply restrictions*

There are many reasons that lead to restrictions on the supply of resource environment, including objective factors as China being in the stage of rapid development of industrialization and urbanization, subjective factors that emphasize development over environmental protection, and at a deeper level, the unclear system of resource property right and imperfect government administrative system and market mechanism.

(1) *Unclear system of resource property rights*

The management of natural resources and their property rights in China is mainly in accordance with the *Constitution*, the *Property Law*, and separate laws on individual natural resources. The *Constitution* establishes two systems of property rights for natural resources, namely, the state and collective ownership of natural resources. From the "Property Law", the right of use, the right of proceeds, and the right of disposition on the basis of ownership are also derived. Land resources in China are divided into state ownership and rural collective ownership. Urban land is owned by the state and rural land is owned by the rural collective. The mineral resources property right is of a mixed decentralized structure, that is, all the state-owned mining enterprises involving national security and natural monopoly belong to the central government and relevant ministries, and most of the other mining enterprises belong to the local government, especially the provincial government. Water resources, except all for reservoirs and resources pertaining to the collective, all other water resources belong to the state, that is, to the whole people.

This shows that the system of resource property rights in our country was characterized by state-owned and collective decentralization, central and local decentralization, and the separation of the rights of ownership and the right of use at the same time. The current system of property rights has not clearly defined direct exercise of ownership by the state government, local government, rural collective, or individuals, nor has it clarified the proxy of the state-owned, collective, central, and local ownership, which leads to inefficient and extensive use of resources, undefined rights and responsibilities, and unreasonable income distribution.

With regard to the environmental property rights, although the state government has carried out pilot trade of pollutant emission right and carbon emission right, at present the *Constitution*, *Environmental Protection Basic law* or *Real Right Law*, and other laws and regulations have not yet clearly stipulated the environmental capacity and the legal right of pollutant discharge. The environmental property right system has not yet been established, giving rise to abuse of environmental capacity and to the "Strategy of the Commons". In recent years, environmental pollution accidents have occurred frequently, the reason for which is the lack of environmental property rights.

(2) *Imperfect government administrative system*

The state ownership shall be delegated to the State Council so that governments at all levels and the relevant resource management departments will exercise the duties of asset management and administrative supervision. There are many problems in the management of resource environment. Horizontally, the National Development and Reform Commission, the Ministry of Environmental Protection, the Ministry of Land and Resources, the Ministry of Water Resources, the Ministry of Agriculture, and the Forestry Bureau have many problems, such as scattered responsibilities, unclear intersection, difficulty in coordination, taking care of one thing and losing the other, and mutually making excuses. Vertically, the local government and the corresponding national sectors exercise multilevel management and allocation of natural resources, respectively, from the local interests and departmental interests. The partitioned management system makes it difficult to improve the efficiency of resource allocation, leading to resource mismatch and resource supply constraints.

At the same time, the management of resource environment is still subject to undefined owners and regulators. In addition to resources owned by the collective as required by law, China's natural resources are owned by the state, that is, the whole people. In practice, the relevant departments of the state and the local governments at all levels have exercised the power of some natural resource asset owners, without distinguishing between owners and managers. In many areas, the government directly allocates or intervenes in the allocation of natural resources, which not only leads to the low efficiency of resource allocation but also affects the performance of its supervisory functions.

(3) *Inadequate market mechanisms*

In the field of resources, China implements the system of paid use of resources, but the market mechanism is not perfect, which leads to malfunction and dislocation of the adjustment function of the natural resources' price lever. The price of resources fails to fully reflect the market supply and demand, the scarcity of resources, the cost of ecological environment damage, and the restoration benefit. First, the formation mechanism of land price is chaotic. In order to attract investment, the actual selling price of industrial land is often lower than the benchmark land price, or even zero land price. In order to make up for the deficit of industrial land, residential land has repeatedly been occupied at a higher price. Second, the price of water resources is on the low side. Due to more stringent price control and monopoly of water supply in regional markets, incomplete information, and other market failures, there are low standards for collecting water fees and sewage treatment fees, so it is difficult to reflect the scarcity of natural resources and its full value. Finally, the price of mineral resources fails to reflect the ecological value and environmental value. Aimed at the problem of ecological environment damage caused by mining mineral resources, the state has issued the *Regulations on Collection and Management of Mineral Resources Compensation Fees*, and clarified that the mineral resources compensation fee is mainly used for mineral resources exploration. However, the mining environment recovery margin system is implemented in some regions. However, both the mineral resources compensation fee and the mine environment recovery margin are too low to fully reflect the cost of pollution treatment and ecological damage caused by mineral resources exploitation, and the problems of predatory mining and extensive utilization of mineral resources are prominent.

In the field of ecological environment and ecological compensation mechanism, there are no perfect emission trading mechanisms and other market-oriented mechanisms. In the current ecological compensation mode, the compensation fund mainly comes from the central financial transfer payment; the cross-basin and cross-regional horizontal ecological compensation is progressing slowly; and the ecological product market trading mechanism has not yet been established. The threshold of ecological environment is low; the external cost of environment is not fully incorporated into the cost of enterprise, and the market mechanism is not perfect. The national unified trading market of environmental property rights has not yet been established, and the trading of pollutant emission rights and carbon emission rights is still at the pilot stage.

IV. Strategic Thoughts of Resource Environment Supply-Side Reform

1. *Guidelines*

We should comprehensively implement the spirits of the 18th Party Congress and the 3rd, 4th, and 5th Plenary Sessions of the 18th Central Committee of the CPC, embody the spirit of the series of important speeches by General Secretary Xi Jinping, firmly establish the concept of innovation, coordination, green, open, and shared development, reform the mode of allocation of resources, improve the efficiency of allocation of resources, promote the efficient and intensive use of resources, and provide sustainable supply of resources for economic and social development; strengthen ecological construction and environmental protection, raise environmental protection standards and thresholds, enforce environmental protection law, upgrade the economic structure, improve the quality and efficiency of economic development, provide more high-quality ecological products for the masses of the people, and promote the formation of a new pattern of modern construction by which people and nature develop harmoniously.

2. *Reform objectives*

By 2020, significant progress will have been made in the construction of resource-saving and environment-friendly societies, the way of resource allocation will have been optimized; the efficiency of resource utilization will have been enhanced, and the capacity of resource supply and security will have been improved. The ecological construction and environmental management will have been further strengthened; the supply of ecological products will have been enhanced; water, atmosphere, soil, and other environmental qualities will have been significantly improved, and the resource environment will have been coordinated with economic and social development.

- The efficiency of resource utilization will have been further improved: the intensity of land development has been effectively controlled; the rate of output of resources has been greatly increased; the intensity of energy consumption has been continuously decreased; the total amount of water used has been controlled within 670 billion cubic meters; the amount of water used for industrial value added has been reduced to below 65 cubic meters; the coefficient of effective utilization of irrigation water has been raised up to 0.55.
- Supply of ecological products will have been significantly increased: the forest coverage rate will reach above 23%; the grassland comprehensive vegetation coverage rate will be 56%; the wetland area is not less than 53.36 million hectares; over 50% of desertified land can be harnessed; the natural shoreline retention rate is not less than 35%; the rate of biodiversity loss is basically controlled; the national ecosystem stability is obviously enhanced.
- The environmental quality will have been generally improved: the total amount of major pollutants discharged will continue to decrease; the quality of the atmosphere environment is improved; the quality of the water environment in key watersheds and inshore areas will be

improved; the rate of water quality in the water functional areas of important rivers and lakes will be raised to more than 80%; the level of drinking water security will be continuously improved; the overall quality of the soil environment will remain stable; the environmental risks will be effectively controlled.

- Significant breakthroughs will be made in institutional construction: decisive achievements will be made in key system construction projects, such as the property right system of natural resources assets, the management system of natural resource environment, and the market mechanism of natural resource environment.

3. *Ways to achieve these objectives*

(1) *Optimize resource allocation and improve resource allocation efficiency*

Theoretically, resource elements are aimed to solve the problem of abuse and ineffective use of resources. With regard to supply of land, water, and mineral resources, the overall idea is to improve the market-oriented allocation mechanism and improve the efficiency of resource allocation.

(i) Optimize allocation of land resources

Land is the basic resource of economic development. First, to optimize allocation of land resources, we will give full play to the decisive role of market allocation of resources and improve the effective supply of land. The root cause for inefficient supply of urban construction land lies in the dual structure of urban and rural land and the management system of planning and distribution index. Reform is aimed to establish a spatial planning system, strengthen the spatial order of land use and planning control, let market play its roles, break through the barriers between rural construction land and urban construction land, allow rural collective-operated construction land to be sold, leased, and invested, implement the same market access as state-owned land, and establish a unified and efficient urban and rural construction land market; promote rational flow of land resources so that the supply of land resources will meet the needs of economic and social development and flow of population.

Second, we will adjust and optimize the structure of land allocation: focus on enlarging effective investment, speeding up examination, approval, and supply of construction land, ensuring land demand for transportation, energy, water conservancy, and information network construction, guaranteeing innovation-driven development strategy and public entrepreneurship, multi-innovative land, support of new industries, new forms of development of land, and ensuring the demand for land for people's livelihood such as education, medical care, and health care, and the demand for ecological and environment-friendly land. On the contrary, we should stop providing land for new projects of excess capacity industries such as coal and steel, abolish the preferential land policy of excess capacity industries, promote the elimination and withdrawal of backward capacity and the annexation and reorganization of enterprises, accelerate the disposal of "zombie enterprises", support the revitalization of enterprises' land resources and assets, and facilitate the transformation and upgrading of industries.

Finally, reform the land examination and approval system, improve the efficiency of land supply, and curb the rising cost of land. Land approval and expropriation will be separated; the State Council and the provincial land authorities are responsible for land approval: simplify the project land approval procedures and content, and verify whether the construction land conforms to the planning plan, land policy, land use standards, and supplementary cultivated land plan. The authority for land approval will be delegated to authorities at lower levels. For the land intended for independent site selection, construction projects approved and examined by the State Council and the investment department under the State Council will be licensed by the land administration department under the State Council, and the land for other construction projects will be authorized by the provincial land administration department. Land expropriation will be subject to examination and approval by the municipal or county people's government. The specific compensation standard and resettlement plan for land expropriation will be determined by the municipal and county governments in accordance with the provisions of the provincial governments after carefully listening to the views of peasants whose land has been expropriated. At the same time, it is necessary to reasonably determine the compensation standard for land requisition and demolition so as to prevent the cost of land requisition from rising too fast.

(ii) Improve the efficiency of water resources allocation

With regard to serious shortage of water resources in China, it is necessary to reform and improve the efficiency of water resource utilization on the supply side, make overall plans, and realize coordination of water resource allocation and economic and social distribution: improve the matching degree of grain production and water resources, reduce the pressure of grain production in water-shortage areas in the north and control or compress the irrigated area in the groundwater overdraft areas in North China and Northwest China; determine the key points and layout of national industrial development according to the conditions of water resources. Water shortage and ecologically vulnerable areas are prohibited from developing high-consumption aquaculture; strictly control the excessive development of cities in water-shortage areas.

It is necessary to improve the formation mechanism of water price. The price of water resources should fully reflect the cost of water supply as well as the cost of environmental protection and the benefit of restoration. Cost is the basis of price setting. The pricing cost of urban water supply includes the cost of water production, transportation, and distribution. The price management department together with the third-party independent organizations should urge enterprises to carry on cost accounting, perfect industry database, calculate average cost of the whole industry, grasp the law of the industry average performance change, and establish the scientific and reasonable cost accounting system; promote reform of agricultural comprehensive water pricing, establish and improve the mechanism for the formation of agricultural water pricing; implement the system of overplanning and over-quota incremental pricing for non-resident water use, and carry out the system of water ladder pricing for urban residents.

Finally, it is necessary to give full play to the role of market mechanism and actively explore ways to optimize allocation of resources through the water rights market; actively explore cross-industry, cross-basin, cross-regional water rights transfer model especially in the northern severe water-shortage areas. The government should establish a relevant system of regional water resources' initial right confirmation, promote pilot national water rights transaction, guide establishment of water rights transaction and water market step by step, clarify initial water rights, regulate behaviors of water rights transfer, reasonably determine the transfer period of water rights, and scientifically determine the transfer price of water rights. Through transfer of water rights, allocation of water resources between urban and rural areas, between regions, and upstream and downstream of the watershed can provide water resources for economic and social development.

(iii) Perfect allocation of mineral resources

In the supply-side reform of mineral resources, first we will perfect the mechanism of ecological compensation for mineral resources development, raise the standard of paid use of mineral resources, and fully reflect the damage of ecological environment and the cost of restoration so as to regulate and control the marginal cost of mineral resources development, reduce the extensive exploitation and overexploitation of mineral resources, and promote the rational exploitation and utilization of mineral resources. Second, increase the reform of oil and gas resources, gradually eliminate monopolies, increase the pace and intensity of private capital entering the field of oil and gas exploitation, expand import and export quota of local oil refining enterprises, and on the basis of improving the formation mechanism of oil product price, release the price of oil and gas market at the right time and give play to the decisive role of market allocation of resources. Finally, encourage scientific and technological innovation to improve the efficiency of mineral resource development and utilization. Encourage mining enterprises to improve technological processes and equipment, enhance the level of comprehensive utilization of resources and the efficiency of output of resources, and extend the life of mines; establish a scientific and technological support platform to improve the comprehensive utilization of mineral resources, give full play to the role of the State Key Laboratory and other research centers, strengthen the introduction, digestion, and absorption of advanced and applicable technologies for the co-occurrence of iron, copper, gold, bauxite, and other important minerals, such as lean ore and refractory metallurgy, and improve the recovery rate of mineral resources, the recovery rate of mineral processing, and the comprehensive utilization through scientific and technological innovation.

(2) *Increase the effective supply of eco-environmental goods and services*

Ecological environmental products are of a public, external, and commodity nature. The theory of externality and property right put forward the way to solve the problem of eco-environment. On the one hand, the government should take the main responsibility of providing eco-environment public goods, and subsidize the behavior of positive and external influence of the environment, that is, eco-compensation, intervention, and correction of market failure and prevention of tragedy of commons. On the other hand, it should clarify the environmental property right, establish the market transaction mechanism, give full play to the decisive role of market allocation of resources, and solve the externality problem of ecological environment through the property right transaction.

(i) Establish a diversified eco-environmental product supply system with government as the main body

To increase the supply of ecological products, it is necessary to fully mobilize the enthusiasm of the whole society and form a multi-subject supply system.

First, give full play to the leading role of the government. The government assumes the main responsibility of providing eco-environmental products and is the most important subject, which is determined by the attributes of public goods and quasi-public goods of eco-environmental products. The government should increase investment in the construction of "mountain, water, forest, field and lake" ecosystem, continually promote comprehensive control of desertification and rocky desertification, continually advance major ecological restoration project, enlarge the area of lakes and wetlands, and protect the biodiversity. At the same time, the construction of environmental infrastructure such as garbage and sewage treatment should be increased, and the treatment of water, atmosphere, and soil should be strengthened. In addition, we should establish and perfect the system and policy system to promote the supply of eco-environmental products, and constantly expand the supply capacity of eco-environmental products.

Second, give full play to the enthusiasm of enterprises. Enterprises are also the main suppliers of environmental products, which will be determined by the commodity attributes of ecological environmental products. On the one hand, vigorously carrying out the third-party environmental pollution control and promoting the government–social capital cooperation (PPP) model will not only effectively solve the problem of insufficient supply of eco-environmental public goods but also help improve the quality and efficiency of eco-environmental products, and help reduce the administrative cost. On the other hand, vigorously cultivate and develop environmental protection enterprises, through scientific and technological innovation, to provide a variety of eco-environmental products. In addition, vigorously publicize and encourage enterprises to support the eco-environmental cause of public welfare behavior.

Finally, play the role of NGOs and the public. We will encourage and develop environmental protection organizations, multilateral aid organizations, poverty alleviation organizations, and other social organizations to play their role in promoting and supervising ecological environmental protection. We will encourage them to invest in and increase the supply of ecological environmental products through taxation and investment policies. We should cultivate and educate the public to participate in and jointly safeguard the ecological environment, cherish and care for ecological products, and consciously supervise the behavior of the government and enterprises.

(ii) Establishing and perfect the mechanism of ecological compensation, encouraging the supply of ecological products and carrying out ecological protection compensation will help arouse the enthusiasm of all parties and increase the supply of ecological environmental products

In recent years, the practice of ecological compensation has been carried out in various departments and regions in China, but there is limited scope of compensation, a low standard of compensation, and imperfect system mechanism of benign interaction between protectors and beneficiaries. In April 2016, the General Office of the State Council issued the *Opinion on Improving the Compensation Mechanism for Ecological Protection*, explicitly proposing that by 2020, all important areas such as forests, grasslands, wetlands, deserts, oceans, currents, and arable land as well as prohibited development areas and key ecological function areas, will be covered by ecological protection compensation. In order to truly implement and establish a sound ecological compensation mechanism, we need to start with and strengthen the following aspects:

First, the scientific approval of ecological compensation standards is needed. According to the difference between ecological function factor and expenditure cost, the scientific compensation standard of ecological products should be formulated.

Second, it is necessary to establish a mechanism for stable investment and reasonable growth. The State Revenue will gradually increase the transfer payment to key ecological function areas and establish the input mechanism of stable growth by raising the balance transfer payment coefficient. The people's governments at the provincial level will also establish and improve the transfer payment system and the mechanism for stable growth of ecological compensation in each province; through ecological compensation, effectively make up for the loss of key ecological function area development opportunity cost and ecological environment protection investment cost, and improve the enthusiasm of ecological environment protection in these areas.

Third, it is necessary to innovate the ways and methods of ecological compensation. The construction of ecological compensation and national key ecological function area will be combined with the establishment of a national park system and other institutional innovation through coordination of all kinds of compensation funds so as to explore comprehensive compensation methods. The establishment of a fund for the co-construction and sharing of ecological products shall consist of social donations and funds invested by governments at all levels; demarcate and strictly abide by the red line of ecological protection, study and formulate relevant policies of ecological protection compensation. We will improve compensation policies for ecological protection in various areas prohibited from development, such as national nature reserves, world cultural and natural heritage sites, national scenic spots, national forest parks, and national geo-parks.

Finally, it is necessary to promote compensation for transverse ecological protection. The horizontal ecological protection compensation mechanism, which is mainly based on local compensation and supported by the central government, is adopted to encourage beneficiary areas and protected ecological areas, and establish horizontal compensation relationships in the upper and lower reaches of the basin through fund compensation, counterpart cooperation, industrial transfer, personnel training, and co-construction of parks. In the Yangtze River, the Yellow River, and other important rivers, we will explore the development of transverse ecological protection compensation pilot. In the Beijing–Tianjin–Hebei Water Conservation Zone, pilot projects for cross-regional ecological protection compensation will be launched in the Jiuzhou River in Guangxi and Guangdong, Tingjiang–Hanjiang Rivers in Fujian and Guangdon, Dongjiang River in Jiangxi and Guangdon, and Xijiang River in Yunnan, Guizhou, Guangxi, and Guangdong.

(iii) Establish and perfect the market trading mechanism of ecological environmental products

Eco-environmental products are of a merchandizing nature, which can improve supply efficiency and balance supply and demand through market trading mechanism. Coase's theory of property rights provides a theoretical basis for the establishment of ecological environment property rights trading mechanism. China's "13th Five-Year Plan" explicitly proposes establishing and improving the paid use and trading system of emission rights, and promoting the establishment of a unified carbon emissions trading market. To promote eco-environmental market transactions, the following aspects need to be taken into account:

- First, clarify the form and attribute of emission right. We should make full use of the successful experience of developed countries in management of pollutant discharge permits, improve the system of pollutant discharge permits, speed up the process of legislation, establish a unified and fair pollutant discharge permit system covering major pollutants throughout the country, and ensure that those who discharge pollutants must discharge pollutants according to their permits.
- Second, establish a fair and reasonable index distribution system. Fair distribution of the primary market is an important basis and prerequisite for the effluent trading to operate effectively. The State Ministry of Environmental Protection, as the main body of government

distribution, and the local environmental protection bureaus should clearly determine the powers, responsibilities, and division of labor for initial allocation of total targets and quotas, and reasonably determine the conditions, procedures, time limit requirements, initial price formation mechanism, and different regions and industries to adjust the equivalent coefficient or correction coefficient, the use and management of funds, and so on.

- Finally, establish the market system of pollutant discharge trade, and improve the efficiency of the allocation of environmental capacity resources of pollutant discharge trade. After enterprises discharging pollutants have obtained the first allocation of pollutant discharge permit, the redistribution of pollutant discharge right property right among polluters will be realized through the market of pollutant discharge right so as to give full play to the role of the market in the allocation of environmental capacity resources.

(3) *Bring into play the restraint and reversed transmission roles of the resource environment*

The resource environment is not only the important content of the supply-side reform but also has an important influence on the supply-side reform in other fields of our country. It helps realize the tasks such as reducing overcapacity and improving weak points during the supply-side reform, and also helps improve the quality and benefit of the economic development in turn

(i) Tighten environmental access and strengthen hard environmental restrictions

Environmental constraints can promote the supply-side reform by reducing overcapacity and improving weak points.

- First, strengthen hard constraints on environment, and promote the removal of backward and excess capacity. Implement a strict environmental protection system, strengthen the constraint on development of the low-end supply side, step up environmental supervision, give prominence to comprehensive treatment of environmental protection

in key industries such as steel and coal, expedite the clean-up and rectification of illegal construction projects, expedite the banning of seriously polluting enterprises, and promote the elimination of backward and excess production capacity.
- Second, promote adjustment and optimization of industrial structure by raising the threshold of environmental access; take into consideration the environmental quality, development status, governance technology, economic cost, management ability, and other factors, formulate pollutant discharge standards scientifically and reasonably, and give full play to the role of environmental standards in leading enterprises to upgrade and restructure their industries; strengthen the linkage between planned EIA and construction project EIA, strictly prohibit addition of low-end backward production capacity, encourage the development of high-quality production capacity, and promote enterprises to accelerate upgrading and transformation.
- Finally, bring in a green supply chain management system to ensure green supply in the whole life cycle, guide green transformation of our industry, and constantly meet the increasing demand for green consumption in the whole society.

(ii) Implement red line control

Implement resource environment ecological red line management and control, limit all kinds of economic and social activities within the scope of red line management, which is conducive to safeguarding the national energy resources and ecological environment security, and inversely promote the quality and efficiency of economic development.

- First, reasonably set indicators for the red line management and control; set the upper limit of resource consumption, control the total consumption of strategic resources such as energy, water, and land, and strengthen synergy between control of total resource consumption and consumption management; strictly abide by the bottom line of environmental quality, set targets for atmospheric, water, and soil environmental quality, strengthen control of the total amount of pollutants discharged in regions and industries, and strictly prevent sudden environmental events; define the red line of ecological protection according to requirements of water conservation, sand fixation, flood storage, biodiversity protection, natural background protection, and ecosystem integrity and stability, to cater to the needs of economic and social development, and to the red line of ecological protection.

- Second, improve red line management and control system. We should speed up establishment of a policy mechanism that reflects the requirements for management and control of ecological red line of resource environment, and form a system of management and control of the red line that is strictly guarded at the source and strictly regulated in the process; set up red line management and control targets, adapt red line management and control to the access system, strengthen implementation of environmental resources and ecological red line supervision, strengthen statistical monitoring of capacity building, establish the carrying capacity monitoring and early warning mechanism of resource environment and the red line management and control responsibility system.

V. Institutional Innovation and Policy Guarantee for Resource Environment Supply-Side Reform

The 3rd Plenary Session of the 18th Central Committee of the CPC put forward establishment of a systematic and complete system of ecological civilization for source prevention, process control, damage compensation, and liability investigation to guarantee and provide impetus for the supply-side reform of resource environment. Because resource environment has dual attributes of public goods and commodities, it is necessary to make a scientific and complete policy system according to its characteristics, which not only guarantees the macro-management and regulation of resource environment but also improves the efficiency of resource allocation and guarantees the supply of eco-environmental products.

1. *Strengthen state ownership of resource environment*

Implement ownership of all natural resource assets by the whole people: Separately set up the State Commission for Administration of Natural Resources Assets to perform agent functions, and authorize it to exercise, on behalf of the whole people, the right to own, the right to use, the right to get earnings, and the right to dispose of such assets, to supervise the quantity, scope, and usage of such assets, and to enjoy rights and interests of the owner.

2. *Perfect the state's power to manage resource environment*

Improve the supervision system of natural resources: Correctly deal with the relationship between state natural resources ownership agents and administrative managers, make the state natural resources managers and state-owned natural resource assets owners independent of each other, and coordinate and supervise each other according to the principle that owners and managers are separate from each other.

Implement use control system and elaborate rules for classification and management of natural resource use control to ensure that resources and ecosystems are not subjected to arbitrary occupation and change. Set up the use control system covering all land space, and implement usage management of natural grassland, woodland, rivers, lakes, wetlands, and other ecological spaces to ensure that ecological area is not reduced.

Establish space control system: The boundary of resources and the boundary of ecological protection are defined by spatial planning. We will reform the planning system to form a national clear-positioned, complementary, and unified spatial planning system, clarify the functional orientation among main functional areas, urban and rural planning, land planning, and ecological environment protection. We will actively explore pilot projects in cities and counties, delimit the development and control boundaries of production space, living space, and ecological space on a blueprint, and define the boundaries of residential areas, industrial areas, urban built-up areas, rural residential areas, basic farmland, and ecological spaces such as woodland, water surface, and wetland.

Implement classified management of resource environment: Differentiate types of pure public goods (or public goods) and pure private goods (or commodities) of resource environment, and implement different management models and examination methods; strengthen management of purely public welfare products, and let purely commercial products play more market roles.

3. *Establish the resource environment transaction system*

First, clarify the property rights, including the right to own, use, get earnings, and dispose of natural resource assets, and implement the paid use system. On the premise of no change in ownership, the rights to use and allocate resources should be vitalized.

Then, improve the paid use system of resources, speed up the price reform of natural resources and their products, promote reform of water price and restrain price of land from rising too fast so that the price of resources can fully reflect the market supply and demand, the scarcity of resources, the cost of ecological environment damage, and restoration benefits. We will promote reform of resource environmental taxes and fees, levy taxes on mineral resources at ad valorem prices, and transform environmental fees into taxes.

It is necessary to establish and improve the market-based trading mechanism, actively explore various market-based transactions of energy-saving volume, emission rights, carbon emissions rights, water rights trading, etc. Meanwhile, we should promote third party governance of environmental pollution, encourage the government and social capital cooperation (PPP) model, and effectively increase the supply of resources and eco-environmental products.

Bibliography

Artak Harutyunyan, A. Massara, G. Ugazio, G. Amidzic, R. Walton, Shedding Light on Shadow Banking, *IMF Working Paper*, 2015.

Bai Chong'en, Government Intervention, Optimal Taxation and Structural Adjustment, *Taxation Research*, Vol. 6, 2015.

Bai Chong'en, Government Intervention, Optimal Tax and Structural Adjustment, *Taxation Research*, Vol. 6, 2015.

Ben S. Bernanke, *The Courage to Act: A Memoir of a Crisis and its Aftermath* (translated by Jiang Zongqiang), CITIC Press Group, 2016.

Blue Hong, Supply-side Reform Policies should Focus on the Rigidity of the Supply of Resource Environment, www.youth.cn, March 9, 2016.

Chang Zhen, Comparative Analysis of Supply-side Structural Reform and Western Supply-side Economics, *Chinese and Foreign Entrepreneurs*, Vol. 21, 2016.

Chen Ning, Theoretical Logic and Practice Approach of Supply-side Structural Reform, *Productivity Research*, Vol. 6, 2016.

Chi Fulin, *Reform Test: Economic Restructure and Structural Reform*, Qunyan Press, 2016.

China Finance 40 Forum, Shanghai New Financial Research Institute, *China Financial Reform Report 2015 — Interest Rate Marketization in China's Economic Development and Reform*, China Finance Press, 2015.

Christophe Freeman *et al. Innovative Economics* (translated by Hua Hongxun), Peking University Press, 2004.

Clarkson, Miller, *Industrial Organization and Public Policy*, Columbia University Press, New York, 1982, p. 119.

Dai Hui, Supply-side Reform and Supply-side Economics, *China Economic Report*, Vol. 3, 2016.

Dai Xiang, Zhang Erzhen, Supply-side Structural Reform and Transformation and Development of China's Foreign Trade, *Guizhou Social Sciences*, No. 7, 2016.

Dang Yang, Construction of Invisible Welfare Constraint Mechanism in Large State-owned Enterprises, *People's Tribune*, No. 11, 2013.

Dani Rodrik, *One Economics, Many Recipes: Globalization, Institutions and Economic Growth* (translated by Zhang Junkuo *et al.*), CITIC Press Group, 2016.

Ding Qijun, A Study on High-profit Sources of Administrative Monopoly Industries — High Efficiency or Monopolistic Pricing? *Industrial Economics Research*, No. 5, 2010.

Ding Zhijie *et al.*, How to Speed up the Reform of Interest Rate and Exchange Rate Marketization, *China Finance 40 Forum*, Website Report, March 25, 2014.

Dwight H. Perkins *et al.*, *Economics of Development*, China Renmin University Press, 1990.

Economic and Social Division of the People's Daily, *Seven Questions about Supply-side Structural Reform*, People's Publishing House, 2016.

Economics Teaching & Research Department of Chinese Academy of Governance, *Supply-side Structural Reform in China*, People's Publishing House, 2016.

Ely, Rely, R.T., *Outlines of Economics*, Macmillan, New York, 1937, pp. 115–120.

Fang Hongsheng, *Chinese Separation of Power, Endogenous Fiscal Policy and Macroeconomic Stability: Theory and Municipal Administration*, Truth & Wisdom Press, 2010.

Farrer, T. H., *The State in its Relation to Trade*, Macmillan, London, 1902, pp. 65–71.

Feng Zhifeng, Theoretical Logic and Practical Path of Supply-side Structural Reform, *On Economic Problems*, No. 2, 2016.

Gao Wenbing, Supply-side Structural Reform Calls for Innovation, *Economic Daily*, July 14, 2016.

Guan Qing-You, Significance of Multi-level Capital Market to the Supply-side Reform, *Netease Finance*, December 26, 2015.

Guan Tao, Seven Major Relationships to be Handled Well to Push Forward the Reform of the Financial Supply Side, *China Economic Guide*, May 25, 2016.

Guo Chunli, *et al.*, Trends and Relevant Suggestions on the Release of Dividend from the Supply-side Structural Reform, Proposals for Investigation and Research, *Journal of Macroeconomic Research Institute*, Vol. 25, 2016.

Guo Lian, Reflections on Financial Innovation and Development under the Condition of Interest Rate Marketization, *China Finance 40 Forum*, October 18, 2014.

He Jun, Li Shaodong, Causes, Hazards and Governance of High Incomes in State-owned Monopoly Industries, *Research of Finance and Accounting*, No. 1, 2013.

Hou Xiaodong, Marxist Political Economics Research on Supply-side Structural Reform from the Comparative Perspective of the Market Supply-Demand Equilibrium Theory, *Contemporary Economics*, Vol. 19, 2016.

Hu Wei-Wei, Zheng Yi-Fang, Exerting the Role of Environmental Protection to Promote the Supply-side Structural Reform — Correct Understanding of the Relationship between the Supply-side Reform and Environmental Protection, *China Environment Journal* (www.cenews.com.cn), May 26, 2016.

Huang Chengliang, Promotion of Ecological Civilization by Supply Side Reform, www.people.cn/theories, March 17, 2016.

Huang Qunhui, Improving Manufacturing Innovation Ecology by Supply-side Structural Reform, *Guangming Daily*, April 27, 2016.

Jia Kang, China Needs to Build and Develop the Reform-Centered New Supply-side Economics, *Journal of Finance and Economics*, No. 1, 2013.

Jia Kang, Essentials of Supply-side Structural Reform, *China Finance*, Vol. 1, 2016.

Jia Kang, Su Jingchun *et al.*, *Economics of New Supply: Innovation and Suggestions*, China Economic Publishing House, 2015.

Jia Kang, Su Jingchun, *New Supply Economics*, Shanxi Economic Press, 2015.

Jiang Chao, Gu Xiao-Hsiao, You'll Understand the Supply-side Reform after Reading these Ten Questions about the Supply-side Reform, *The Wall Street Journal*, December 1, 2015.

JiRui and Wang Huaifang, Financing Constraints and Land Finance & Local Government Investment Behavior. *Statistical Research*, Vol. 12, 2015.

Joseph A. Schumpeter, *Schumpeter: Theory of Economic Development* (translated by Guo Wujun), Huaxia Publishing House, 2015.

Joseph E. Stiglitz, *Economics*, 4th edition (translated by Huang Xianfeng and Zhang Fan), China Renmin University Press, 2013.

Kong Weiyan, A Study on Income Distribution of China's Monopoly Industries — From A Perspective of Comparison with Competitive Industries, *China Price*, No. 10, 2012.

Kou Tiejun, My Opinions on the Reform of China's Finance and Tax System. *Taxation Research*, Vol. 1, 2016.

Li Guojun, Establishment of a List of Government Purchases of Basic Public Services for Environmental Protection, *China Environment Journal* (www.cenews.com.cn), January 23, 2015.

Li Jinjin, The Strategy of Supply Side Reform Based on China's Economic Reality, www.drcnet.com.cn, March 11, 2016.

Li Ruiming, Shi Lei, Double Efficiency Loss of State-owned Enterprises and Economic Growth, *Economic Research*, No. 1, 2010.

Li Xiangmao, Wang Yixin, Analysis of Income Distribution of China's Monopoly Industries, *Reform of Economic System*, No. 11, 2011.

Li Yan, Tang Zhuo, Profit Distribution of State-owned Enterprises and Improvement of State-owned Assets Operation Budget — Based on Analysis of Sharing the Revenues on Public Resources, *Journal of the Central University of Finance and Economics*, No. 6, 2013.

Li Zhiqing, Green Development from the Perspective of Supply-side Reform, *China Environment Journal* (www.cenews.com.cn), December 23, 2015.

Li Zuojun, Let Supply-side Reform Back to Common Sense, *Economic Information Daily*, December 22, 2015.

Li Zuojun, Supply-side Reform Promotes the Construction of Ecological Civilization System, *People's Daily*, April 5, 2016.

Lin Feng, Direct Measurement for Contribution of Administrative Monopoly Industries to National Income Distribution Gaps, *East China Economic Management*, No. 1, 2013.

Lin Yifu, *New Structural Economics: A Framework for Rethinking Development and Policy* (translated by Su Jian), Peking University Press, 2014.

Liu Fang, Coordinating Analysis of Structural Tax Reduction and Tax Reform. *Modern Economic Management*, Vol. 3, 2015.

Liu Shijin, Production Factor Market — The Main Battlefield of Supply-side Reform, *New Financial Review*, Vol. 6, 2015.

Liu Si-Yu, China's Capital Market to Better Serve the Supply-side Reform, *China Network*, June 22, 2016.

Long Guoqiang, Opening-up Strategies for China's Economy under the New Normal, *Foreign Economic Relations and Trade*, No. 4, 2015.

Lu Feng, *Structural Contradictions Resolved by Structural Reform*, Vol. 7, Qiushi, 2016.

Luiz De Mello, Pier Carlo Padran, Promoting Potential Growth: The Role of Structural Reform, OECD Economics Department Working Papers, No.793, OECD Publishing, 2010.

Luo Deming, Li Ye, Shi Jinchuan, Factor Market Distortion, Resources Misallocation and Productivity, *Economic Research*, No. 3, 2012.

Ma Xiaohe, Analysis of Economic Development Trends and Supply-side Structural Reform in the Second Half of the Year, www.71.com, July 28, 2016.

Ma Xiaohe, Current Economic Situation and Supply-side Reform, hexun.come, April 10, 2016.

Ma Xiaohe, Grasping the Key to Supply-side Structural Reform, *Economic Daily*, July 28, 2016.

Ma Xiaohe, The Real Connotation of Supply-side Reform Needs to Be Clarified Urgently, *Xiao Kang* (*Insight China*), July 2016.

Meng Chun, Implementing Financial Policies to Support the Supply-side Reform. *Henan Social Sciences*, Vol.1, 2016.

Ministry of Environmental Protection, Guidance on Active Environmental Protection Role to Promote the Supply-side Structural Reform, No. 45, 2016.

Nie Huihua, Jia Ruixue, Productivity and Resources Misallocation in China's Manufacturing Industry, *World Economy*, No. 7, 2011.

Niu Ximing, On the Supply-side Reform of Commercial Banks, *Bankers*, Vol. 10, 2016.

OECD, *National Innovation Systems*, 1997.

Outline of the 13th Five-year Plan for National Economic and Social Development (2016–2020) of the People's Republic of China, March 17, 2016.

Pan Fanfan, Strengthening Environmental Protection to Promote Supply-side Reform, *China Environment Journal*, July 27, 2016.

Pan Shengwen, Measures to Standardize Income Distribution in Monopoly Industries, *Economic Review*, No. 7, 2009.

Paul A. Samuelson, Willian D. Nordhaus, *Economics*, 18th edition (translated by Xiao Chen), Posts & Telecom Press, 2008.

Pei Changhong, Difference between China's Supply-side Reform and the US Supply-side Economics, in *The 5th CF40 — PIIE Sino-US Economists Symposium*, May 21–22, 2016.

PuYufei, *Development Pressure and Institutional Elasticity*, Economic Science Press, 2013.

Qiao Weibing, *China's State-owned Assets Supervision and Administration Yearbook (2014)*, China Economic Publishing House, 2014.

Ren Zeping, How to Conduct Supply-side Reform on the Capital Market, Sina.com, January 2016.

Research Group of the Institute of Economics, Chinese Academy of Social Sciences, Research on the Mechanism of Monetary Policy Regulation in the Condition of Interest Rate Marketization and Financial Diversification, Report of the Institute of Economics, 2015.

RuiMingjie, Industrialization Innovation Promotes Supply-side Structural Reform, Science-Pie, July 22, 2016.

Shao Ping, Supply-side Reform of Commercial Banks, *China Finance*, Vol. 2, 2016.

Sheng Chaoxun *et al.*, Research on Key Areas Reform Nodes: Supply Side and Demand Side, *Reform*, Vol. 1, 2016.

Shi Jinchuan, Zhao Zifang, Ownership Constraints and Factor Price Distortion — An Empirical Analysis Based on China Industry Database, *Statistical Research*, No. 6, 2007.

Song Li, *et al.*, Research on Deepening the Reform of Fiscal and Taxation System (Internal Report), a Key Research Project of the Macroeconomic Research Institute in 2014.

Stephen H. Sosnick. A Critique of Concepts of Workable Competition, *American Economics Review*, Vol. 42, No. 5, 1974, 10–14.

Tao Xiaoma, Xing Jianwu, Huang Xin, Zhou Wen, Studies on Energy Price Distortion and Factor Substitution in China Industrial Sectors, *Quantitative and Technical Economics*, No. 11, 2009.

Teng Tai, Fan Bi *et al.*, *Supply-side Reform*, People's Oriental Publishing & Media, 2016.

The Central Committee of the Communist Party of China and the State Council, Outline of the Strategy for National Innovation-Driven Development, 19 May 2016.

The State Council, *The 13th Five-Year Plan for Scientific and Technological Innovation*, No. 43, July 28, 2016.

Tong Hangjian, Supply-side Economics — Not the Theoretical Origin of Supply-side Structural Reform, *Economic Research Guide*, Vol. 10, 2016.

UNCTAD, *World Investment Report 2015*, August 2015.

Unirule Institute of Economics: Causes, Behaviors and Removal of Administrative Monopoly in China, http://www. unirule.org.cn/xiazai/2012/20120803.

Unirule Institute of Economics: Nature, Performance and Reform of State-owned Enterprises, http://www. unirule.org.cn/index.php? c=article&id=295,2011-05-29.

Wang Chunfa, Thoughts on the Theory of National Innovation System, *China Soft Science*, Vol. 5, 2003.

Wang Chunlei, Tax Policy for Promoting Structural Adjustment of Demand and Expanding Household Consumption. *Economic and Management Review*, Vol. 6, 2012.

Wang Fengchun, Recommended Management of Natural Resources by Public Welfare and Operating Assets, *Economic Report for the 21st Century*, September 23, 2014.

Wang Xiaolu, Thoughts on Status Quo, Tendency and Reform of China Income Distribution, *China Market*, No. 20, 2010.

Wang Yiming, Chen Changsheng, Li Chengjian, Correct Understanding of the Supply-side Structural Reform, *People's Daily*, March 29, 2016.

Wang Yiming, Chen Changsheng, *Reconstructing New Balance: Macro-Economic Situation Outlook and Supply-side Structural Reform*, China Development Press, 2016.

Wang Zhixuan, Deng Liping, Optimization of Tax System Structure and Consumption Growth in China, *Taxation Research*, Vol. 9, 2015.

Wei Liao, S. J.-A. Tapsoba, China's Monetary Policy and Interest Rate Liberalization: Lessons from International Experiences, IMF Working Paper, 2014.

Wei Liqun, *Retrospect and Prospect of China's Economic System Reform in the Past Three Decades*, People's Publishing House, 2008.

What exactly is the supply-side structural reform? *People's Daily*, December 1, 2015.

Wu Jiansheng, Li Dawei, Chen Changying, Promote Transformation and Upgrading of China's Processing Trade, *China Development Observation*, No. 6, 2014.

Wu Jiansheng, Li Dawei, Chen Changying, Promoting Transformation and Upgrading of China's Processing Trade, *China Development Observation*, No. 6, 2014.

Wu Jinglian *et al.*, *Supply-side Reform: Economic Restructure Remodels China's Layout*, Chinese Culture & History Press, 2016.

Wu Jinglian, Li Yining *et al.*, *The "13th Five-Year Plan" Led by Supply-side Reform*, CITIC Press Group, 2016.

Xi Jinping, Speech at the Seminar on Study and Implementation of the Spirit of the 5th Plenary Session of the 18th Central Committee of the CPC (January 18, 2016), *People's Daily*, May 10, 2016.

Xi Jinping, Struggle to Build a Powerful Country of Science and Technology — A Speech at the National Congress of Science and Technology Innovation, the Congress of Academicians of CAS and CAE, and the Ninth National Congress of the Chinese Association for Science and Technology, May 30, 2016.

Xia Maosen, PengQisi, Jiang Lingling, Wang Yumei, Relationship between Factor Price Distortion — Base on Sample Date During 1991–2010, *Technical Economics*, No. 12, 2013.

Xu Jianbiao, Evaluation and Prospect of the Pilot Tax System Reform in China, *Taxation Research*, Vol. 1, 2016.

Xue Lan, Zhao Jing, Contemporary Significance and Strategic Thinking of Innovation-Driven Development During the 13th Five-Year Plan, *Journal of National School of Administration*, Vol. 5, 2016.

Xue Xiaoguang, Song Xuchao, Literature Review of National Innovation System, *Industrial Economic Review*, Vol. 9, 2016.

Yan Ping, Discussion about Influence Factors of Capital Misallocation, *Economics*, No. 11, 2012.

Yang Dongde, Teng Xinghua, A Strategic Study of the National Innovation System and Strategy in the United States, *Journal of Beijing School of Administration*, Vol. 6, 2012.

Yang Weimin, *Establishing a Systematic and Complete System of Ecological Civilization*, and *Decision of the Central Committee of the Communist Party of China on Several Major Issues Concerning the Comprehensive Deepening of Reform*, People's Publishing House, 2013.

Yang Weimin, Promoting Harmony between Man and Nature, *Qiu Shi* (*Seeking Truth*), Vol. 23, 2015.

You Quan, Innovation Throughout the Supply-side Structural Reform, *Fujian Daily*, March 5, 2016.

Yu Liangchun, Jian Minjie, Analysis of Influence Factors for Industrial Monopoly and Difference of Resident Income Distribution, *Research of Industrial Economy*, No. 2, 2013.

Yuan Zhigang, Xie Dongdong, Analysis of Influences of China's Labor Misallocation on TFP, *Economic Research*, No. 7, 2011.

Yue Ximing, Li Shi, Shi Taili *et al.*, Discussion of High Income Problems in Monopoly Industries, *Social Sciences in China*, No.3, 2010.

Zeng Guoping, Gou Youzhao, Liu Lei, From "Innovative Systems" to "Innovative Ecosystems", *Science Research*, Vol. 1, 2013.

Zhang Shifei, Supply-side Reform Leads Financial Management into a New Era. *China Finance*, Vol. 2, 2016.

Zhao Zhiyun, Essence of Supply-side Structural Reform: Promote Innovation, *Science and Technology Daily*, July 4, 2016.

Zheng Jingping, Several Opinions on Supply-side Structural Reform in China, *China Opening Herald*, Vol. 2, 2016.

Zhou Wen, Supply-side Structural Reform and Economic Theory Innovation in China, *Theory and Reform*, Vol. 4, 2016.

Zhu Keli, *Supply-side Reform During the 13th Five-Year Plan*, CITIC Press, 2016.

Zhu Xi, Shi Qinghua, Gai Qing'en, Factor Allocation Distortion and Agricultural Total Factor Productivity, *Economic Research*, No. 5, 2011.

Zong Liang, Give Play to the Role of Financial Support and Promote Supply-side Reform, *Financial Times*, August 4, 2016.

Index

Lightning Source UK Ltd.
Milton Keynes UK
UKHW022030160720
366664UK00004B/176